INTERACTIVE
MULTIMEDIA

Visions of Multimedia for
Developers, Educators, & Information Providers

INTERACTIVE MULTIMEDIA

Visions of Multimedia for
Developers, Educators, & Information Providers

Foreword by John Sculley

Edited by
Sueann Ambron and Kristina Hooper

PUBLISHED BY
Microsoft Press
A Division of Microsoft Corporation
16011 NE 36th Way, Box 97017, Redmond, Washington 98073-9717

Library of Congress Cataloging in Publication Data

Interactive Multimedia.

   1. Audio-visual education.   2. Educational
technology.   I. Ambron, Sueann Robinson.   I. Hooper,
Kristina.
LB1043.I566   1988   371.3'3   88-1449
ISBN 1-55615-124-1

Printed and bound in the United States of America.

1 2 3 4 5 6 7 8 9 MLML 8 9 0 9 8

Distributed to the book trade in the United States
by Harper & Row

Distributed to the book trade in Canada by General
Publishing Company, Ltd.

Distributed to the book trade outside the United States
and Canada by Penguin Books Ltd.

Penguin Books Ltd., Harmondsworth, Middlesex, England
Penguin Books Australia Ltd., Ringwood, Victoria, Australia
Penguin Books N.Z. Ltd., 182-190 Wairau Road, Auckland 10, New Zealand

British Cataloging in Publication Data available

CONTENTS

FOREWORD

The book you are holding is a beacon illuminating an exciting future for American education. Technologies described in this book will give us the ability to explore, convey, and create knowledge as never before. Teachers and students will command a rich learning environment that, had you described it to me when I was in school, would have seemed entirely magical.

Imagine a classroom with a window on all the world's knowledge. Imagine a teacher with the capability to bring to life any image, any sound, any event. Imagine a student with the power to visit any place on earth at any time in history. Imagine a screen that can display in vivid color the inner workings of a cell, the births and deaths of stars, the clashes of armies, and the triumphs of art. And then imagine that you have access to all of this and more by exerting little more effort than simply asking that it appear.

It seems like magic even today. Yet the ability to provide this kind of learning environment is within our grasp. The environment builds on technologies already emerging from corporate and academic research centers. Powerful computers, high-speed telecommunications, and optical storage devices such as CD-ROM and videodisc will provide the hardware platforms. Simulations, artificial intelligence, and multimedia engines such as HyperCard will provide the software platforms. And a new breed of multimedia storytellers, enchanters, and guides will build for us pathways and superhighways through banks of information and libraries of sights and sounds.

I believe that all this will happen not simply because people have the capability to make it happen, but also because people have a compelling need to make it happen.

One of the challenges in designing an educational system is in recognizing that the system must prepare students to take their place in a world that has not yet come into existence. Girls and boys who entered kindergarten this fall will enter college in the twenty-first century. What can we teach them now that will serve them well in the future? The sobering fact is that we don't know.

Thinking of education as simply the transfer of knowledge from teacher to student, pouring from one vessel into another, is no longer possible. It is not as though we can give young people a ration of knowledge that they can draw on throughout their careers. We don't even know what their careers will be. Students today cannot count on finding one smooth career path because, by the millions, jobs that exist today will change radically in the near future. To succeed, individuals will need tremendous flexibility to be able to move from one company to another or from one industry to another. What tomorrow's students need is not just mastery of subject matter, but mastery of learning. Education cannot be simply a prelude to a career; it must be a lifelong endeavor.

Although we cannot predict what jobs today's students will hold in the new century, a look at what is happening to the United States in the world economy provides a clear idea of what these students will need to accomplish.

The move from the Industrial Age to the Information Age is not just technological, but also entails a major shift in the political economy of the world. The global economy has shifted from a hierarchical order to one of deep interdependence. Where the United States once was at the pinnacle of an economic hierarchy, we are now just one node along an economic network. Our once exclusive know-how is available in many newly industrialized nations such as Korea, Taiwan, Singapore, Mexico, and Brazil.

The massive institutions that the United States built to drive our prosperity in the Industrial Age are failing to keep up with these changes. As the flow of world trade shifts, it is clear that as a nation we are living beyond our means. We no longer are creating enough value to sustain our lifestyle, and we are falling deeper into debt.

The only way to halt this slide is to find new ways to create value in the world. That means that our education system and our businesses must foster innovation and discovery. Yet innovation has never come through bureaucracy and mass institutions; it has always come from individuals. For that reason, our institutions must focus on individuals.

Our ability to renew ourselves as a society depends on our ability to renew ourselves as individuals. We will serve our students best, therefore, if we give them the skills they need to continuously renew their understanding of a changing world. Preparing students for success in the twenty-first century is a matter not of teaching a particular body of knowledge but rather giving students the skills to explore their environments—discovering and synthesizing knowledge for themselves.

That is why I believe that the technologies described in this book are not simply engaging and intriguing but, more than that, they are a key to our future prosperity and renewal.

The transformation I am calling for—shifting focus from the institution to the individual—has a close parallel in history. In medieval Europe, people were subservient to the institutions of the church and to feudal hierarchies. Then came the Renaissance, which redefined the individual as the center of intellectual activity.

The Renaissance did more than change people's perspective of the world; the movement literally invented perspective. The medieval painter depicted great religious events with the most important figures appearing the largest. Composition reflected ideology. Then the composition style changed. The Renaissance artist drew figures and buildings in "perspective" the way they would appear to an observer. For the first time, "point-of-view" was introduced to the world.

One key technology—printing—galvanized the many forces that converged to bring about the Renaissance. The rise of printing led with astonishing speed to an explosion of literacy. The result was a tremendous and unprecedented exchange of ideas, a wealth of invention, and a new sense of personal worth for the individual.

We are, today, in need of a second Renaissance, which like the first also can be galvanized by technology.

Let us remember, however, that the printing press never wrote a single book: Authors write books. So, too, will it be with the new technologies described in this book. The most exciting developments will be the contributions of creative individuals who will provide tours, presentations, and limitless opportunities for teachers and students.

The multimedia learning environments you will read about here are stimulating, exciting, and within reach. They represent an expansive vision, but not a distant one. They are the tools of a near tomorrow and, like the printing press, they will empower individuals, unlock worlds of knowledge, and forge a new community of ideas.

John Sculley

PREFACE

This book is based on one of a series of *Learning Tomorrow* publications produced by Apple Computer, Inc., to provide information on how technology can be used in education. Our hope is that the book will be of interest and value to researchers, to developers, to teachers, and to students.

This collection of articles was compiled after an invitational conference on Multimedia in Education held June 19 and 20, 1986. Participants were selected because they are leaders in writing about and building examples of multimedia presentations.

The participants in this conference represented many different traditional perspectives, including computer science, engineering, education, publishing, and television. In addition, each individual brought a multidisciplinary perspective— something that seems critical in creating multimedia products.

While we are excited about the results of the meeting, the views expressed by the participants do not necessarily represent Apple's point of view. They are instead the diverse views of some of the best people in the field of educational technology, presented to give readers an overview of the opportunities in multimedia.

We believe that education can benefit from the new kinds of multimedia presentation discussed during the 1986 conference. We hope that our children and yours will learn differently in the very near term using these new materials. We hope that teachers soon will be able to integrate technologically enhanced multimedia in an easy, everyday way in their classrooms.

And we hope that this book plays an important role in helping this all to happen.

Sueann Ambron, Ed.D.
Manager of Market Development
Apple Computer, Inc.

Kristina Hooper, Ph.D.
Senior Researcher
Apple Computer, Inc.

Introduction

Sueann Ambron

SUEANN AMBRON

Sueann Ambron, Ed.D., is the Manager of Education Market Development at Apple Computer. Her responsibilities include investigating new technologies for the education market and building prototype products that demonstrate the promise of new technologies. The National Geographic Society–Lucasfilm collaboration is among the multimedia projects she manages.

Ambron completed her doctorate from Columbia University with honors in 1973 and joined the education faculty at Stanford University. She has been active in the use of technology in education since the early seventies when, as a professor of education, she was faculty sponsor for human-factors students at Stanford University and XEROX PARC. Later, she was responsible for new education product development as a product manager at Atari.

As Manager of Software Products, she was responsible for several award-winning educational software products. Ambron has continued to work in technology and education, including work in artificial intelligence as it relates to multimedia.

Ambron has authored a number of professional books and articles, including a best-selling college textbook on child development.

Ambron's main professional interest is creating superior educational products using new technology. As an educator and futurist, she believes that "a great product is one that makes learning a compelling experience."

NEW VISIONS OF REALITY:
MULTIMEDIA AND EDUCATION

> Fifteenth-century Europeans "knew" that the sky was made of closed
> concentric crystal spheres, rotating around a central earth and carrying the
> stars and planets. That "knowledge" structured everything they did and
> thought, because it told them the truth. Then Galileo's telescope changed
> the truth.
>
> As a result, a hundred years later everybody "knew" that the universe was
> open and infinite, working like a giant clock. Architecture, music, litera-
> ture, science, economics, art, politics—everything—changed, mirroring
> the new view created by the change in the knowledge.
> (Burke, p. 9)

Multimedia, like Galileo's telescope, is a powerful tool; it will change the way we look at
knowledge and give us a new vision of reality. The change in our view of knowledge
brought about by multimedia will not take one hundred years as it did with Galileo's
telescope. The changes are already happening. They started with the wide acceptance of the
microcomputer and continue as we move toward videocomputers, interactive television, and
electronic books. Three industries—computers, television, and publishing—that were quite
separate during the sixties started to overlap in the seventies and eighties. By the nineties the
three industries will be even more intertwined. The products of these industries provide the
content and media for education. Consequently, the new reality of multimedia will change
education.

The purpose of this book is to give you a glimpse of multimedia in education. Conference
participants from the fields of computer science, television, and publishing will share their
vision of multimedia with you.

How do you explain something new for which the words have not yet been invented? One
way is to show it! That is why this book is basically a collection of examples. Computer-
controlled multimedia is new, so examples are necessary to define the medium, develop the
vocabulary, and explore new dimensions of content, software, and hardware. When you
have finished reading the book you should have a better idea of what multimedia is and why
it is likely to have a major impact on education as well as business.

WHAT IS MULTIMEDIA?

We'll start with a short history and a working definition of multimedia.

Multimedia without computer enhancement is not new. For example, cave drawings in France are a record of early man's images of animals. These records were made with various media, probably using stick tools.

A more recent and varied example of multimedia is found in a kindergarten class, where you'll find paints, crayons, filmstrips, books, records, and clay—all examples of media, and all tools for multimedia production. The products of this media-rich environment can include a picture of ladybugs made with thumbprints, a green clay frog, and felt-pen illustrations for stories.

What is new and exciting is the innovation of mixing text, audio, and video with a computer. Computer-supported multimedia is a new technology-based medium for thinking, learning, and communication. Users can browse, annotate, link, and elaborate on information in a rich, nonlinear, multimedia data base. Going beyond the traditional pencils, crayons, chalk, paint, clay, books, and the other traditional classroom paraphernalia, computer-based multimedia learning stations will allow students and teachers to explore and integrate vast libraries of text, audio, and video information.

Automated nonlinear text was first described by Vannevar Bush as a "memex" device in which an individual could store books, records, and letters in a form such that specific information could be retrieved rapidly. Theodor Nelson used the term "hypertext" in the early 1960s to describe the idea of nonlinear reading and writing implemented on a computer system for annotating and connecting ideas; Doug Engelbart developed a number of hypertext systems in his SRI lab during this time. The term "hypermedia" extends hypertext to include video, audio, and animation in addition to text. As used in this book, multimedia, hypermedia, and intermedia refer loosely to the same class of presentations. I will use the term multimedia in this chapter.

Multimedia can be examined in three parts: media, technology, and products.

MULTIMEDIA ELEMENTS

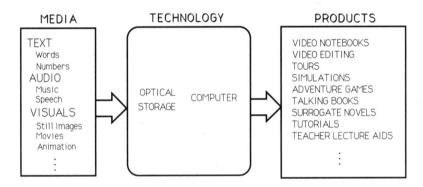

Media include text, audio, and visuals. The *technologies* that make multimedia possible are optical storage and computers. Multimedia *products* are just emerging; they include video notebooks, video editing, tours, simulations, adventure games, talking books, surrogate novels, tutorials, and teacher lecture aids. Users and developers will start with conventions that they understand—television, books, films, computer games, computer-aided instruction—and then discover new ways to use the multimedia environment.

Not only will there be new products emerging from multimedia uses, but multimedia also may change the way we think and solve problems—just as in recent years, word processing, spreadsheets, and data bases have changed how we think about writing, accounting, and information access. Multimedia will enable new ways of analyzing information to evolve and new insights to be achieved in many disciplines. Some of these insights may come from relative novices in the fields, because of the easy access to basic content. Users can communicate with each other easily, so compound documents can be created by many authors working simultaneously. Or a single author may produce a very rich visual presentation. In addition, the results of the work can be displayed in print, disc, or video form.

The technology components of multimedia will change with time. Today, a multimedia application typically requires a computer-controlled videodisc and/or a CD ROM player. Eventually, there will be video computers with many multimedia capabilities built in or available as modules. Multimedia will only get faster, less expensive, and more capable of doing useful activities. What are some of the useful activities for multimedia in education—how will multimedia be used in education?

HOW WILL MULTIMEDIA BE USED IN EDUCATION?

I have presented what multimedia is and how it may change with time. Now I would like to describe a few examples of what multimedia could be like for students, teachers, university professors, and business people. More detailed examples of multimedia applications are the subject of this book. My purpose here is to suggest what is possible with multimedia.

A sixth-grade science student is asked to do a science project. The student is very interested in the astronomical phenomenon of "eclipses," and decides to do her report about them. Instead of merely summarizing the encyclopedia article on the subject, all too often the time-honored approach for preparing a written report, the student collects various texts about eclipses from sources on a CD ROM. In addition, she views an astronomy videodisc and copies a diagram of eclipses of the sun and moon, and a short movie clip of a total eclipse of the sun, taken in Bolivia in 1966, that dramatically reveals structural details of the sun's corona. She then uses off-the-shelf software to write title and credits, to create an animation sequence for the path of a total solar eclipse, and finally to dub in Star Wars music. Putting all the elements together with a computer, the student creates her own multimedia video science documentary. With multimedia, the student has a new way of communicating vividly what she has learned about eclipses.

A high school history teacher is preparing a lecture on civil rights. Instead of just lecturing to his students about civil rights, the teacher really makes the subject come alive with a multimedia videodisc that includes video news clips of the civil rights marches of the sixties, and Dr. Martin Luther King's famous "I have a dream" speech. The teacher selects the text of relevant court cases from a CD ROM, and visual and audio information from a videodisc, to create a powerful, animated educational experience for students.

A university professor of developmental psychology is writing a textbook. The professor and the publisher decide that a companion videodisc of milestones in human development would be a useful research and learning aid for students, because the subject matter of early human development is so rich visually—and is difficult to communicate with traditional text and still-image forms alone. Furthermore, the existing vast quantities of film and sound information on the subject have historically been difficult to access. Multimedia is an ideal way to show students, for example, the differences among one-year-olds in motor behavior. The professor proceeds to develop a videodisc that is integrated with the textbook. Since the material covered by most textbooks is overlapping, the videodisc has broad appeal as a lecture aid and can be used with many different textbooks. In fact, the market for the videodisc extends beyond college courses—it's an ideal product for new parents.

A data communications company hires a new sales engineer. Instead of sending him back to the factory for two weeks of individual product training, the company gives him a computer-controlled videodisc of new products and applications. The salesman could further use the training material to create a videotape for a key customer sales presentation. His locally produced videotape would stress particular product applications of interest to his customer, edited from the company-produced training videodisc. Multimedia can save time and money in field training, and give a field sales engineer a highly visual, customized, and persuasive way to communicate with a customer.

In sum, multimedia will provide instructors, students, and others with a dramatic new environment for presentations. They will no longer be bound by the limits of illustrating processes on a chalkboard or in slide collections. Vast libraries of audio, visual, and text material will be easily accessed by the computer. In addition, the user can integrate such existing computer programs as word processors, graphics, and data files. Instructors and students will have the opportunity to create their own classroom videos for presentation and personal video notebooks. Students and teachers alike will be able to become "video producers" or "video publishers" utilizing the vast data bases at their command for images, sounds, and text.

Researchers will use multimedia for new approaches to scholarship. Multimedia will allow a level of analytic control not possible in viewing traditional film, audio, or print materials. Multiple scholars will be able to work on the same multimedia data base simultaneously, combining their analyses of different aspects of the field.

The business world will discover that "desktop video" is a powerful method of communicating within the company and to customers. For example, businesses will have an efficient method of delivering consistent training at off-site locations.

WHY IS MULTIMEDIA IMPORTANT IN EDUCATION?

Multimedia is important in education because it holds great promise for improving the *quality* of education. People have been dreaming about easy access to information that has the richness of multiple images and sounds, and multimedia begins to deliver on the dream. Multimedia provides the ability to illustrate ideas with visual, audio, text, or any combination of media, so users can create new ways of communicating ideas. For example, instead of just using text to teach about the Constitution, teachers can enliven class discussion with rich visuals such as paintings of the drafters of the Constitution, maps of colonial America, political cartoons, and a film clip from the play "1776." Of course, the visual information can be linked to text from the Magna Charta, the Federalist Papers, or current court cases. In short, teachers and students can have a great learning experience exploring the Constitution.

Teachers can break free from the constraints of textbooks and the chalkboard. They can back up their imagination with classroom materials they have been dreaming about. Concepts that are difficult to explain, such as meiosis, become clear when you can freeze a frame on a videodisc and discuss it with the students.

Students who have difficulty expressing ideas in writing can now have a new way to communicate and a new class of material to learn from. Children who are used to watching television, listening to music, and playing computer games find multimedia a more compelling learning tool than the book-and-chalkboard educational media of their parents' generation. Finally, multimedia allows the user to be an active learner, controlling access to and manipulating vast quantities of information with a computer.

I trust the examples in this book will help us all to begin to envision the possibilities of multimedia in education. The first chapter is by Doug Engelbart, who began many of the discussions addressed in this book years ago, well before most people understood what he was saying. Our hope is that this book does justice to elaborations and developments of the foundation he provided for us all.

REFERENCES

Burke, J. *The Day the Universe Changed.* Boston: Little, Brown and Company, 1986.

Bush, V. "As We May Think," *Atlantic Monthly* : 176, pp. 10–108; July 1945. Reprinted in *CD ROM: The New Papyrus;* Microsoft, 1986.

Section I:
Computer Science
and Engineering

Doug Engelbart brought the perspectives of an engineer and societal visionary to the task of providing computer support for human activities many years ago, taking a different view of the problem from what was popular at the time. He did not consider "the computer as technology" central to the effort, as most engineers did (and typically still do). Instead, he thought that computers could be keys in bringing communities together to solve particular tasks and to form effective teams by providing communication links. It was inspiring at the Conference, for example, to see Engelbart's slides of multiple mice used by different participants at a meeting, as well as to watch hypertext structures used casually in the context of other tasks, but then to realize that even these ideas and implementations have not yet been made widely available. Amidst all the hoopla of rediscovery of Engelbart's early work, much of his simple and profound message has been missed.

Norm Meyrowitz and his colleagues at Brown University, Steve Weyer and Frank Halasz, have taken many of Engelbart's developments and have used the computer tools now available to make explicit how certain systems might work. **Meyrowitz** takes the concept of linkage systems into "hypermedia," linking images and text in an educational framework. In this sense, his work will eventually be evaluated by just how well it functions in a learning framework with individuals who are not professional knowledge workers looking for tools for their work; students will need to see clearly how the system will work for them, and the tools will need to be quite accessible. **Weyer** focuses his analysis directly on the learning process, which is the basis for the browsing systems he designs. His task is not simply to retrieve particular "facts" or even categories of concepts. Instead, he has made explicit the notion that information be provided in a way that the user can learn new things, not just find descriptions of them. Stated simply, his emphasis has to go beyond linking everything and describing reasonable pathways between items; his perspective demands that he provide tools that engage users and provide them what they need to approach tasks cognitively. He must provide "an interface to knowledge," not simply the structuring of knowledge or the tools for this structuring (each of which is a mighty task in itself).

Frank Halasz has designed a system titled "NoteCards" which provides knowledge workers with a framework in which to organize their ideas as they are developing them, not "after the fact," when they have figured out what they might want to present about a particular idea. This system is currently commercially available, making it one of the few powerful tools for the "augmentation of the human intellect" which have moved from research laboratories into the "real world."

The Augmentation System Framework

Doug Engelbart with Kristina Hooper

DOUGLAS C. ENGELBART

Douglas C. Engelbart is a senior scientist with McDonnell Douglas/ISG, Cupertino, California. His professional focus is on the application of computer and communications technologies with an aim toward bringing exceptional new capabilities to individuals and organizations that are heavily dependent upon knowledge work.

A pioneer in office automation, Engelbart's innovations at SRI International in the '50s and '60s included the mouse, two-dimensional editing, multiple-window screens, cross-file editing, outline and idea processing, formatting directives, integrated help systems, and a full-scale electronic mail system. Other Engelbart innovations currently being implemented include shared-screen teleconferencing, composite text-graphics files, in-file addressing and cross-conference links, multiple viewing modes for text, and the universal user interface front-end module.

In recent years, Engelbart's studies have expanded into strategies for organizations facing rapid changes in technology, competition, and operating environments.

This paper has been put together in two stages. The first involved compiling notes of conversations in November 1986 between Doug and me. The second was influenced greatly by conversations during 1987, and relies particularly on quotes from a presentation Doug made at the Hackers' Conference in October 1987. I quote liberally from this presentation so that Doug can make his complex ideas accessible directly to the reader.

The focus of this paper is on "augmentation." "Augment" is a transitive verb which is defined by Webster's as meaning "to make greater, as in size, quantity, strength, etc.; to enlarge." Doug uses this term to emphasize the role of technology in a human context; technology is to be designed to increase human capabilities, to extend them in imagined and unimagined ways, to change the basic character of communities, and to make these more effective.

This perspective on computer technologies has been acknowledged widely in recent years, in theoretical work as well as in marketing slogans. Our widespread use of computers for word processing and "diagram organization" to assist in human expression and to aid in human work—to "augment the human intellect," in Doug's terms—demonstrates this approach directly. Similarly, the papers included in this book typically take as an assumption this human-centered perspective.

It is noteworthy, however, that in the early 1960s these concepts were quite unfamiliar to the computer science community with whom Doug was working. The general approach, then, as it oftentimes still is, was toward the development of technologies for their own sakes, or for the replacement (or minimization) of human involvement.

The approaches described throughout this book were made possible by the questioning of the uses of computer technology pursued by Doug and others early in the development of this technology. Hypertext systems, for example, are important and useful only when one takes an explicitly human view of the reading process in an information environment. It is a set of examples generated twenty years ago by Doug's lab that serve as central prototypes for the linking systems described in this book. Similarly, the entire notion of multimedia presentations—the central focus of this book—assumes a human viewer who is benefiting from the richness of these presentations. From the standpoint of technology, such presentations bring on a range of processing problems that clearly should be avoided unless these presentations are judged to be of value.

There are now widespread examples of Doug's influence in our computer environments— not the least of which are the direct manipulations made possible with the mouse, which he invented, and the simultaneous views of information provided in windowing systems, which he first demonstrated. Yet the crispness of Doug's analyses continues to invite innovation and inventive implementation. Much remains to be done in the context of Doug's analyses to explore the nature of the human communities and the opportunities for changes in these communities that are brought to our attention in a careful consideration of computer technologies. My hope is that this chapter can help people to understand the basic approach taken by Doug so that they can work to expand his investigations in a range of contexts.

In the following transcript, my comments are printed in italics. Doug's comments—either made in the first stage of our preparation, in 1986-87, or quoted from his October 1987 presentation—are in plain text. His comments from the October 1984 presentation are enclosed in quotation marks.

Kristina Hooper, November 1987

AN AUGMENTATION FRAMEWORK:
AN INTRODUCTION

"I had this kooky thing happen to me in 1951 where I decided to commit my career to trying to help mankind be able to cope better with complexity and urgency and the problems of the world. I had an image of sitting in front of a display and working with a computer interactively. I had been a radio and radar technician during World War II, so I knew that any signals that came out of a machine could drive any kind of hardware—they could drive whatever you wanted on a display. But I really didn't know how a computer worked. Still, I thought, 'Boy! That's just great!' The images of the different symbologies that you could employ, and other people sitting at workstations connected to the same complex, and working in a close, collaborative way. And I just said, 'Well, that's something I can pursue as an electrical engineer, and maybe try to follow that goal.' So it was about eight years later, after I'd gotten a Ph.D. and had gone to SRI to work, that I got a chance to start sitting down to really put it together, saying, 'Just exactly how would I pursue that?'"
(Engelbart 1987)

Many of us just start working as hard as we can when we feel that there is a lot to do. What Doug did instead was to very self-consciously build a framework for his analysis, so that he could be sure of the context in which he was working and so that he wouldn't be distracted by interesting work different from his that was going on around him.

"So I sat there for two years building a framework. And out came this picture that showed that if you really want to improve how people cope with the world, you sort of peel off a lot and realize that there's a huge system already provided for you as you grow up within a given culture. You're indoctrinated in all sorts of unconscious things. You're taught explicitly conceptual and symbolic things, and a spoken language and eventually a written one. And you're given lots of tools and lots of methods and lots of organizational structures. And all of this constitutes one big system that augments human capability."
(Engelbart 1987).

Doug described this framework for analysis succinctly in November 1986:

The components of an augmentation system are the bundle of all the things that can be added to what a human is genetically endowed with, the purpose of which is to augment these basic human capabilities in order to maximize the capabilities that a human or human organization can apply to the problems and goals of human society. Augmentation systems have always existed; they have often been developed unconsciously. Throughout history, augmentation systems have emerged as a result of continuing socio-cultural evolution.

A broadbrush categorization of the components of an augmentation system includes three distinct but interacting elements: language, artifacts, and methodology. Society must train humans to use the three augmentation components in an integrated way.

This analysis of the context in which technologies exists led Doug to posit that an augmentation system framework must consider two types of system contributions. It must involve both _human_ _system_ contributions—the social and cultural frameworks that have evolved at any time in history to support human activities, as well as the basic human capabilities and their possible extensions through training—and the _tool_ _system_ contributions—the capabilities that are provided to enable human activities.

Figure 1 makes explicit these two kinds of system.

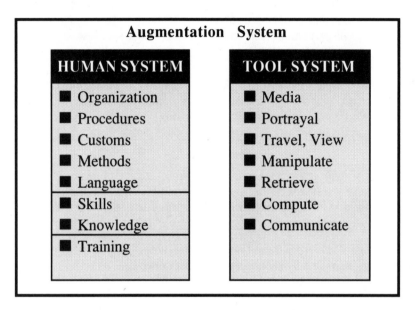

Figure 1. It is important to consider a two-part augmentation system: the human system and the tool system.

Figure 2 shows how these two systems might interact to provide an individual with a particular capability—some "example capability." For each capability—for example, programming a computer, setting up a conference, wiring a piece of hardware, or writing an understandable document—can be thought to result from a combination of existing human capabilities and existing tool capabilities, where individuals must have the skills and knowledge to take advantage of these two systems to augment their activities.

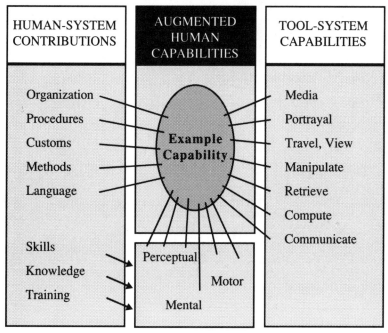

Basic Human Capabilities

Figure 2. *Most of our capabilities are composites: any "example capability" can be thought of as a combination of human-system and tool-system contributions. These capabilities come from the human having the necessary skills and knowledge to employ these augmentation systems.*

The complexity of this analysis becomes clear when one acknowledges that each new capability interacts with the wide range of existing capabilities. A new set of example capabilities will continually evolve from the interaction of the human and tool systems. Figure 3 shows a way to think of this.

Advanced Capability Hierarchy

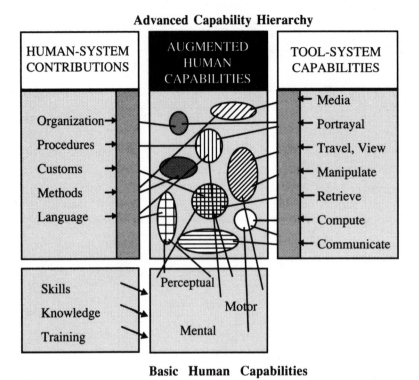

Basic Human Capabilities

Figure 3. Our capabilities grow hierarchically: Each new capability interacts with the wide range of existing (interrelated) capabilities.

Doug argues that we need to focus on a systematic way to understand this evolution, without oversimplifying it and "losing the phenomenon." For computers can provide critical new capabilities to support some of the most human of human endeavors.

"And so I said, 'Gee, that means this little computer toy coming along isn't all that different anyway; it's just another category of tool.' But then if you start thinking about how all of this evolved in the first place, you realize that one doesn't just suddenly evolve a bunch of tools. It is the co-evolution of all of these different aspects of what it is that helps augment a human. And so I thought, 'Well, I guess that's right....'

"So what's going to come out of all of this in the way of real changes, in the way people can think, formulate, conceptualize, portray, manipulate, communicate, collaborate—all of that? And so I thought, 'Well, I'll just start with a fresh start in a few dimensions.' And one of them was: 'Alright, what would I do to show things in a data structure? Since the hierarchical ways in which we organize thoughts are very basic, you should start out with explicit hierarchical stuctures in multimedia. So as fast as we can, let's get graphics with these, and let's scale and move around quickly with these, and the cross-linkages will help us.'"
(Engelbart 1987)

In his lab at SRI, Doug provided extremely cogent demonstrations of just how systems like those he specified in his written descriptions of augmentation systems might appear. For he realized even then that without specific examples—and the lessons that were to be learned in putting together these examples—his analysis would remain far too abstract for most people to understand.

A classic demonstration of this is one that Doug made before a large audience at a Computer Conference in 1968 in San Francisco. Fortunately for us all, it was filmed (Engelbart 1968). In this presentation, Doug showed very explicitly, among other things, how facilely a mouse and a special keypad might be used to directly manipulate and display structured documents. He also showed how multiple individuals—connected via both audio and video links— could work collaboratively on a single document.

These elements, described and demonstrated so clearly 20 years ago, slowly have been showing up in commercial products, often as the direct result of the work of alumni of Doug's lab who went on to work for research labs and computer corporations such as Xerox, Apple Inc., and Sun Computer when SRI closed the Augmentation Lab more than ten years ago.

And there will be more examples of Doug's influence as people begin to understand his analyses, and as we all rise to the challenges and opportunities that computers provide us. For, as Doug asserts, the potential impacts of the computer on our culture are too great for us to let augmentation systems evolve haphazardly. He argues that we as a culture must focus our resources on the formulation of a <u>methodology</u> for addressing complex human-tool interactions—a language system that lets us analyze the current situation in terms that can enable us to develop better and better augmentation systems.

At the same time, Doug makes it clear that it is quite hopeless to design something as complex as an entire augmentation system. And so he suggests a number of direct strategies we might employ in shaping augmentation systems—to influence their co-evolution— while we simultaneously develop methodologies for understanding them.

A brief description of Doug's analysis of methodologies and strategies is set forth in the next two sections of this chapter.

An Augmentation Framework: Methodologies

"Now you're bringing in, in terms of the computer, something very, very radical in the way of tools. I'd learned enough about scaling physical devices to realize that if a quantitative change in some system environment changes past a certain threshold, you get an immediate qualitative change—very much a qualitative change. You change the scale of an airplane and suddenly it won't fly—things of that sort. So I went, 'Well, the impact of all of this technology could just be very, very dramatic.'" (Engelbart 1987)

The complexities of his analysis were clear to Doug very early on, as were the complexities of the computer and human systems he was anticipating. To address this, Doug called very directly for the formulations of very new methodologies for coping with these issues, a call which is still very timely, as our culture has still failed to address these issues directly in our considerations of the impacts of computers on our societies. In our 1986-87 meetings, Doug stated this in the following terms:

We need methodologies and skills directed toward software, toward tools. For in any given knowledge-work domain, there is a special set of concepts, terminologies, and portrayals. The tools developed have an impact on the language. Understanding these dynamics is key. This requires explicit exploration; currently this topic does not get this exploration.

For instance, software designers are the subjects of such potential augmentation, but they are not themselves the researchers equipped to create it.

If not the software designers, just who are the people who work with methodologies and training? Who are the people who consider languages for augmentation that are not concretely programming languages?

What seems necessary to me is the development of a completely new discipline that embraces the whole augmentation system. Think of it as similar to architecture, a whole-system discipline that integrates in a coordinated way the specialty fields of structures, heating, electricity, plumbing, and more.

It is indeed amazing that we have no such focus on the efficient use of our own ideas and communications, even though we often do acknowledge their importance to our goals! As Doug notes, we all struggle with haphazard ways to organize our own thoughts, rarely even able to think of how the ideas of groups might be effectively combined:

What are the methodologies that I apply in collecting ideas and organizing them? Currently, I have a set of haphazard ways to organize things. And we all have haphazard ways of piecemealing methodologies of organizations together.

Why not put together a whole "academic department" on this subject? Or a specific department in a "work environment"? Why not think of augmentation as a system, and provide it with formal tools of analysis as well as extensive settings for experimentation?

Historically, one of the few settings that have been made available for this kind of experimentation was Doug's lab at SRI, a lab that was closed in the mid-1970s.

In this lab, Doug developed a very systematic way in which a group of workers could exchange information with the assistance of electronic technologies. And he tried his ideas out in the lab. Doug organized the document linkage system shown in Figure 4 —The Collaborative Information Domain—which formed a critical focus for the "Community." The document linkage system was intended to add more and more powerful opportunities for individuals to collaborate in this community.

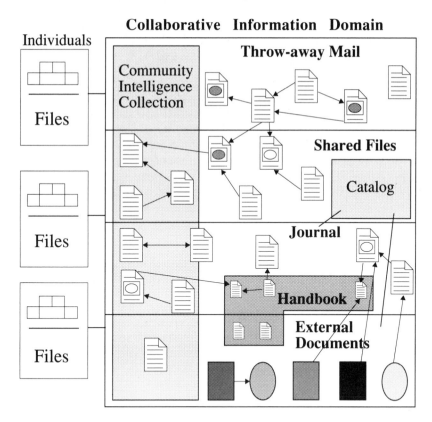

Figure 4. *A document linkage system forms a critical focus for the community; it adds more and more power to how individuals in a community can collaborate.*

The basic unit for this system was a single document. However, as shown in Figure 4, there were four different classes of document:

- *Throw-away Mail included those files that were not of long-term value. These files stayed within the system, to be linked to other files; this added value to throw-away mail, making it relevant explicitly to other elements in the shared domain.*

- *Shared Files were the typical units in the document linkage system. They were contributed by many individuals, and were linked more and more extensively with each use, acting often as references to new documents.*

- *The Journal included the set of online "published works" of the community. Individuals would commit themselves to write these documents, and they would deliberately make them available to everyone for reading and for comment (much as one does when one publishes an article in a print publication). Since documents in the Journal could refer to other relevant documents directly, readers could quickly obtain the context for considering new presentations. This provided for very rapid and condensed recorded dialog on these new idea presentations.*

- *A fourth primary element in the Collaborative Information Domain was labeled External Documents. These were documents not in electronic form—books on individuals' desks, articles in the library, and so forth—that were referred to in other files.*

There was a Catalog in this system, in addition to these four other elements. This Catalog gave users access to the External Documents. It also provided easy access to files in the Journal.

- *Two other elements in this document system are worthy of note: The Community Intelligence Collection was the group of documents (some in each of the four basic categories) that dealt with ongoing activities outside the community. Provided by the community for general information, this community-specific view of relevant outside activities was judged critical for the survival and adaptation of the community in the outside world.*

- *The Handbook described the status of the community at any time. It was produced by individuals charged with the task of deliberately sifting through the activities of the community, evaluating and integrating these activities for general consideration.*

This general framework for collaborative exchange provided an excellent setting for watching the activities of the community in Doug's lab, and it provided an efficient mechanism for information exchange.

"After that, a big part of that framework got to be what kind of strategic approach one would use if one were pursuing something that offered a revolutionary change. This thing looked to me like the biggest revolution you had ever seen for humanity, in the sense of people being able to connect their brain machinery to the world's problems. And it was going to go on for many, many decades. Even the resources of everybody in here with all the money you could get will be just a drop in the bucket." (Engelbart 1987)

Unfortunately, there are few, if any, organizations currently set up for this kind of analysis. The call for the development of a new methodology for considering human exchanges of information in groups, as well as for establishing centers for the systematic investigation of these exchanges, is very relevant today.

An Augmentation Framework: Strategies

Doug has again and again raised the issue of considering the possibility of a maximally augmented organization. This issue involves a consideration of just what capabilities might be involved in a fully augmented system. It also raises the issue of how this full augmentation might be established. Doug's position is that the process will be evolutionary, that activities that both enhance the current status of augmentation and assist in self-consciously bootstrapping on each incremental gain should be pursued immediately. The use of small groups, particularly in facilitation roles, becomes critical, in his analysis:

First, just where are we now in terms of maximum augmentation? How can we get to the maximum? What are the approaches and strategies that will work?

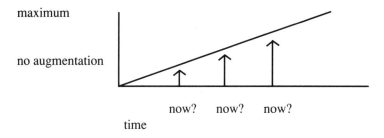

Evolution is the only viable strategy; we must get the evolutionary process going, directing it at "climbing the hill."

During any period of time, there is a limited set of resources that can be applied to directly exploring the "ascent." Various targeted outcomes/goals that have several dimensions of value can be expected. In simple terms, there are two ways to assess the value of an outcome, and hence to determine a strategy:

(1) How much would the outcome boost our capability in some specified "in-line work"? For example, how might one use available resources to boost the ability of people to do their work?

(2) How much will the outcome boost the capability to "climb the hill"? In other terms, what bootstrapping and evolutionary support are provided by a particular outcome?

Doug then suggests immediate actions, as well as long-term planning to enhance future activities, combining both of these classes of value. And, he provides some specific ideas for

leveraging resources effectively for both classes of outcome:

What are the practical strategies that will allow our society to pursue high-performance augmentation?

My strategy is to begin the "pursuit" with small groups. Small groups are preferable to large groups because of shorter evolutionary cycles, more economical scale of experiments, and more "cultural mobility." Small groups are preferable to individuals because exploring high-performance, augmented collaboration is at the center of opportunity.

These small groups would be the "scouting parties" sent ahead to map the pathways for the organizational groups to follow. I have come to call these exploratory groups "high-performance teams."

One early candidate for these teams' role would be to support working conferences; this would provide a very valuable service and match well with early augmentation possibilities. The approach would provide exploration projects of limited duration, and its cyclic nature would allow for debriefing and system updates. Since there would be a new set of participants for each cycle with this approach, more (key) people would gain new perceptions of what high-performance augmentation can bring to their organizations.

Another closely related role for a high-performance support team would be as an "integrator" for a large project within a special-interest community. In this role, the team would support dialog, analyze the contributions, integrate them into a Handbook (see Figure 4), and generate special "portrayals" (presentations or documents).

Figure 5 suggests a framework in which facilitation teams can provide training and coaching to a community (in the context of the document system shown in Figure 4). This group can enhance and make explicit the activities of the community, relating these to the document linkage system of this community. In addition, this group can add value by enabling records to be sorted in standardized formats for later easy access and analysis, principally in the Handbook.

This facilitation allows for the effective evolution of the community. This organizational evolution can affect outcomes positively, as well as influence other organizational units positively. It is therefore an excellent focus for the immediate investment of tools, according to Doug's analyses.

This notion of investment becomes key as one tries to make these issues "realities." Specifically, Doug calls for well-supported "outposts" that can try out some of these notions and then send back "lessons learned" systematically to new organizational candidates:

You need high-performance teams. You also need "outposts" for these teams.

There are some teams currently scattered about by accident, but they typically are not carrying out the systematic exploration that is needed "out there"; we need a plan for putting

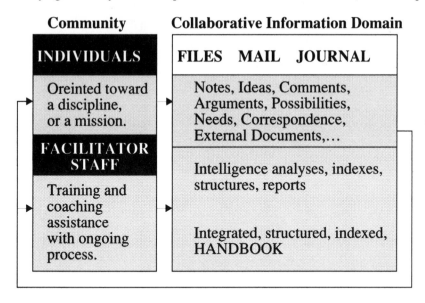

Figure 5. *Facilitation teams provide training and coaching to the community. In addition, they enhance and make explicit the activities of the community, relating these to the document linkage system of this community. This group can also add value by enabling records to be sorted in standardized formats for later easy access and analysis, principally in the Handbook.*

the teams out, and we need a large number of teams.

The first expenditures should be toward the development of outposts. The initial task would be to determine what people would do at these outposts. Another central task would be to determine just who would employ these teams.

The question of who should employ these "experiments" has been a real show stopper for the past few decades, particularly in the U.S. technology business and research environments, in which most of the serious considerations of augmentation systems take place. Doug has weathered this situation for years. His optimism prevails. He has the plan; he just needs to find a way to fund a few outposts and a few teams to get on with the evolution:

"Lots of what we've done since 1968 has to do with the evolution of these things, and especially large organizations all over the place, where the architecture of computer systems has to provide for the concurrent evolution for lots of users—their peripheral hardware, their skills, their methods....

"So it's an absolute thrill to see some of this stuff move like this. It's sort of like being able to come back out of some kind of funny exile and just say—I don't know—'Can I still talk with people about this?' [Laughter and applause from audience]

"There's just an overwhelming amount to do, and we're just getting started. And it's going to be, I think, just the most exciting intellectual thing that anybody's ever been able to participate in historically. The early emergence of language itself was very, very exciting, but it took a long, long time. But here things are just going to catapult." (Engelbart 1987)

Welcome aboard, everyone!

BIBLIOGRAPHY

Engelbart, D.C., "A Conceptual Framework for the Augmentation of Man's Intellect," in Vistas in Information Handling, Howerton and Weeks (Editors), Spartan Books, Washington, D.C., 1963, pp. 1–29.

Engelbart, D.C., "Coordinated Information Services for a Discipline—or Mission-Oriented Community," Proceedings of the Second Annual Computer Communications Conference in San Jose, California, Jan. 24, 1972—also, Published in "Computer Communication Networks," R.L. Grimsdale and F.F. Kuo editors, Noordhoff, Leyden, 1975. (AUGMENT, 12445,)

Engelbart, D.C., "Evolving the Organization of the Future: A Point of the Stanford International Symposium on Office Automation, March 23–25, 1980, edited by Robert Landau, James Bair, Jeannie Siegman, Ablex Publications Corporation, Norwood, N.J. (AUGMENT, 80360,)

Engelbart, D.C. "Collaboration Support Provisions in AUGMENT," Proceedings of the AFIPS Office Automation Conference, Los Angeles, California, February 20–22, pp. 51–58. (OAD, 2221,)

Engelbart, D.C., "Toward High-Performance Knowledge Workers," Proceedings of the AFIPS Office Automation Conference, San Francisco, California, April 5–7, 1982, pp. 279–290. (AUGMENT, 81010,)

Engelbart, D.C., "Authorship Provisions in AUGMENT," Proceedings of the 1984 COMPCON Conference, San Francisco, California, February 27–March 1, pp. 465–472. (DAD, 2250,)

Engelbart, D.C., "Workstation History and the Augmented Knowledge Workshop," Conference Proceedings of the ACM Conference on the History of Personal Workstations, Palo Alto, California, January 9–10, 1986, pp. 73–83. (AUGMENT, 101931,)

Engelbart, D.C. Speech presented to "Hackers' Conference," October 1987

Engelbart, D.C. Presentation to the Fall Joint Computer Conference, San Francisco, 1968

Issues in Designing a Hypermedia Document System

The Intermedia Case Study

Nicole Yankelovich, Karen E. Smith, L. Nancy Garrett, and Norman Meyrowitz

NORMAN MEYROWITZ

Norman Meyrowitz, manager of IRIS's Scholar's Workstation Group, graduated from Brown University in 1981 with a degree in computer science. His major research interests are in the areas of text-processing, user-interface design, and object-oriented programming. He was the senior author, with Andries van Dam, of the most up-to-date and widely referenced article on computer-based text editing, "Interactive Editing Systems." Under a contract with IBM, Meyrowitz has completed research in integrated page-makeup systems and object-oriented programming under Smalltalk-80. He has authored over a dozen technical publications and several major IRIS proposals, including one in 1984 to the Annenberg/CPB Project, which granted $1.5 million to IRIS's Educational Software Project. In 1980, Meyrowitz designed one of the first window systems based on UNIX®.

At IRIS, Meyrowitz manages a group of 12 charged with the design and development of end-user software, and provides technical management for the Intermedia, Educational Software, and Signifier Projects. He also serves as Brown's technical liaison with Apple Computer, Inc. and several other vendors.

ABSTRACT

A hypermedia document system provides a set of tools that allow authors to share a network of linked documents, link their own and others' documents together, leave notes for one another, and retrieve information stored in documents of different types. This paper describes the Intermedia system developed at Brown University's Institute for Research in Information and Scholarship and then uses Intermedia as a case study to explore a number of key issues that software designers must consider in the development of hypermedia document systems. The major issues we address include a variety of design options for linking together multimedia documents, the contexts in which those links exist, and the need for visual representations of the links that exist within a given context.

INTRODUCTION

Annotating existing work and forging links between writings has long been an important undertaking of knowledge workers. Today, computer-based *hypermedia* systems model traditional handwritten margin notes, annotations in illuminated manuscripts, and conventional "see also" references in encyclopedias [Enge68, Meyr85, Nels81, and Yank85]. Such systems provide an electronic equivalent of the cooperative processes of knowledge workers by allowing authors to create, annotate, and link together information from a variety of media such as text, graphics, timelines, video, audio, and spreadsheets.

Hypermedia systems differ from the traditional methods in several important ways. Where the traditional methods imply sequential access, hypermedia systems aim to allow multiple authors to add commentary to the same corpus at the same time. And where the traditional methods are limited to paper media, hypermedia systems are free to exploit the worlds of electronic information access. Where the traditional methods are associated with static textual documents and manually created indexes, hypermedia systems are able to present visualizations of a complex, changing, dynamic world.

The design and implementation of a system with such potential power, flexibility, and a wide-ranging audience encompass many degrees of freedom. For a given audience, what is the best way to organize links? What is the best way to symbolize links? What is the best way to present visual renderings of the entire network of links?

This paper catalogs many issues associated with building a hypermedia system. It draws on our experience in designing and building *Intermedia*, a framework for a collection of tools that allow authors to link together the contents of text, timeline, graphics, three-D models and video documents over a network of high-powered workstations [Meyr85, Meyr86, Garr86, Yank88]. First we describe Intermedia. Next, to present the basic problem domain, we discuss issues involved in the most elementary hypermedia system, one in which a single user is able to link together read-only documents. We then explore many of the same issues as they are complicated by the ability to edit documents, and examine these issues in a multiple-user environment. We then explain the uses of Intermedia, and finish by discussing some of the problems associated with hypermedia systems.

DESCRIPTION OF INTERMEDIA

2.1. Hypertext and Hypermedia

In the early 1960s, Theodor Nelson coined the word *hypertext* to describe the idea of nonsequential writing. A hypertext system is one that allows authors or groups of authors to *link* information together, create *paths* through a corpus of related material, *annotate* existing texts, and create notes that point readers to either bibliographic data or the body of the referenced text. With a computer-based hypertext system, students and researchers are not obliged to search through library stacks to look up referenced books and articles; they can quickly follow trails of footnotes without losing their original context. Explicit connections—links—allow readers to travel from one document to another, automating what one does when following references in an encyclopedia. In addition, hypertext systems that support multiple users allow researchers, professors, and students to communicate and collaborate with one another within the context of a body of scholarly material. For a survey of early hypertext systems refer to Yankelovich 1985.

Hypermedia is simply an extension of hypertext that incorporates other media in addition to text. With a hypermedia system, authors can create a linked corpus of material that includes text, static graphics, animated graphics, video, sound, music, and so forth. Examples and descriptions of existing hypermedia systems can be found in Backer 1982, Bender 1984, Feiner 1982, Halasz 1987, and Weyer 1985.

2.2. Architecture

Intermedia is both an author's tool and a reader's tool. The system, in fact, makes no distinction between types of users providing they have appropriate access rights to the material they wish to edit, explore, or annotate. Creating new materials, making links and following links, are all integrated into a single, modeless environment.

The Intermedia system is built on top of the 4.2 BSD UNIX operating system and runs on IBM RT/PC and Sun workstations that support Sun's Network File System (NFS). To create Intermedia, the software-development team adapted an object-oriented preprocessor to the C programming language licensed to Brown University by Bolt, Beranek, and Newman as well as Apple's MacApp facility for creating generic Macintosh applications [Tesl85] and Cadmus's CadMac tool box, both under special agreement with Apple Computer, Inc. With an object-oriented development environment and a UNIX-based implementation of the Macintosh Toolbox, the Intermedia programmers constructed a system that began with a conceptual application framework similar to the Apple Lisa [Appl83] or the XEROX Star [Xero82] environments, to which they added full hypermedia capabilities. For a more detailed description of the underlying Intermedia architecture, refer to Meyrowitz 1986.

2.3. The Applications

Five applications currently exist within the Intermedia framework: a text editor (*InterText*), a graphics editor (*InterDraw*), a scanned-image viewer (*InterPix*), a three-dimensional object viewer (*InterSpect*), and a timeline editor (*InterVal*). Any number of documents of different types may be open on the desktop at one time, along with the folders containing the documents. These applications conform as closely as possible to the Macintosh interface standards detailed in Apple 1985. Both programmer-level tools and well-defined user interface concepts contribute to the high degree of consistency exhibited across all Intermedia applications.

The InterText word-processing application is similar to Apple's MacWrite [Appl84a], but with *style sheets* for formatting text rather than MacWrite-style rulers. Using style sheets, the user can define a set of styles for a particular document (for example, paragraph, title, subtitle, indented quote, numbered point) and apply those styles to any unit of text between two carriage returns, called an *entity*. When the user edits the definition of a style, all the entities to which that style is applied reformat accordingly.

With InterDraw, a structured graphics editor similar to Apple's MacDraw [Appl84b], users can create two-dimensional illustrations by selecting tools from a palette attached to each InterDraw window.

InterPix is a utility program that displays bitmap images entered into the system using a digitizing scanner. These images can be cropped, copied, and pasted into InterDraw documents. The InterPix application is being extended to provide full bitmap editing capabilities.

Like InterPix, InterSpect is a viewer rather than an editor. It converts files containing three-dimensional data points into three-dimensional representations of that data. Users can manipulate the three-dimensional image by rotating it, zooming in or out, or hiding parts of the model.

The fifth application, InterVal, provides interactive editing features for creating chronological timelines. As the user enters pairs of dates and labels, the application formats them on a vertical timeline according to user-defined styles. As with a charting package, the display of the data is determined by a certain set of parameters that the user can modify.

2.4. Hypermedia Functionality

The hypermedia functionality of the Intermedia system is integrated into each application so that the actions of creating and traversing links may be interspersed with the actions of creating and editing documents.

The act of making links between Intermedia documents has been modeled as closely as possible on the Smalltalk/Macintosh *copy/paste paradigm* [Appl85, Gold84] in an effort to fit the link-making process into a conceptual model already familiar to users. If links are to be made frequently, they must be a seamless part of the user interface. The smooth integration of this new function into an already ingrained user interface model is apparent in the sample session later in this section.

Unlike some other hypertext or hypermedia systems that allow links to be made only to entire documents [Know86, Shne87], Intermedia allows users to create links from a specific location in one document to a specific location in another document. These "anchor points" in the documents are called *blocks*. In designing the Intermedia linking functionality, one of the development team's design goals was to allow anything that could be selected to be made into an anchor for a link. The size of a block, therefore, may range from an entire document to an insertion point, depending on the selection region a user identifies as the block's extent. For example, in an InterText document, a block might consist of an insertion point, a single character, a word, a sentence, two paragraphs, and so forth. Small marker icons are placed near the source and destination blocks to indicate the existence of a link.

To help manage a large corpus of linked documents, links and blocks are assigned a set of descriptive *properties*. Some of these, like user name and creation time, are assigned automatically, while other properties are user-defined. Users access and edit link and block property information through *property sheet dialogs*. A dialog contains a field in which the user enters a one-line *explainer*, similar to the subject field in some electronic-mail programs. Link explainers are particularly important from a reader's perspective. If a single block has more than one link emanating from it, users choose the path they wish to follow from a list of link explainers presented in a dialog box.

Property sheets also contain fields for adding keywords. Although still under development, these keywords, along with the default information assigned to links and blocks, will provide users with a mechanism for searching the document corpus. The result of a keyword search will be a list of explainers associated with all the blocks or links meeting the search criteria. Each item in the list will automatically be linked to its corresponding block, or, in the case of links, to the corresponding source block of each link. For example, a student would be able to search for all the links created by a particular professor after a certain date that contain the keywords "Browning" and "Dramatic Monologue."

Some users may want to enter both block and link properties during the link-creation process, while others may not want to take the time to fill them in at all. Property sheets are *not* automatically presented to the user by default. Intermedia provides a *Viewing Specifications* dialog as a utility for setting user preferences. To change the default behavior, users alter settings in the Viewing Specifications dialog, turning link and/or block creation to "verbose." With the verbose setting, the property dialogs are presented to the user immediately upon completion of the block or link creation. If users have created links with the "fast" rather than the "verbose" setting, they can still edit block and link properties after a link has been established, by selecting a marker icon and choosing the "Link Properties" or "Block Properties" command from the menu.

Link and block properties help to manage complexity within the Intermedia environment, but the notion of *context* is even more crucial. In some systems, links are global; all links are available at all times to all users. In such systems, links become an integral part of the documents. In Intermedia, block and link information is not stored within individual documents, but rather is superimposed on them. *Webs* are provided to maintain the block and link information, allowing users to work within their own context undistracted by documents, blocks, and links created by others sharing the same computing resources. In the future, webs will also serve as the focus for filtering operations. Opening a web causes a particular set of blocks and links to be imposed on a set of documents for as long as the web is open. Thus, webs allow different users to impose their own links *on the same document set*. For example, an academic department might purchase all of Shakespeare's works in electronic format. Rather than duplicate every work each faculty member wants to link to, Intermedia's webs allow multiple users to create their own links to the same documents, without having to see each other's links. Although only one context may be viewed at a time, users can easily switch contexts by closing one web and opening another. Of course, if users *do* want to work together, any number may share a single web.

In addition to webs, Intermedia also has a system of user access rights that helps to manage multiple users sharing large bodies of connected material. Due to the hypermedia functionality of Intermedia, the access-right scheme is slightly more complex than that of other UNIX environments where users may have either *read permission* or *write permission* to files and directories. Intermedia adds *annotation permission* to the other two forms of access rights. This allows students to add links to a document that they are not allowed to edit.

2.5. Common User-Interface Concepts

Several user-interface concepts stressed throughout Intermedia enable users to learn new applications quickly and predict the behavior of features they have never used before. Like copy and paste operations in the Macintosh and Smalltalk programs, some operations in the Intermedia system behave identically across all applications. The linking functionality is a prime example. Users can specify a selection region in any document, choose the "Start Link" command from the menu, define another selection region in any other document, regardless of type, and choose one of several "complete link" commands. Likewise, to follow a link, a user exploring a web can select a marker icon in any type of document, and choose the "Follow" command from a menu. As a shortcut, a user can double-click on a marker icon to initiate the Follow, just as he or she might double-click on an icon in a folder to open a document. Since following a link usually entails opening a document, we anticipated that users would *expect* to be able to follow a link by double-clicking on the marker icon. In a system that encourages rapid transitions between applications, it is essential to limit the amount a browser must learn in order to be a successful user of the system, in part by capitalizing on those conventions with which he or she may already be familiar.

Other features in the system, while not exactly identical to one another, are conceptually similar. Most applications, for instance, allow users to control the format or the display characteristics of data. The interface techniques for conceptually similar operations have been designed to capitalize on the similarities. One such example is the *style paradigm* [Inte86, Smit82]. Styles are sets of properties or characteristics that govern the appearance of data within a document. Users can define or modify a style by filling out or editing a "form" called a *style sheet* (sometimes referred to as a *property sheet*). Both the InterText application and the InterVal application contain style sheets that can be used to specify different text formats such as paragraphs, indented quotes, lists, and titles, or different timeline formats such as position of dates relative to tick marks and position of labels relative to dates. In the graphics editor, different styles may be applied to shapes such as line width, pen style, or fill style. Although not yet implemented, InterDraw will also allow users to "borrow" the style of one shape and "apply" it to any others. This means that the combination of line width, pen style, and fill style can be defined once and then applied as a unit to any existing objects or to any new objects. The concept of styles will also be included in the InterSpect three-dimensional viewer in the future. In this case, users will be able to define a set of viewing parameters that specify a particular camera position. Just as styles in the text editor do not alter the content, but simply the presentation, of the text, styles in InterSpect will be used to define the manner in which the data is viewed. By storing all presentation parameters in style sheets, it is possible to substitute styles with the same name but different parameters for all types of data in the system.

Related to the use of styles is the frequent use of *palettes* —sets of controls attached to a document window. Along with style-sheet dialogs, palettes provide a means for defining and applying styles. In InterText, for example, all the styles defined for a particular document are stored in a style palette. Two mouse clicks are all that is necessary either to change the style of an existing text entity or to change from one style to another before beginning a new entity. With a large screen and the ability to have a large number of windows open at one time, it is essential that all the tools needed for common operations be close at hand rather than in the menus. When they are not needed, however, all palettes can be hidden from view to unclutter the screen and to improve the manner in which material is presented to a person browsing through the system.

Another example of a standard user interface concept that permeates the system and is made possible in a workstation environment with virtual memory capabilities is the use of "infinite" *undo* and *redo* commands. Instead of being able to retract only the last action performed, the user is able to incrementally undo the effects of all actions performed since the last time a document was saved. Any single action or set of actions that the user has undone may then be incrementally redone. There are no content-modification actions in any Intermedia applications that cannot be undone. This fosters a sense of security in users, permitting them to experiment freely with their document with the knowledge that they can return it to its former state at any time.

To aid programmers in incorporating the standard features mentioned above (such as "undo" and "redo") consistently throughout all Intermedia applications, the software-development team first extended Apple's object-oriented application framework, MacApp, and then implemented two general-purpose, programmer-level *building blocks* within the extended framework. The building blocks, one for text and one for graphics, allow programmers to reuse text and graphics objects either "as is" or in slightly modified forms, cutting down on duplication of programming effort as well as enforcing consistent user-interface techniques. With only MacApp and the building blocks, programmers would be able to implement applications that conform to the Macintosh user-interface standards; however, the requirements for the Intermedia system include a uniform method of linking together the contents of documents created with any application within the system. To meet this requirement, the development team extended MacApp to include a set of features necessary for supporting linking functionality. In this way, applications not only inherit window, menu, mouse, and other generic application functionality from MacApp, but also inherit linking functionality from the MacApp extensions, and text and graphic editing functionality from the building blocks.

2.6. Sample Session

To illustrate the user interface features and the linking functionality discussed above, this section of the paper takes the reader on a tour of the system. The tour is designed to simulate the interaction that takes place during a hands-on Intermedia session. The figures should aid in visualizing the system, while the text supplies the action.

Figure 1 shows the Intermedia desktop. Initially, the display includes a window manager, a graphical folder system, a menu bar, and a mouse interface. The contents of the folders reflect the underlying hierarchical UNIX directory structure.

Unlike the Macintosh, Intermedia does not store application icons in the same folders with documents; instead, they are stored with several other special-purpose tools in an application, or *New*, window. The reason for this is twofold. First, users do not have to search through folders to find the applications. Even if overlapping windows hide the New window, selecting the **New** command from the **File** menu reveals the window again. Second, in a networked environment, it is easier to store a single set of applications in an agreed-upon place so that a system administrator can easily maintain and update.

The contents of the active folder in Figure 1 include a web icon, an InterDraw document icon, and a set of folders containing material from the corpus of material called *Context 32: A Web of English Literature* [Land87]. These materials were created for the course English 32: A Survey of English Literature from 1700-Present.

Before opening documents and following or creating links, we must define a context by opening an existing web or by creating a new one. If a web is not open, we can still open

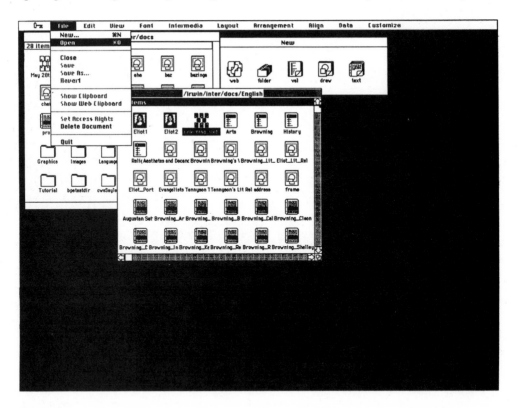

Figure 1.

and edit the documents; however, no link and block information will be visible. Rather than begin a new web, we select the icon titled "Context32" and choose the **Open** command from the **File** menu.

When the web opens, Intermedia displays a *local map* view, as is shown in Figure 2. Local maps are used to *track* the user's progress through the corpus, displaying the active document and the links that emanate from it. When the user activates a different document, either by following a link or by opening one from a folder, the local map updates to display the new current document and its direct predecessor and successor links.

In Figure 2, the local map shows the InterDraw document Browning OV in the center. After opening the web, we returned to the folder containing the web icon, opened the folder called Brownings, and then opened the overview document containing an image of Robert Browning.

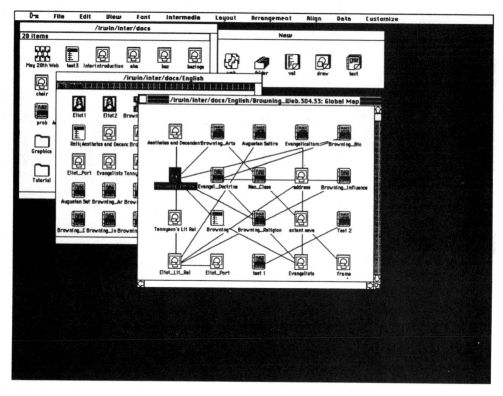

Figure 2.

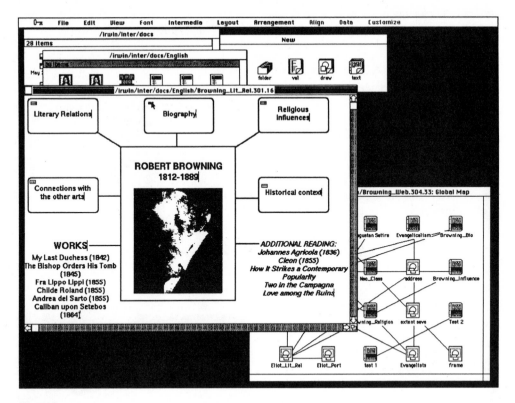

Figure 3.

Notice that several of the boxes in the overview diagram contain *marker icons*—tiny arrows enclosed in boxes. These markers indicate the links that exist. To follow a link in the display, we first select the marker above the text "Biography" by clicking once on it.

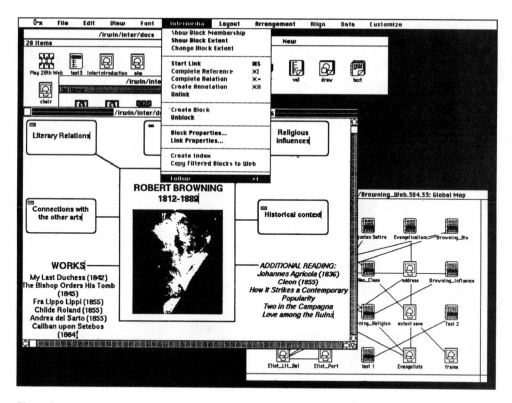

Figure 4.

After selecting a marker icon, we pull down the **Intermedia** menu and select the **Follow** command, as shown in Figure 4.

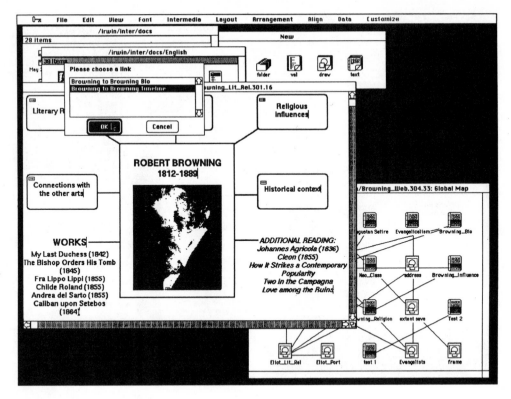

Figure 5.

The dialog box that appears above immediately tells us that two links emanate from the marker we selected. One leads to a biography of Browning (Browning Bio) and the other to a timeline (Browning Timeline). Both titles are displayed in a links list box. We select the second link explainer in the dialog box and click on the **OK** button to confirm our selection.

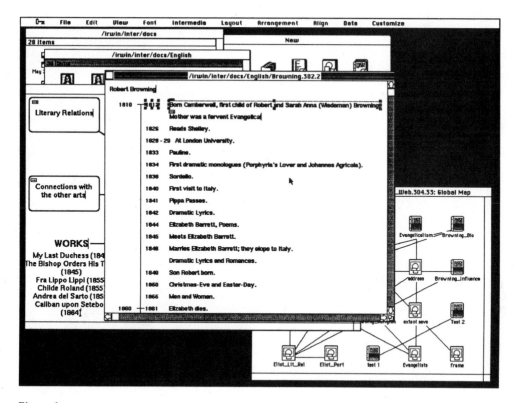

Figure 6.

The traversal of the link is now complete and the timeline document, which lists important events in Browning's life, appears in the right bottom quadrant of the window, as shown in Figure 6. The events in Browning's timeline are clustered in 50-year intervals, each of which fits neatly into the timeline window. In other words, all events between 1810 and 1859 are clustered under the tickmark by 1810, and all the events between 1860 and 1919 are clustered under the tickmark by 1860.

Notice that Intermedia marked the extent of the block at the other end of the link. The system does this when a link is traversed to indicate a particular scope of information to the reader. In this case, our attention is drawn to the first event in the timeline.

We can now opt to recluster the timeline, but instead, we notice another marker icon above the second event on the timeline and decide to follow the link. We do so by double-clicking on the marker.

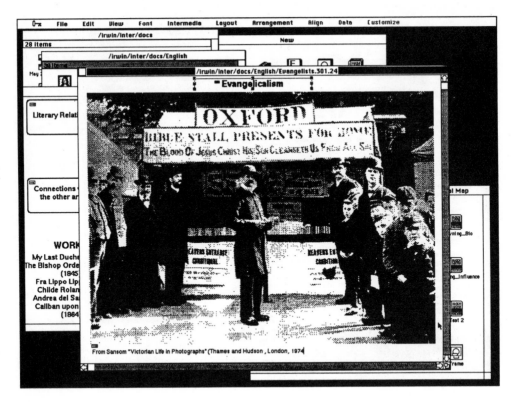

Figure 7.

Another InterDraw document opens—Evangelists, as shown in Figure 7. Notice that no dialog box appears this time. When we select a marker icon from which only one link emanates, the document at the other end of the link opens immediately, because no alternative paths are available.

Like the portrait of Browning in Figure 3, the illustration in Figure 7 was entered into the system using a scanner. The bitmap was then displayed by the InterPix application and was cropped and pasted into this InterDraw document. After looking at the picture, we decide to close the document by clicking in the *close box* located in the window's upper left corner. Next we close the InterVal timeline in the same manner.

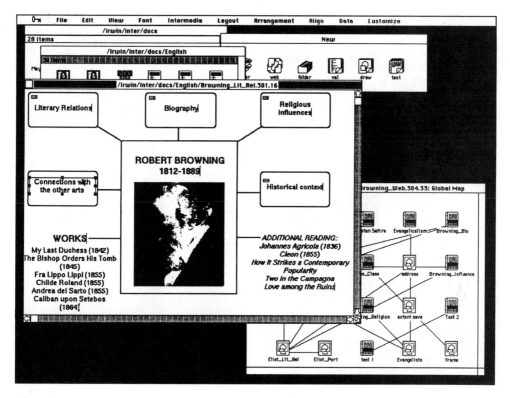

Figure 8.

This returns us to the original Browning overview diagram. After our brief exploration, we decide to fill in the diagram by creating a new link. The first step for creating a link involves defining a block to serve as the *anchor* for the link. We select the text "Connection with the other arts" as the link's source block (see Figure 8) and then choose **Start Link** from the **Intermedia** menu (as shown in Figure 9). While a link is pending, we may perform any number of other actions unrelated to link-making. As with the Copy operation common to all Macintosh-like applications, the Start Link operation is completely modeless.

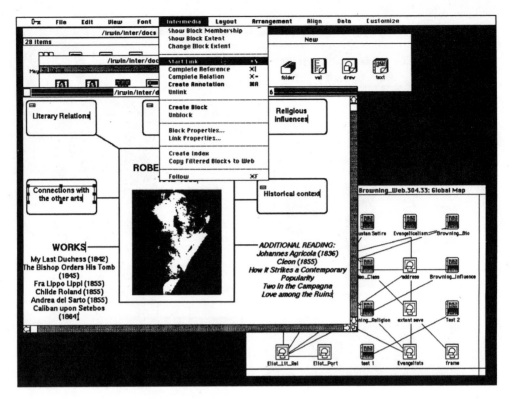

Figure 9.

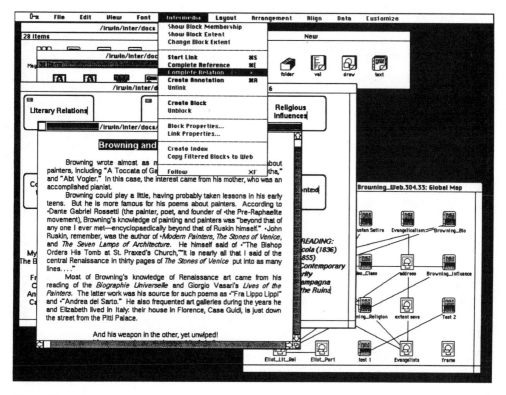

Figure 10.

Before completing the pending link, we return to the folder (not pictured) and open an InterText document called RB Arts. Once the text is displayed, we select the heading of the document as the destination block of the link, as shown in Figure 10. To complete the link, we choose **Complete Relation** from the **Intermedia** menu. You will notice two complete commands on the menu. Their functions are similar, but each creates a different type of link. The **Complete Relation** command, which we chose, indicates a *primary path;* the **Complete Reference** command signifies that the information contained in the source block is of more importance than the information contained in the destination block.

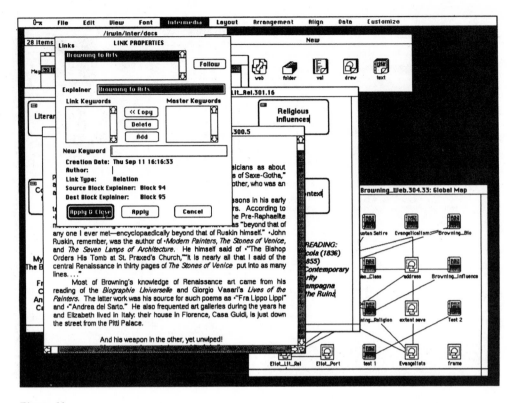

Figure 11.

After we choose the complete command, a Link Property dialog box appears, in which we can type descriptive information about the link we're creating. We replace the default text, "Link 35," with the more meaningful explainer shown in Figure 11. (Before this session, we changed the default setting for link creation in the Viewing Specifications dialog box so that a Link properties dialog box would automatically be opened each time we create a link.)

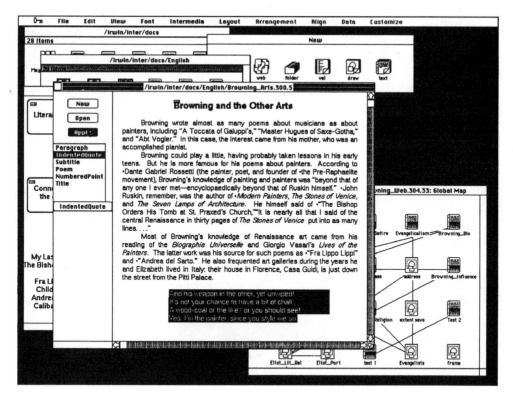

Figure 12.

Once a link is established, markers indicate both ends of it. In some applications, these markers are enclosed in boxes for better visibility, but the markers themselves are identical in all applications. We'll make another link, but before doing this, we add a quotation to the InterText document. After typing the text of the quotation, we select the text, display the *style palette* with a menu command, choose the IndentedQuote style from the palette located to the left of the text, and click the **Apply** button, also in the palette.

With a simple text selection followed by a palette selection and a button press, we have easily reformatted the text without resorting to the more complex series of steps necessary in other word-processing programs.

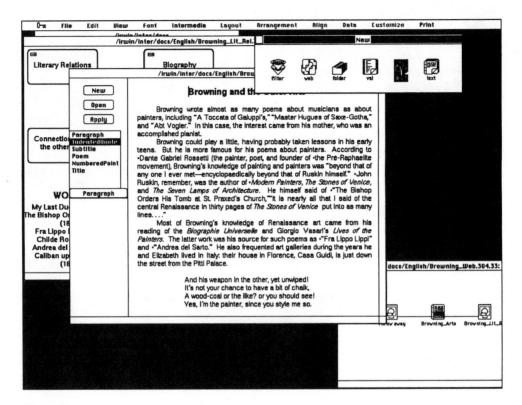

Figure 13.

Now we decide to make an additional link to a new InterDraw document. This link will contain an overview diagram of Renaissance art. The destination block of the previous link is appropriate for the source block of our new link. So we select the existing marker next to the title by clicking on it, and then we choose **Start Link** from the Intermedia menu as we did before. Now, to create a new document, we activate the **New** window and then double-click on the InterDraw application icon (the draw icon shown in Figure 13) to open the application.

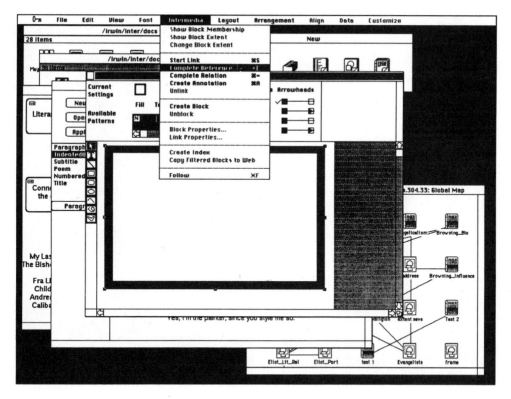

Figure 14.

A new InterDraw document opens. We draw the beginning of the new overview diagram. For the drawing, we use tools from both the tool and style palettes attached to the top of the window. When we finish our drawing, we can hide one or both of the palettes. When a document is saved, InterDraw preserves the size of the window and the state of the palettes along with all editing changes.

Remember that a link is still pending. We select the text "Overview of Renaissance Art" as the destination block of the pending link and then choose **Complete Reference** from the **Intermedia** menu. This time, Intermedia adds a new marker only to the destination block, since the source block is already marked.

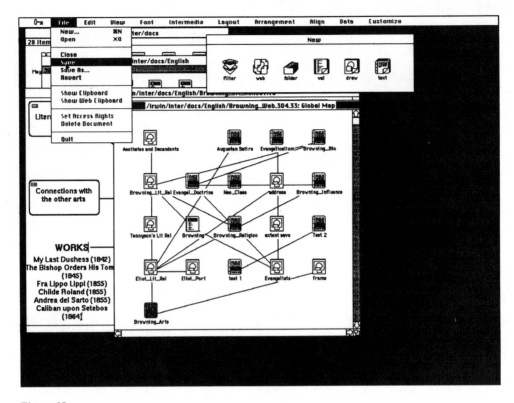

Figure 15.

Before we end our session, we save the new diagram. Notice that the new document icon now is added both to the local map in the right-hand corner of the screen and to the current folder. We select the icon in the folder and choose **Access Rights** from the **File** menu to display the Document Access Rights dialog box shown in Figure 15. Using this dialog box, we change the default access rights settings so that all users can *annotate,* or create links to the diagram. We do not change the remainder of the settings, which allow all users to read the document and the owner and others in the owner's group to edit the document.

The tour through Intermedia illustrates the functionality of only one of several hypermedia systems under development today. We have designed a user interface that we believe creates an easy-to-use but powerful environment for both the reader and the author. Yet that user interface was the result of much enumeration of possibilities, heated discussion, comparison of choices, and consideration of what could be accomplished given today's technology.

The second half of this paper discusses the issues that we and other designers face in determining the hypermedia capabilities of our systems. We begin the discussion by examining what the most elementary read-only hypermedia system might look like and considering which design issues are involved. We then move to a system in which a single user can edit the multimedia corpus. Finally, we explore the issues of multiple users accessing a shared set of documents.

A SYSTEM OF READ-ONLY DOCUMENTS

The simplest hypermedia system is one in which a single user at a stand-alone workstation examines read-only documents and creates and follows links among these documents. This section explores some of the concerns that appear in designing such an environment, including the issues of providing appropriate (1) contexts for webs of links, (2) anchors for individual links, and (3) visual representations of the linked corpora.

3.1. Providing Contexts

When an author links to a destination document that contains links from previous sessions, either all of the links of the destination document can be incorporated into the set of links on which the author is working, or the system can display the destination document as if it has no links at all.

In the first situation, the author would automatically inherit all of the connections anchored in the destination document; all of the links would exist in the same "plane" (Figure 16). By making links, an author would thereby provide bridges to other worlds of links. This bridge is appealing in systems where the fundamental goal is to encourage the maximum interconnectedness of information. This would, however, prevent authors from presenting a limited corpus.

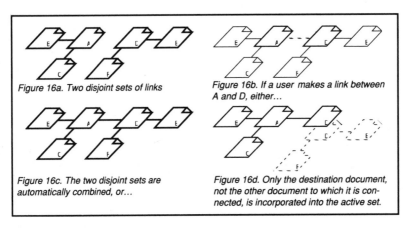

Figure 16a. Two disjoint sets of links

Figure 16b. If a user makes a link between A and D, either...

Figure 16c. The two disjoint sets are automatically combined, or...

Figure 16d. Only the destination document, not the other document to which it is connected, is incorporated into the active set.

Figure 16.

The second option solves this problem by enabling the user to partition links into private worlds, or separate contexts. Such contexts would be useful to a scholar who wants to organize material for a variety of research projects, each of which may reference the same document.

Intermedia designers opted for the second solution with a construct called *webs*. Until the user opens a web, all opened documents appear without any links. To view documents with the links that belong to a particular web, a user opens a web and then opens one or more of its documents. Although other webs may also reference the documents, only the links that were made in the current web are available. As a result the user does not have to sift through the connections of multiple contexts.

3.2.   Linking
3.2.1. The Link Anchors

Textual anchors are currently limited to insertion points and are represented internally by only one pointer. In Intermedia graphics applications, the user specifies an anchor by selecting any number of graphics objects, regardless of their proximity, and issuing the appropriate command. A graphics anchor is represented internally by a list of objects included in the anchor rather than by the start and end points of a sequence.

Anything from entire documents to precise insertion points could serve as anchors for links, depending on the purpose of the system under development. Between these extremes lie other possibilities: a link might be anchored to any number of user-defined text segments or graphics objects or to a single word or graphics object.

The designers may make the decision between these alternatives by balancing implementation and functional concerns. A system that allows a user to link only to entire documents is easier to implement than the other options, but it does not allow the user to reference specific contents. Being able to link to insertion points is an improvement over linking to entire documents, and it involves a manageable increase in implementation complexity. With insertion points, however, references may be ambiguous. Some authors might place the link at the beginning of a reference to signal that what follows is important, while others might place the link at the end, as they are used to doing with conventional footnotes. If text segments or graphics objects could be the link anchor, the author would be able to indicate the reference clearly.

For some purposes, such as a system for indexing or for organizing encyclopedia information, yet another design might be appropriate. Such a system might provide automatic linking so that each link would be characterized by a single keyword on one end and an entire document on the other.

As designed, an Intermedia anchor may typically be any legitimate selection in that application, such as a user-defined sequence of characters or a combination of graphics objects. With this design, a textual anchor could be represented internally as pointers to the start point and end point in the underlying model. However, due to complications caused by providing text editing functionality (see Section 4), and time constraints in implementation, we were not able to implement this design fully in the first version of Intermedia.

3.2.2. Indicating Links

For users to be able to follow links, the system needs to indicate to the users where the links are anchored. The system could indicate the links in a number of ways, including marking the beginning, end, or extent of the anchor. The marking might consist of (1) a single icon at each anchor, where there may be more than one link per anchor; or (2) highlighting the extent of the anchor with font or color changes, outlining, or reverse video. The indication of links could be done automatically by the system or upon the user's request. In deciding how to indicate links, designers must consider the purpose of the system, the desirability of user control, and the potential problems of display clutter and ambiguity.

Icons are an appropriate way to mark links in some systems. Systems that require or allow anchoring links to insertion points would benefit from icons because they provide a tangible link anchor. Furthermore, icons can be designed to convey additional meaning such as whether they are the origin or destination of the link and whether the link leads to text or graphics. For example, imagine Penny Straker creating a hypermedia mail-order catalog of traditional hand-knit sweaters. She wants to link from a picture of a sweater to information on price, ordering, size, yarn, and the history of the sweater. If all of the icons had the same design, the shopper might have to follow each link to find the desired information. If, however, the icons were designed to indicate graphically the various kinds of information, the shopper would know which to follow (Figure 17).

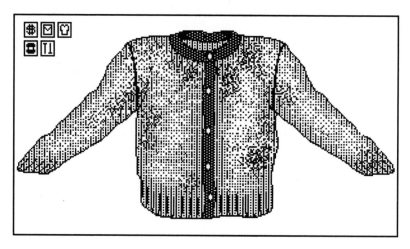

Figure 17.

However, there may be problems with excessive or ambiguous icons. Readers might find the icons intrusive, especially in a document with many links. With one icon per link, many icons might need to be displayed at the same location. For example, an article on Pennsylvania might mention Gettysburg. An author might have linked from Gettysburg to articles on Presidents Lincoln and Eisenhower, a description of the Battle of Gettysburg, and a copy of the Gettysburg Address. Four similar icons would be clustered at the same place, and the user would have no way to tell which one to follow. Even with the different icon design strategy mentioned above, the display could still become cluttered. Another strategy is to allow the user to control whether icons are displayed. The user could turn off the icon display to concentrate on the content of the document and subsequently turn it on to examine linked references. A third possibility is to limit each anchor to one icon, thereby uncluttering the display. However, because information might be lost, the system would need to provide more information about the links that emanate from an anchor. Such additional information might include how many links exist and to what kind of document each one leads.

Icons are sufficient for marking the ends of links when anchors are just insertion points. However, if anchors can themselves have contents, icons alone cannot give complete visual information about the anchor. A supplement to icons is the display of the extent of the anchor. Highlighting could consist of font or color changes, outlining boxes, or reverse video. Not only would such highlighting accurately show the extent of nonoverlapping anchors, but it could also show the individual extents of overlapping anchors (Figure 18).

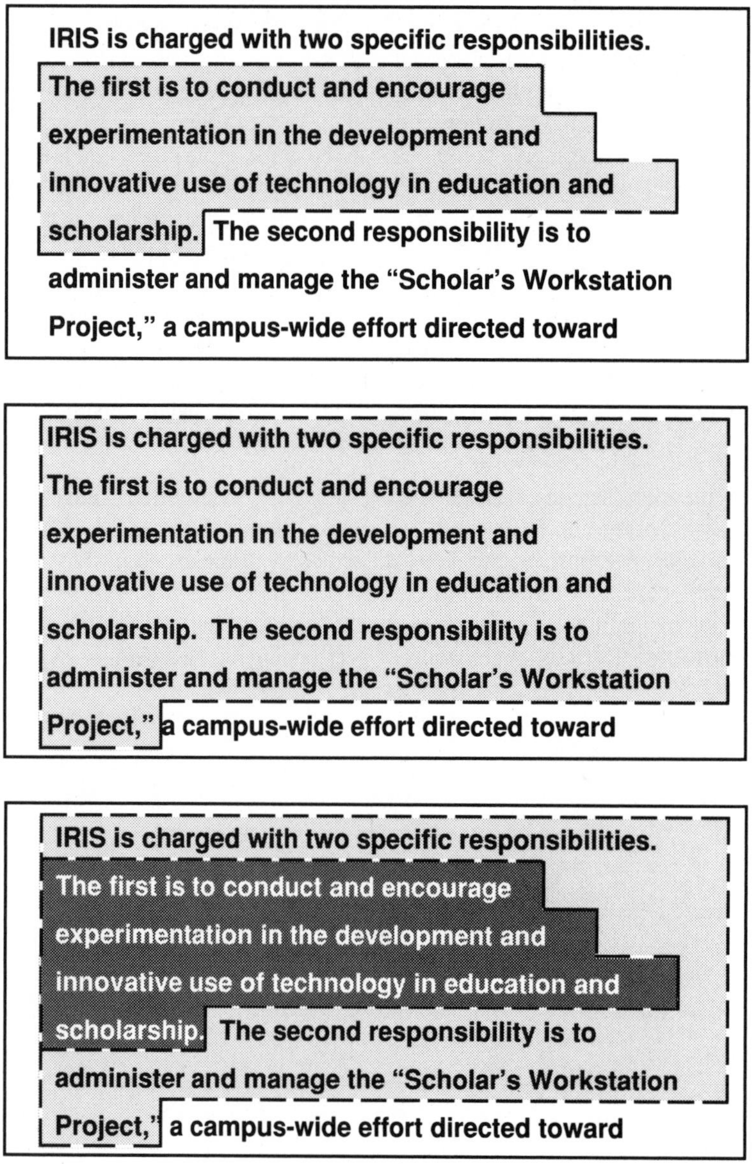

IRIS is charged with two specific responsibilities.
The first is to conduct and encourage
experimentation in the development and
innovative use of technology in education and
scholarship. The second responsibility is to
administer and manage the "Scholar's Workstation
Project," a campus-wide effort directed toward

IRIS is charged with two specific responsibilities.
The first is to conduct and encourage
experimentation in the development and
innovative use of technology in education and
scholarship. The second responsibility is to
administer and manage the "Scholar's Workstation
Project," a campus-wide effort directed toward

IRIS is charged with two specific responsibilities.
The first is to conduct and encourage
experimentation in the development and
innovative use of technology in education and
scholarship. The second responsibility is to
administer and manage the "Scholar's Workstation
Project," a campus-wide effort directed toward

Figure 18.

Although highlighting might provide some improvement over icons, it might still clutter the display. As with icons, the user could control when the anchor highlighting is displayed by toggling the appropriate switch. In addition, the system could provide a context-sensitive cursor that would invoke highlighting only when it moved to a point within an anchor.

Intermedia uses a combination of icons and anchor highlighting to show links and anchors. Each anchor has one icon, regardless of the number of links attached to it. In graphics documents, icons mark the existence of anchors, and highlighting indicates anchor extent. The user may select any number of icons and ask that their extents be highlighted. Currently, text-document anchors are limited to insertion points that are marked by icons. Because each icon may indicate more than one link, when the user selects an icon and gives the "Follow" command for an anchor with more than one link, Intermedia presents a list of the links that are attached to the anchor. The user can then choose which link to follow.

Plans for future versions of Intermedia include allowing the user to control icon display. Text will mirror graphics by allowing the user to attach links to arbitrary selections rather than just to insertion points.

3.2.3. Names, Keywords, and Keyword/Value Pairs

If a document has many links, the user would benefit from having additional information for each link before choosing which one to follow. Imagine a poem with links leading to the poet's biography, to the poem's location on the poet's timeline, to a document that describes the style of the poem, and to a related poem by an earlier poet. All of the links are marked by identical icons. If a reader who wanted to see only related poems had a way to know which links were relevant, choosing and following links would be more efficient.

The system could allow authors to attach titles, keywords, and arbitrary keyword/value pairs to their links. The title would be an arbitrary character string attached by the author. The user might select simple keywords from an available list or might enter each keyword freely without matching against existing keywords. Keyword/value pairs allow more precise, detailed keyword searching; for example, a professor creating material for a poetry course might add a keyword/value pair *meter=iambic* to one link and *meter=dactylic* to another link. The professor could later ask the system to retrieve links only where *meter=iambic*.

For all links, the system might also have common, predetermined keyword/value pairs to which it assigns values automatically. Possible keywords include the kind of document at the other end of the link, the title of that document, and the creation date of the link. Such information not only could provide additional information on all of the links, but could also be available for querying. A sample query might be, "Show all links created after September 1986."

Currently, Intermedia incorporates three of these features: titles, keywords, and system-defined keyword/value pairs. The system fully implements titles by providing a default title that the user can edit. A menu command provides access to the title of any link. The functionality is partially developed for both keywords and automatically attached information. Automatically attached data include the date of creation and author's name (since, in Intermedia, more than one author may have access to the same document). Authors can enter an arbitrary number of keywords for any link. Whereas titles and keywords may be edited, the automatic information is fixed.

The use of keyword/value pairs attached to an anchor or link can vary. The issues essentially can be broken into two areas: (1) definition of the search criteria, and (2) feedback of results.

Defining the search criteria is itself a two-part problem: It involves (1) deciding the extent of queries that will be allowed and the domain on which those queries can operate, and (2) determining the appropriate user interface to generate such queries.

Users must be able to specify the *scope* of the queries that use keywords as a criterion. At its simplest, a search for block or link keywords could be limited to the currently active document. At the other extreme, it could extend to all documents in the system. Alternately, it could be limited to all open documents. Or it could be limited to those documents that reside in the currently opened web. Additionally, the user may be able to specify whether the search domain should include keywords attached only to links, anchors, or both.

Document and web owners might want to apply some permanent constraints to the search scope. For example, the web owner might want to dictate that links with the keyword "confidential" are never to be viewed by anyone except him/herself. In the simplest scenario, a set of global web keywords could be established that would always be added to whatever queries an individual makes. In a more complex system, each user might have his or her own "global" keywords that are added to the web owner's keywords, and an owner might be able to apply permanent keyword constraints to each document. On top of all of these owner constraints, a user would want to add his or her own constraints. For most queries, these would likely be per-session temporary query constraints, but for some, the user would want to have the personal constraints applied automatically each time a web or document was opened.

Discussion of the type of user interface needed to specify queries with appropriate scope and content involves a set of extremely complicated issues. In short, these issues include ease vs. power of query language, temporary vs. permanent queries, and graphical vs. textual specification of scope, among others. Many of these issues are the same as those that have troubled designers of data base management systems for years. To that end we will not delve further into these issues in this forum.

Assuming a system designer can bind upon an interface that allows a user to specify the scope and content of a query, the next issue is how to apply the query, and next, how to present the results back to the user. In particular, the query can be applied for one of two purposes: (1) to *filter* the user's domain of links and blocks, or (2) to *collect* the results that satisfy a particular search criterion.

In a multimedia document system, a *filtering* query would typically result in the removal of block and/or link markers in the documents contained in the query's scope. For instance, the query "Show only the link markers for the links created by 'kes' for all the documents in the current web" would result in the "hiding" of all the markers in all documents, other than those that had been created by the user "kes." In a *collection* query, that same request would result in a list of all link explainers of all links for all documents in the current web that met the criterion. Where a filtering query changes the user's view of the active corpus, a collection query enumerates the results without changing the state of the work.

Hypertext can be used in a clever way to aid the user interface for a collection query. In many data base systems, the result of a collection query is, too often, a list of "hits" quickly typed out on the screen—which must be quickly copied by the user, or, sometimes, captured in a file; users must then manually enter the document name to browse each item discovered. In a current unimplemented Intermedia design, the results of collection queries would themselves be collected in a hypertext document. Each "hit" referencing a block or link would be identified by a text line that includes the document name and block/link explainer. Most important, that line would itself be linked to the block or link destination that was discovered. With this system, a user could simply scroll through the collection list, choose "Follow" for each of the hits that seemed interesting, and travel to exactly the proper place in the corpus, using the same user interface that he or she is familiar with for traversing in the hypermedia.

3.2.4. Enhancing Link Functionality

What kinds of links are appropriate for a particular hypermedia system? An on-line encyclopedia might have only automatically created links from keywords to other articles. There may be no need to have more than one link type. However, in a more general-purpose hypermedia system, users might create links for different purposes. One user might create links only to connect footnotes to their sources, while another user might want to link vocabulary words in a text to their definitions.

With the basic manual link type—a simple tie between two anchors—users can still perform basic linking tasks, such as linking footnotes and dictionary entries. But, by specializing links to do a specific task, the system could make it easier to create certain kinds of links. One such type of link is a *numbered link*. For example, a footnote link type might be represented by a special automatically numbered icon that appeared in the source document.

Automatic links would be generated by the system rather than the user, based upon the contents of the target documents and the algorithms supplied by the user. For instance, a vocabulary link type might automatically link each word in a document to the appropriate location in a dictionary file; each word in the user's files essentially becomes a source anchor while each entry in the dictionary becomes a destination block pointed to by one or more source anchor words.

Additional link types could provide functionality that is not possible with just a simple tie between two anchors. For example, link destination could depend on such factors as the user's level of expertise, the actual content of the source or destination anchors, or whether the user had previously taken the same path. These *conditional* links would be useful in some educational and training situations.

An *action* link, rather than bringing up a new document, could cause a certain operation or computation to be performed each time it was followed. Essentially, the link is attached to an action formula, like that of a spreadsheet cell, that is evaluated on the follow; it can use the content of the source or destination anchors as values if desired. In a more complex system, the formula could allow references to other links/link computations. If parts of the formula could themselves be references to hypermedia commands, each one of these action formulas could be thought of as a potential system macro.

The first implementation of Intermedia does not provide numbered, automatic, conditional, or action links. Future plans include both footnote and automatic dictionary links as described above.

3.3. Visualizing Connectivity

Additional tools could be useful in helping the user understand the information structure of the linked network. One such tool might be a graphic representation, or map, of a web of links.

The scope of such maps is an important consideration. A *global map* could portray the entire linked structure, similar to a highway map of the United States. However, global maps become difficult to display in a way that is helpful to the user—both in systems without partitioned contexts and in systems with partitioned contexts but with a large number of documents. These "flat" representations often become tangles of lines. Three-dimensional global maps could untangle the lines somewhat to clarify the linking structure. However, users might be confused when viewing such a map.

Alternatively, many systems show a global map by picking some document as the root and representing the network of links as a hierarchical tree. If there are cycles in the network, these schemes either duplicate the relevant subnode of the hierarchy (since the maps are typically generated only for what is currently in view, infinite recursion is prevented) or draw lines back to a previously drawn node. In the latter case, a tangle can again result, so many systems have viewing modes that allow users to see the hierarchy both with and without cycles.

In all of these systems, the notion of fish-eye views [Furn86] allows the user to focus in detail on the most important information while seeing, in less detail but in spatial context, much of the information that surrounds the main information.

A subset of a global map could simplify the user's cognitive world model. A *local map* could show those links that emanate from the current document, like an inset of a road map that shows only the roads that lead directly from Providence to other cities. A local map might exist as a static snapshot of the possible links from one anchor or document or as a tracking map that updates itself as the user moves from one document to the next, always keeping the current document as the central focus.

In a system in which links can lead to anchors inside documents, system designers need to determine what level of detail is appropriate to show in a map: a document linked to all of its related anchors or to only its related documents, or an anchor to related anchors or just to related documents. Global and local maps have different potential levels of detail. A global map could show how anchors are linked together or how documents are connected. Furthermore, a global map could provide both levels of detail and illustrate how both anchors and documents are connected (Figure 19). With local maps, there are more possibilities. As with global maps, local maps could show links between anchors, links between documents, or a combination showing both levels of detail; but unlike the global maps, the connections would be shown only from the focus, the current document, or the anchor. In addition, because local maps have a focus, they can show the documents that are linked to or from the current anchor, or the anchors that are linked to or from the current document (Figure 20).

Additional map features could include a label on each link and an indication of the direction of each link. If filtering is implemented, the map could represent a subset of the web as processed through the active filters. The user could control these features, or the system could impose them.

Intermedia provides both global and local maps showing document interconnection. Future versions will provide additional map functionality.

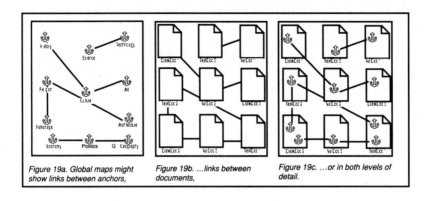

Figure 19a. Global maps might show links between anchors,

Figure 19b. ...links between documents,

Figure 19c. ...or in both levels of detail.

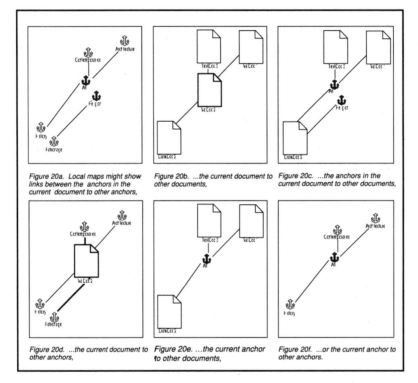

Figure 20a. Local maps might show links between the anchors in the current document to other anchors,

Figure 20b. ...the current document to other documents,

Figure 20c. ...the anchors in the current document to other documents,

Figure 20d. ...the current document to other anchors,

Figure 20e. ...the current anchor to other documents,

Figure 20f. ...or the current anchor to other anchors.

Figures 19 and 20.

A SYSTEM OF READ/WRITE DOCUMENTS

To be effective for cooperative work, a hypermedia system must provide an authoring as well as a browsing capability. Adding this capability to a hypermedia system increases its complexity. Designers need to determine how the system should respond to editing outside of the confines of anchors, changing the contents of an anchor, and deleting anchor contents.

The effects of editing are influenced by the cognitive model of anchors that the designer decides to present to the user. An anchor can be either a list of distinct objects or a boundary that the user specifies at link creation. The former scheme means that the user can clearly define the anchor, but the system has to store more information per anchor. The latter is more efficient as far as storage is concerned, but the potential for ambiguity is greater. Different media might benefit from different schemes for representing anchors. For example, anchors in a text editor are well represented by all of the text falling between two endpoints. In a structured graphics editor, on the other hand, anchors are better represented as a list of graphics objects. Even with a defined cognitive model, the designer must anticipate and resolve conflicts that can occur during normal editing. The remainder of this section discusses the details of these concerns.

4.1. Editing Content Within Anchors

With a pure boundary scheme, a text editor would represent an anchor made from the string "green eggs and ham" as all of the characters between the "g" in "green" and the "m" in "ham," regardless of what might be changed between these two endpoints. When the user inserts the word "fried," the phrase would read "green fried eggs and ham," and the anchor would now reference the entire phrase. Therefore, by editing, the user could change the anchor contents. In many cases such simultaneous changes of document content and anchor content would be appropriate.

However, the integrity of a link could be at stake if the change is at the boundary of the anchor or if there are substantial changes to the anchor contents. If the user links "eggs and ham" to a recipe, then later inserts "green," so that the phrase now reads "green eggs and ham," the link may no longer be appropriate. Similarly, if the user links "I do not like green eggs and ham" to a biography of Dr. Seuss and then substitutes "scrambled" for "green," the link might not be valid. Instead of automatically updating the link anchor to include the editing changes, the system could eliminate the link on the assumption that any changes to the anchor would invalidate the link. A more flexible system could alert the user to changes to an anchor and allow him or her to determine whether the link should remain.

The list scheme may solve some of these ambiguity problems, but it introduces new problems. With the pure list scheme, the user can select two wheels in a picture of a jeep and link them to a description of snow tires. If the user then added an axle between the wheels, the axle would not automatically become part of the anchor; the system would appear to be correctly anticipating the user's intention. However, this scheme presents new design problems, such as how to let the user add objects to an existing anchor and how the system should respond to changes in any of the anchor's objects. For example, the user might want to add the other two wheels to the anchor. And, if the wheels were replaced by cement blocks, the author would probably not want the link to remain.

In Intermedia, anchors in graphics documents are object lists, and the addition of a graphics object does not automatically change existing anchors. Currently, anchors in text documents are limited to insertion points. Future versions of Intermedia will implement the endpoint paradigm for anchors in text documents.

4.2. Editing Content Outside of Anchors

A system with read/write documents needs to ensure that editing changes outside of anchors do not change what is referenced by the anchors (Figure 21). This is a problem only in editors of linear data, such as text, that use the boundary scheme. In such editors the insertion of new data "bumps" existing data. Therefore, the system might need to adjust its internal anchor representation to ensure that the proper part of the document is presented as an anchor to the user. By contrast, under the list scheme, editing changes outside of an anchor would not affect the identification of the objects to which a link is anchored.

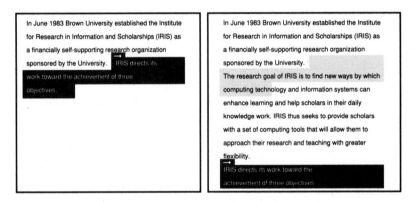

Figure 21. *(a) The user has established a link anchor. (b) When the user inserts a new paragraph, the system needs to adjust the location of the anchor highlighting.*

4.3. Deleting the Entire Contents of an Anchor

When the user deletes the entire contents of an anchor, should the system also delete the attached links? Although it would be possible to implement such a scheme by leaving the link information attached to an insertion point anchor, it might not be appropriate to maintain a reference to something that no longer exists. For example, if a reference to Dylan Thomas's "A Child's Christmas in Wales" linked to a copy of the poem itself, an author would probably not want to maintain the link if the reference were eliminated. Alternatively, if the user wanted to cut the reference only to replace it with more accurate information, it might be appropriate for the system to attach the link to the new content. There is no way to predict whether the link would still be relevant. A modification to the above alternatives (in which the system arbitrarily maintains or eliminates link information) is to leave the decision to the user on a case-by-case basis.

Intermedia retains the link even when all of the anchor's contents are cut, to avoid being destructive. The user can then explicitly remove the link if necessary. This solution allows the user to control what links are left in each instance and recognizes that actions on content and actions on link information are different.

A MULTIUSER ENVIRONMENT

If a hypermedia system is to be useful for cooperative work, it must provide ways for multiple authors to read, link to and from, and even edit the same set of documents, while also allowing authors to protect their work from unauthorized access or changes. At its simplest, this functionality could be implemented in a system that gives authors sequential access to documents. However, it would be more useful for cooperative work to have a fully networked environment in which multiple authors would have simultaneous access to documents.

The possibility of multiple users examining and editing documents simultaneously introduces complexity to any system. In hypermedia systems the complexity is increased because the user might not need to edit a document but might want to link to or from the document contents. Interactive linking adds another dimension to the traditional read/write access-rights paradigm. The issues involve control of access to documents and webs, data storage design for both document and link data, contention management, and update schemes for propagating editing changes.

5.1. Access Control

In a system that promotes shared, cooperative work, it is important to control access to document contents and link information. Appropriate access control assures the integrity of information, allows individuals working together to have full access to their shared data, and prevents unauthorized users from viewing or modifying such data.

5.1.1. Document Access

Typically, systems provide two categories of document-access privileges. *Read access* allows the user to view data, while *write access* allows the user to modify data. These categories are still important in the hypermedia world, but they are complicated by the hypermedia notion of *annotate access*. Such a category would be appropriate for systems that encourage users not only to read documents and follow links, but also to create new links as they browse. With annotate access, users could create links without having the right to make changes to the content of the document. Presumably, these access rights are additive, meaning that write access encompasses annotate and read access, and annotate access includes read access.

The annotate privilege could be: (1) limited to writers of documents, (2) assigned to all those with read access, or (3) designated as a separate category. The first case is most appropriate when it is necessary to prevent readers from changing the system in any way, such as in delivery of training materials. The case in which it is appropriate for everyone with read access to make links is in a system that encourages maximum connectivity of information, as in a university course that emphasizes discovery of meaningful relationships among data. The third case provides the flexibility and protection necessary for effective cooperative work.

Intermedia provides all three document-access categories. *Readers* may examine the contents of a document and follow links. *Annotators*, in addition to having readers' rights, can add links and can modify their links, but cannot alter the contents of the document. *Writers* have all of the capabilities of annotators and can also modify the contents of a document.

5.1.2. Web Access

A system with webs, or separate link contexts, could also control access to the webs. The web-access paradigm might follow the document-access categories of read, annotate, and write. Users would need *read access* to navigate the links associated with a web. As in the document-access paradigm, users would need *annotate access* to add links to a web. *Writers* would have all read and annotate rights plus the right to delete or rename the web. To determine if the user could access or change any document and follow or establish any link, the system would need to match the web-access rights against the particular document-access rights of the user. For example, to browse a web, the user would need both read access to the web and at least read access to each document that he or she wanted to view.

5.1.3. Assigning Access Rights

After designers specify the categories of access rights, they need to determine how these privileges should be assigned. One possibility is that the creator of the document or web be the only person with rights to modify any contents or links, and all other users have only read access. Another possibility is to designate a document as either private or public; once a document is launched into the public domain, all users would have all rights to it. Alternatively, users could have only "constructive" rights, as opposed to "destructive" rights, allowing them to add information but not to remove any information from the system.

Intermedia designers addressed the problem by designating one *owner* for each document and web and allowing the owner to designate individuals as having read, annotate, or write access to that document and web. Such users may be referred to individually, by specified lists of users, by groups, or by default as the remainder of the *universe*. When a document opens, its access rights are combined with the rights of the currently open web to create an access rights *capability* for that document. For example, if the document-access rights allow annotation but the web-access rights allow only read access to the web, the document capability would be set to allow only read access. This allows individual owners to specify the rights they desire for their document, while allowing the owner of the web to set limits for that web.

5.2. Storing Document Content and Anchor Information

Between sessions, anchor information could be stored with document content or separately. Because the anchor information is closely related to the content, it seems natural to store the two kinds of data together. In a system in which only one user at a time can annotate or edit a document, this approach might be appropriate. But if the hypermedia system allows (1) multiple simultaneous annotators, (2) different webs imposed on the same document at the same time, or (3) static documents such as those available on compact disks, the system designer must consider a different approach.

If the system allows multiple simultaneous annotators, it would be unwise to use the one-file system; allowing multiple users to write to the same file simultaneously presents potential concurrency problems that are not handled by most operating systems. Rather, the system should provide a way for multiple individuals to access and update the anchor information without fear of write collisions. Furthermore, in the one-file scheme, the document would have to store anchor information for all webs. Each application would need to filter the link information on a per-web basis.

The approach that we have taken is to store the link data independently from the document contents that they reference. Such data is stored by a data base management system on a per-web basis. When a document opens, the data base is queried for all of the document's link information in the currently opened web; the links are then dynamically added to the document's internal data structure. The data base management system provides concurrency management at the record-locking level over a network of workstations, so that no two individuals can update the same link information at the same time. Updates to the data base are not made at the time of link creation/deletion, but are batched together using a transaction-based scheme and are added to the data base when the web is saved. Because the link information is stored independently from a document, user A can have web A opened on a set of read-only documents, user B can have web B opened on the same set of documents, and both can add or delete links and save their respective webs without modifying the document files at all. Additionally, we anticipate that such a scheme will facilitate adding hypermedia structure to large-scale CD-ROM document sets.

5.3. Contention Management

If the system does not limit the number of users with write access at the document level, it must provide a scheme to manage simultaneous users with equal rights at run time to assure data integrity. Plans for contention management, which are well known for conventional read-write access situations, are complicated by the addition of annotate access to the system. For each document there are eight possible combinations of current status: below, s = single, m = multiple.

writer	annotate	reader
s	s	s
s	s	m
s	m	s
s	m	m
m	s	s
m	s	m
m	m	s
m	m	m

On this table, "s s s" denotes a single user accessing with write, annotate, and read capabilities, and "s s m" denotes a single user accessing with write and annotate capabilities, but multiple-user access for reading.

The hypermedia system designer needs to determine which combinations are acceptable. Some are far more difficult to implement than others. Of the first four, "s s s" and "s s m" are the easiest to build. "s m s" and "s m m" are significantly more difficult to implement than the previous two because of the concurrency problems involved with multiple simultaneous annotations. They require that the access to information in the web stay synchronized while multiple users add and delete links from the web and another user simultaneously makes changes to the document contents. The last four include multiple writer privilege and require complex chalk-passing and synchronization protocols to enable multiple individuals to edit simultaneously.

In Intermedia, when a user opens a web or opens a document from within a web, the system computes a capability for that user for that session for that object. For this computation, the system matches the user's rights to access the object (document or web) against the system's maximum allowed access level (one version of the system, for instance, might not allow multiple simultaneous annotation even if the individual has those rights). Once this capability is computed, the document is opened on a read-only basis if the user has read rights. If not, the user is presented with a dialog that signals the lack of rights, and is unable even to read the document.

If the document is opened on a read-only basis, the user is free to browse through the document and follow links. The first time the user attempts to make a change that affects the contents or the links of the document, the system checks first to see if another individual has locked that document for writing/annotation. If so, the user is told that he or she is unable to make changes to that document currently, but is free to read it and follow links from it. If the document is not locked, the system checks to see if the document capability allows writing/annotating. If not, the user is told that he or she is unable to edit/annotate, and appropriate menu items are disabled. If the document does have the appropriate capability, it is locked in the data base to alert other users who may be trying to annotate or edit it. The user interface is such that individuals attempting simply to read documents and follow links in a corpus that gives them appropriate read rights never see any signs of an existing access-rights scheme. Only individuals annotating or editing the corpus are aware of potential contention conflicts, and this only when there are actual locks or version mismatches that the author wants to be aware of.

5.4. Annotating/Editing Effects on Documents

Notification of updates is another issue to consider in a multiuser environment. There are four possible ways the system could respond to a user's changes: immediate update, immediate notification, passive notification, or no notification. The complexities of these options differ depending on whether the underlying documents are read-only or read/write.

The basis for immediate update is that a user should always have current information. Every new link could be broadcast across the network and would appear immediately whenever that document is open. In a read-only environment this would cause little disruption for the user. The appropriate indication of the new link would appear, and the user could then access the link. However, in a read/write environment this option would pose not only severe implementation problems, but also several conceptual problems. Presumably, if the system were to update links immediately, it should also update the document contents immediately to preserve the integrity of the information. It could be extremely distracting to a reader if the contents of a document were to change automatically because of editing by another user currently accessing the same document.

Immediate notification differs slightly from immediate update in that changes to an open document would result in a message being sent to all current readers of the document, letting them know that someone had changed the document. Users could then request to have their version of the document updated. This would give the reader more control over the changes presented, thereby preventing the problem of unexpected display changes.

Passive notification would inform users, via a facility such as electronic mail, that there had been changes to documents since they last opened them. Such notification would be particularly helpful to users who had made links to these documents; they could then determine whether or not the links should remain, considering the changes in the document.

The simplest solution for implementation is not to provide any notification of changes. Open documents would remain as opened, but the next time the document opened it would reflect the changes. These last two alternatives, passive notification and no notification, imply that most link information is not so timely that it needs to be known immediately.

Intermedia currently provides the no-notification scheme as an interim solution. We are investigating ways of allowing users to determine the level of notification they would prefer.

FUTURE RESEARCH

There are other issues in hypermedia that we are anxious to explore in future versions of Intermedia. One such issue pertains to sophisticated navigational tools. Such tools could show what links the reader followed to get to the current document, could allow the author to define paths for readers to follow, and could let the user leave a "bookmark" in the corpus to make it easy to "jump" to that place later. We also want to implement filtering so that the user could concentrate on links of particular individual interest in the current document and perhaps throughout an entire web. Furthermore, we are planning on looking into "hot links" that would force an instance of the information at one end of the link into the document at the other end. A hypermedia system that would automatically keep track of versions of documents [Nels81, Deli85] is also an area for future exploration.

APPLICATIONS OF INTERMEDIA

To assess the power and utility of hypermedia, IRIS is conducting a series of experiments at Brown that introduce the Intermedia system into existing courses. As in the English literature course, students in a plant cell biology course are using Intermedia's editors, utilities, and linking functionality to write term papers and to explore a corpus of material about the cell and its processes. Prior to the beginning of the semester, the professor wrote, collected, organized, and linked together primary source material for the corpus, including current research papers, digitized electron micrographs, diagrams, lecture notes, and three-dimensional models of cells. In writing their papers, students use the same editing tools used by the professor, including links to relevant primary source material in the corpus. The professor annotates student papers at various stages in the writing process, beginning with the outlines. These annotations consist of notes about the content of the paper and links to material that the professor feels the student should read, examine, or explore before committing to a particular assertion or argument. Finally, after the papers are "submitted" for a grade, the students in the course are asked to read and comment on each other's papers. Like the professor's comments, the students' annotations include reactions and criticisms, or point to other student papers or to primary source material. Since the comments become part of the corpus, each student has the opportunity to read any or all of the comments left by others and comment on the comments, thus engaging in an electronic dialog. At the end of the course, the professor evaluates the quality of each student's research paper as well as the quality of his or her comments.

In the cell biology experiment, the Intermedia system is being used throughout the authoring process, providing facilities to create, organize, reorganize, and cross-reference free-form text and graphics. The experiment also illustrates how a group of authors and editors can use a hypertext or hypermedia system to work collaboratively, using the tools to communicate as well as create.

In the Intermedia system, hypermedia functionality is incorporated into an integrated work environment with consistent, modeless, direct-manipulation applications. Strict adherence to predefined user-interface paradigms throughout the system eases the difficulty of learning a set of different applications. The ability for users to apply what they have already learned from using one application is particularly important in an environment, such as Intermedia, that encourages frequent transitions from application to application.

PROBLEMS WITH HYPERMEDIA SYSTEMS

Hypermedia is a powerful concept for multimedia communication. The goal of presenting a "seamless" environment—one in which a reader can become an annotator or an author—presents interesting user-interface problems. The goal of presenting the same seamless environment over a large corpus of documents that can be read, annotated, and edited simultaneously by multiple users over a communications network presents comparably difficult implementation issues. And the goal of presenting a new paradigm for sharing information in such an integrated fashion poses similarly difficult questions of social interaction and the management of such systems. With Intermedia, we have made a first attempt at resolving some of these issues, and we hope that this paper will help us and others as we continue to look at the complicated but fascinating unanswered questions of hypermedia.

ACKNOWLEDGMENTS

We wish to thank Helen DeAndrade for designing the figures for this chapter as well as many of the icons, palettes, and dialogs within the Intermedia system.

The development of Intermedia has been the culmination of over a year of intense, coordinated effort by the members of a large team, all of whom equally share the credit for the determination and resolution of the issues explored above. In particular, Charlie Evett developed a large part of the Intermedia architecture, the graphics building block, and the InterDraw application. Ed Grossman, Matt Evett, and Tom Stambaugh developed the text building block and the InterText application. Steve Drucker and Bern Haan developed the Intermedia framework. Page Elmore developed the web data base and the web map capability. Ken Utting added printing capability to the system.

In addition, Mike Braca, Dave Bundy, Dan Stone, and Scott Bates provided the base operating system, the data base, and the operating system extensions that enabled Intermedia to run. Brian Chapin and Sam Fulcomer configured the systems countless times. Eric Wolf developed the program for decompressing scanned images. George Landow, David Cody, Glenn Everett, Rob Sullivan, and Suzanne Keen Morley produced the enormous corpus *Context 32: A Web of English Literature* and heroically subjected themselves to the ordeal of teaching an English literature course with the system in its infancy. Andy van Dam, Marty Michel, Bill Shipp, and Don Wolfe provided advice and support throughout the project. Kate Archambault translated much gibberish into English.

This work was sponsored in part through a grant by the Annenberg/CPB Project and a joint study contract with International Business Machines Corporation. In addition, we greatly acknowledge Larry Tesler of Apple Computer, Inc., Jeff Singer and Stan Fleischman of Cadmus Computer, Inc., and Mark Nodine of Bolt Beranek and Newman for their assistance in making available key software that made Intermedia viable.

REFERENCES

[Appl83]   Apple Computer, Inc. *Lisa Office System.* Cupertino, CA, 1983.

[Appl84b]   Apple Computer, Inc. *MacDraw.* Cupertino, CA, 1984.

[Appl85]   Apple Computer, Inc. *Inside Macintosh.* vol. 1, 2, and 3. Addison-Wesley
             Publishing Company, Inc., Reading, MA, 1985.

[Back82]   D. Backer and S. Gano. "Dynamically Alterable Videodisk Displays." *Proc.
             Graphics Interface 82.* Toronto, May 17–21, 1982.

[Beem87]   W. Beeman et al., "Hypertext and Pluralism: From Lineal to Non-Lineal
             Thinking," *Hypertext '87 Papers,* Chapel Hill, NC, November 1987.

[Bend 84]   W. Bender, "Imaging and Interactivity," *Fifteenth Joint Conference on Image
             Technology,* Tokyo, Nov. 26, 1984.

[Deli85]   N. Delisle and M. Schwartz. "Neptune: A Hypertext System for CAD
             Applications." Tektronix Laboratories Technical Report no. CR–85–50.
             Beaverton, OR, 1985.

[Enge68]   D. Engelbart and W. English. "A Research Center for Augmenting Human
             Intellect." *Proceedings of FJCC,* vol. 33, no. 1. AFIPS Press, Montvale, NJ,
             Fall 1968, pp. 395–410.

[Fein82]   S. Feiner, S. Nagy, and A. van Dam. "An Experimental System for Creating
             and Presenting Interactive Graphical Documents." *Trans. Graphics*, vol. 1,
             no. 1, 1982.

[Furn86]   G.W. Furnas. "Generalized Fisheye Views." *Proc. CHI '86* Boston, MA,
             April 13–17, 1986, pp. 16–23.

[Garr86]   L. Garrett and K. Smith. "Building a Timeline Editor from Prefab Parts: The
             Architecture of an Object-Oriented Editor." *Proceedings of OOPSLA.*
             Portland, OR, September 1986.

[Gold84]   A. Goldberg. *Smalltalk-80: The Interactive Programming Environment.*
             Addison-Wesley Publishing Company, Inc. Reading, MA, 1984.

[Hala87]   F. Halasz and R. Trigg, "Notecards in a Nutshell," *CHI & GI '87 Conference
             Proceedings,* Toronto, Canada, April 1987.

[Inte86]   Interleaf. *Workstation Publishing Software: User's Guide.* Ten Canal Park,
             Cambridge, MA, 1986.

[Know86]   KnowledgeSet Corporation. *Laser Facts*. Monterey, CA, 1986.

[Land87]   G. Landow, "'Context 32,' Using Hypermedia to Teach English Literature," *IBM AEP Conference Proceedings*, 1987

[Meyr85]   N. Meyrowitz et al., "The Intermedia System: Requirements." IRIS Report, Institute for Research in Information and Scholarship, Providence, RI, September 1985.

[Meyr86]   N. Meyrowitz, "Intermedia: The Architecture and Construction of an Object-Oriented Hypermedia System and Applications Framework." *OOPSLA '86 Proceedings*. Portland, OR, September 1986.

[Nels81]   T. Nelson. *Literary Machines*. Swarthmore, PA, 1981. Available from author.

[Shne86]   B. Shneiderman, "User Interface Design for the Hyperteis Electronic Encyclopedia," *Hypertext '87 Papers*, Chapel Hill, NC, November 1987

[Smit82]   D.C. Smith, C. Irby, R. Kimball, and B. Verplank. "Designing the Star User Interface." Byte Publications Inc., April 1982.

[Tesl85]   L. Tesler. "An Introduction to MacApp 0.1." Apple Computer, Inc., Cupertino, CA, Feb. 14, 1985.

[Weye85]   S. Weyer and A. Borning. "A Prototype Electronic Encyclopedia." *ACM Trans. Office Information Systems*, vol. 3, no. 1. January 1985.

[Xero82]   Xerox Corporation. *8010 Star Information System Reference Guide*. Dallas, TX, 1982.

[Yank85]   N. Yankelovich, N. Meyrowitz, and A. van Dam. "Reading and Writing the Electronic Book." *IEEE Computer*, vol. 18, no. 10. October 1985, pp. 15-30.

[Yank87]   N. Yankelovich, D. Cody, and G. Landow. "The Creation of a Hypermedia Corpus for English Literature." *SIGCUE Bulletin*, vol. 19, Spring/Summer 1987

[Yank 88]   N. Yankelovich, B. Haan, N. Meyrowitz, and S. Drucker, "Intermedia: The Concept and the Construction of a Seamless Information Environment," IEEE *Computer*, January 1988

As We May Learn

Stephen A. Weyer

STEPHEN WEYER

Stephen Weyer has worked since 1970 to enhance learning environments on computers, improve access to knowledge, and provide advanced programming tools. At Stanford University, he developed and tested Logo environments involving animation, sound, and model trains. Over the next nine years Weyer worked for Xerox PARC, he taught and extended Smalltalk and developed information retrieval tools, browsing interfaces, and applications for the office, library, and school. For his dissertation project at Stanford, Weyer designed an online world history book and evaluated students' use of it to answer questions. This dynamic book had many hypertext qualities: subject and content bookmarks, search path highlighting, hierarchical subject links, and hierarchical text.

In contrast to this emphasis on structure and search techniques, Weyer worked on a prototype electronic encyclopedia at Atari, exploring issues related to dynamic information: active objects (measurement conversion, abbreviations, and cross-references), videodisc images, and simulations. During two years at Hewlett-Packard, he worked on natural language access to data-bases and managed an artificial intelligence programming environment project. Currently, he works at Apple, where he is balancing and combining these themes of exploratory and guided learning environments, information browsing and creation, and artificial intelligence for the purposes of representing and presenting knowledge.

Vannevar Bush's classic article of more than 40 years ago, "As We May Think" (Bush 45), describes an ambitious vision for information researchers—one that is only now being realized. The problem then was an increasingly specialized "growing mountain of research" that, ironically, might hinder further scientific progress because of difficulties in sifting through this mass of material. Bush's proposed Memex would have been a library-in-a-desk containing typed items, photographs, and longhand annotations recorded on microfilm. More than just an extensive and efficient storage medium, however, Memex would also have provided powerful ways to consult and modify the human record. Information would be accessible through association as well as through indexing. The user could join any two items, including the user's own materials and notes. Chains of these associations would form a "trail," with many possible side trails. Trails could be named and shared with other information explorers.

"Wholly new forms of encyclopedias will appear, ready-made with a mesh of associative trails running through them, ready to be dropped into the Memex and there amplified," Bush predicted. In addition to scientists, lawyers, patent attorneys, chemists, and historians, he said, "there is a new profession of trailblazers, those who find delight in the task of establishing useful trails through the enormous mass of the common record. The inheritance from the master becomes not only his additions to the world's record, but for his disciples the entire scaffolding by which they were erected."

In closing, Bush ponders not only whether a Memex might be necessary for our complex civilization to survive and understand itself, but also whether the storage medium and mode of interaction might more directly involve the brain, bypassing the tactile, oral, and visual levels of representation. Neural input and output as replacements for multimedia user interfaces still seem distant possibilities (except in science fiction novels such as Vernor Vinge's *True Names* or William Gibson's *Neuromancer*).

Beyond Memex

In addition to Memex's filing-cabinet functions, its description hinted at its use for numeric and logical manipulations. With the benefit of hindsight, we might have asked Bush to add further symbolic processing so that an automatic file clerk of sorts might have assisted us in searching, organizing, and interpreting the data. We might also have asked: If Memex became indispensable to the work of Bush's professional scientists, how might it revolutionize the work of amateur scientists, artists, and learners of all ages and abilities?

With the advent of inexpensive and powerful personal workstations, CD-ROM and writable optical storage, high-bandwidth networks, and hypertext-like software systems (Conklin 87; Yankelovich 85; Hypertext 87), much of Bush's vision has begun to materialize. As we build and experiment with such information systems, it's important to look beyond Memex and beyond browsing, not only because browsing breaks down when there are too many trails, but also because the importance of a trail often relates to educational purpose; instead of hypertext systems, we need to consider "hyperknowledge assistants."

The title of this paper (which I hope is not too pretentious in its extension of Bush's title) is meant to draw attention to the educational potential and artificial intelligence (AI) requirements of such a system—"learning" in addition to "thinking" for both human and computer partner. The name Memex suggests memory and storage; perhaps we should call our system Mimex to emphasize simulation and learning from examples.

The theme of this paper is that the system, instead of being only a passive tool or repository of information, should become a partner with the learner in searching, interpreting, and creating knowledge. Equally important, we should look at information from the perspective of the learner and his or her needs, rather than only from the perspective of what the technology can do or what the information industry currently provides. Considering such symbiotic systems and information needs should help us to rethink many of our assumptions about electronic information systems. We need fundamentally new organizing principles for knowledge, and we need new navigation and manipulation tools for the learner.

Intelligent Hypermedia Knowledge Systems for Learning

In this section, I will touch briefly on the importance of the aspects of *multimedia, learning,* and *intelligence* in broadening our perspectives of information systems. Most current information systems deal only with text. They retrieve information but provide no help in analyzing or synthesizing it. They treat the learner's query and stored data and information as "just bits" rather than as "meaning." Literal retrieval and exhaustive browsing are sometimes necessary, but more often a learner wants to define the similarities among concepts in more personal or intuitive ways and to filter and conform the information to suit personal needs.

Life in general and learning in particular are *multimedia,* multimodal experiences—perception and experience are highly dynamic and personal, not well portrayed by static text. To provide flexible access to information, a knowledge base must describe textual, visual, and aural images with more than a name—it must identify, classify, and match important characteristics of the images. In addition to providing for the representation of content, a multimedia perspective should change the style in which we present and organize knowledge—how we combine text, animated pictures, music, and speech to explain a principle of physics or to organize a roadmap to a new subject area. The knowledge base must include advice such as when to use a still image with voice-over instead of a full-motion video for particular purposes and learners. Thus, a multimedia approach is important both to convey recorded content and to make effective interfaces. In the spirit of next-generation "hyper-knowledge" systems, the reader should link discussions of "multimedia" or "hypermedia" in the other papers in this collection to the concepts of "knowledge" and "interface" discussed throughout this paper.

A *learning* perspective implies exploring conceptual understanding as well as modifying the practical application of knowledge to include academic education, informal lifelong learning, and professional and industrial training. Besides helping to mine information from library-like repositories, an intelligent system must help refine and create knowledge—it should have many of the qualities of coach, tutor, and colleague, encouraging the learner to question, conjecture, create, and experiment. Although an educational information system still must help us find "the answer" more efficiently, the emphasis must be on creating questions, proposing solutions, and contributing to understanding. Talking about "learners" instead of "users" should help make these information needs primary in our minds over information sources.

Adding *intelligence* to a multimedia educational information system can mean many things. We could build expert systems in many narrow domains or try to create an autonomous intellect equal or superior to our own. In its more widespread interpretation, artificial intelligence is the augmentation of human intelligence by means of better development and authoring environments. Instead of regarding an intelligent system as a human replacement, we can consider the system as an adaptable tool, an intelligent medium, or a helpful assistant or partner (Lenat 83; Stefik 86; Fischer 86). This means, in part, improving the organization of information—thus conveying knowledge as part of a neighborhood of concepts rather than as isolated facts. Intelligence in filtering or guiding means taking advantage of the relationships between concepts (for example, inheritance and ordering) to begin to guess what the learner understands (or misunderstands), to anticipate the learner's next action, or to prescribe a preferred path. To be intelligent, a system must grasp something of the purpose of the knowledge—what it can be used for—even if it does not deeply understand the information itself. To be intelligent, a system should be prepared to explain its actions (a general expert-system characteristic), and also be able to take advantage of explanations that the learner offers. Human learner and system learner should be able to converse at the level of examples, make inferences and guesses, develop analogies, and propose generalizations.

Learner Intentions and Needs,
or Information in Isolation *vs* the Real World

In our initial attempts to supply electronic information, we have often modeled some of the artifacts of early information systems, such as books and libraries, and little of the context that is such a vital part of the learning process. For example, a teacher, a written teacher's guide, or a discussion group can add much to a learner's understanding of a book. A library's card catalogs can be useful, but wouldn't you rather have access to a knowledgeable librarian or research assistant?

What is the educational intent of searching? A helpful electronic assistant must know something beyond "the learner is collecting information"—something more like "the learner wants information to answer the following question" or "the learner wants information to help test the following hypothesis." A good tutor should have a grasp of a student's understanding and know why and when to offer knowledge that could be relevant or helpful. This is easier said than done, yet it is a critical step in solving a problem of interest. Simpler approaches typically give us answers to the wrong problems.

In some situations and for some learners, a quick, small dose of facts may be exactly what is desired. However, the information retrieved can suit many purposes, depending on how the system presents it. For example, the system might supply the following forms of information:

Learner's goal	System's interpretation
Tell me.	Give me the facts, no embellishments.
Inform me.	Give me facts plus optional background and other points of view.
Amuse me.	Find me interesting connections or perspectives.
Challenge me.	Make me find or create creative connections.
Guide me.	Let me browse, but give me over-the-shoulder advice.
Teach me.	Give me more step-by-step guidance, fewer irrelevant links.

These needs, among others, often are not considered in designing information systems. Dervin (1983) succinctly contrasts "...two perspectives for looking at information transfer—one, an observer construction, sees information as a brick to be tossed from system to person (an empty bucket); the other, a user construction, sees information as clay to be molded and shaped by the perceiver. The observer construction has been and still is the dominant perspective in the social science literature relating to information transfer and in the practice and design of information systems.... In the context of such [absolute information] assumptions, an emphasis on information takes precedence over an emphasis on users. In the context of relativistic information assumptions, we would expect our information systems to look different. For one thing, the user would become the emphasis, the raison d'être. Instead of an emphasis on factualizing, there would be an emphasis on personalizing.... Instead of an emphasis on document transfer, there would be an emphasis on sense making."

Figure 1 illustrates the differences between these two perspectives of information systems and user activities. Current on-line systems are heavily biased toward the tidier, central, one-way view of information. In contrast, hypothetical users of Memex would be encouraged to annotate, interpret, collaborate, and personalize. The figure shows that information is not a nicely compartmentalized and static commodity—it is a shared experience. Information changes us: In addition to accumulating more of it, we may restructure what we know and think differently.

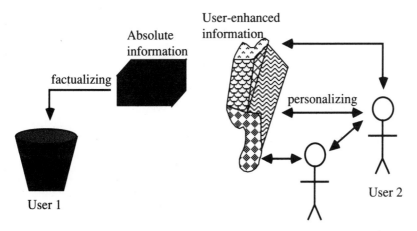

Figure 1. Two perspectives of information systems: absolute information 'brick' delivered to user vs user creates meaning in information 'blob'

In analogous fashion, Winograd and Flores, in their 1986 book *Understanding Computers and Cognition*, question the prevailing AI "information processing model" of the world. This book is difficult to summarize—briefly, it discusses fundamentally different ways to think about constructing human-computer interfaces. The authors state that symbolic/logical/conceptual approaches prevail, yet these approaches fail to acknowledge and explain what people do in the real world. Human communication is difficult to express or understand through words alone—context and common sense are essential. How can we use "the meaning" inherent in a piece of text (or in a multimedia sequence) for communication or learning without knowing something about the context in which the author and the learner/reader see the information? (Also, hypertext systems increasingly are considered for use by groups in collaborative interaction [CSCW86].)

As we begin to construct hyperknowledge systems that give access to large amounts of information for many different individuals, will we be able to maintain a balance between personalized access and efficient access? In addition to providing "the facts," can we help learners understand how to request and interpret them? In addition to helping the learner to better ask "What?" can we make more explicit such questions as "When is this information appropriate?" and "Why is it important?" and "From whom did it come?" and "With what effect?"

Learning Filters

Who is in the best position to articulate the needs and intentions of learners? Ideally, the learners themselves are, even if inexperienced; however, what of the judgments of teachers, AI-based tutors, parents, the local community, and national or global committees? Choice of curriculum materials raises controversy when the decisions touch on such issues as creationism *vs* evolutionism, the banning of certain novels for teenagers, sex education, and so on. Ironically, electronic information systems can provide broader access to information (assuming we can provide equal access to systems and avoid the widening social and informational gap between "have-nets" and "have-nots") at the same time they provide increased control for narrowing access. Censorship is really a form of filtering, imposed by someone else, that is difficult to discover or to undo. A key question is whether an electronic assistant should be somewhat subversive in making us aware of other points of view and the bias (perspective) of each, even if we have deliberately chosen to ignore them in our dedication (or close-mindedness). At the same time, how can we avoid being deluged with multitudinous perspectives and opinions, some of which are more important or relevant to our needs than others? (See the later discussion of whether all links are created equal.) In many situations, the constraining guidance offered by editorial and tutorial assistants may best serve the learner otherwise overwhelmed by complete freedom of choice. Clearly, the dialog between system and learner to describe the right kind and the right amount of information is never really complete and must periodically be reexamined and refined.

In order to adapt to the learner's needs, the system will need to build a model of preferences, skills, and information the learner has previously looked at (including how long ago and how well understood). For example, what constitutes "news" is closely related to importance, uniqueness, and incremental value. I will likely consider the first several stories about the Chernobyl nuclear disaster highly important regardless of my stated interests, thus overriding a narrow information filter. Assuming that subsequent stories are frequent and highly redundant in background information, a filter should then yield the significant differences that develop or periodic summaries, not entire hourly stories. Many such "important" stories or subjects may compete for the learner's (or the informed citizen's) attention. What is an important or unusual story or an interesting interdisciplinary connection, though somewhat the decision of the editor or author, depends largely on the learner's background.

Information *vs* User-oriented Organization

Some types of knowledge organization will certainly reflect conceptual relationships—for instance, multiple classifications of the world's knowledge (such as Encyclopaedia Britannica's *Propaedia* or the CYC project [Lenat 86]) to suit different cultural and learning styles. These correspond to the "observer constructs" or "absolute information" (Dervin 83) discussed earlier. Conceptual relationships involving entities and events seem factual: biological taxonomies (the family of mammals), royal genealogies, sequences of events in world history (not necessarily implying cause-effect relationships), geographic relationships (for example, France is in Europe, next to Belgium), and widely accepted scientific relationships (such as that between mass and energy).

Beyond the no-nonsense "tell me the facts" uses lie pedagogical uses and organizations of information based more on "user constructs"—that is, learner perceptions and needs. Pedagogical relationships between concepts admit to less of an absolute classification or agreement among experts; they are more closely related to order and style of presentation, to personal interpretation, perception, and belief. In contrast to structuring the content itself, user-oriented organizations address questions of intent, function, appropriateness, source, and implication. A user-oriented system might provide the following responses:

> Here is how Walter Cronkite might have described X.
>
> These provide increasingly complicated and graphic examples of X.
>
> Here are a series of experiments that can be used to prove (or disprove) X.
>
> This argument supports proposition X under assumption Y.
>
> This is a criticism/annotation of X.
>
> Here are parameters to cause simulation X to fail in the following situation.
>
> If X hadn't occurred, here's what might have happened.
>
> How is person X similar to you?
>
> This is analogous to X if we emphasize aspect Y.
>
> This situation is similar to (different from) X in the following ways.

Dervin (1983) lists some possible practices in a "user-based information system":

- Frequent use of question-answer formats, as in the so-called "Dear Abby" format.

- Frequent reporting of values, motives, and frameworks for observing, along with the results of observing.

- Frequent reporting of conflicting observations resulting from different frameworks.

- Frequent use of case studies in presenting information.

In addition to organizing the information itself (the "answers"), a user-oriented approach provides a structure for the possible approaches to the information (the "questions"). Simple lists (as above) are not satisfactory; reverse links from information (as answers) to possible questions are not enough. We would like a question browser or problem browser that would relate types of questions and suggest appropriate strategies. How can types of questions be classified? Which typify the philosophic or pragmatic approaches of certain disciplines, scientific paradigms, or individual practitioners? For example, what interesting questions would a biologist see in this situation, or how would Einstein (Newton, Galileo, Aristotle) have addressed this question? Creating a taxonomy of learner needs, styles, and problem-solving approaches may seem like an overwhelming task, but it is a necessary one if future systems are to help the learner use information more intelligently.

An Example Question: Making Historical Comparisons

For example, if the learner wants to make comparisons by identifying similarities and differences, this goal suggests certain strategies for locating information, whether the learner is researching which is the best refrigerator or spreadsheet to buy or seeking related work in a scientific survey article (for example, how is Memex like X?).

In previous work (Weyer 82), I gave students history problems such as "Compare the falls of the Roman and Han (Chinese) empires" and provided electronic search and bookmark aids so that the students could flip back and forth easily between the appropriate sections of an on-line history book. "The Huns attacked both empires" may not really be an adequate response to the question, even though this fact may be discussed for each empire near the date of actual downfall. A more serious analysis would identify many earlier factors— social, economic, and geographical—that may have led to weakness and then would compare these factors for the two empires in a static table format. An intelligent assistant might help us generalize the question to other empires or related problems. "Fall of an empire" is really a special case of "change in government" and "culture shock." What factors differentiate it from "civil war" or "scientific paradigm shifts"? Beyond providing answer templates or tools to transform the question, an intelligent assistant might test deeper understanding by encouraging the student to try to influence the course of history in games such as Chris Crawford's Eastern Front (an Atari 800 game that aids in understanding the failure of Hitler's invasion of Russia) or Balance of Power (a Macintosh game that explores political influence and intrigue in the modern nuclear world). Or perhaps learners might be encouraged to create their own simulations of civilization, to predict revolutions or declines.

Similarity-based Searching

Learners should be able to use their own concepts and words when searching in a user-oriented information system. To interpret these phrasings, natural language parsing, thesaurus tools, or graphical concept organizations must be available. In many situations, a particular example is at hand and the learner would like to find more information "just like it, almost." For example, after reading about the fall of the Roman Empire, the learner might be interested in "similar" events. Finding related events may be easy if the author of the materials has provided explicit links to the declines of other empires—how much more powerful if these links could be declared in terms of the attributes the author considered important in suggesting the connection.

If indexing is adequate to identify significant concepts such as "Hun invasion," "political corruption," "mercenary army," and "immorality," then the information system can match other events that involve some of these concepts. However, manual indexing is time-consuming and the results are often inconsistent, either between different trained indexers or for the same indexer over time. Automatic indexing is usually based on word frequency; it can be improved by grouping words into index phrases. Current systems do not collapse synonymous references to a single term, handle proper names properly, or suggest terms that do not occur in the document. Without indexing, it's easy to find a few relevant items by using free text on most on-line systems, but it's very difficult to conduct a more exhaustive search. A promising demonstration where most of the words in a document are used to match similar documents has been done on the massively parallel Connection Machine (the 64,000 processor machine from Thinking Machines) (Stanfill 86).

Several problems complicate the task of finding similar items in current on-line systems. Syntax is often cumbersome and query dialects often differ between information systems. These problems have been partially solved by search intermediaries or information gate-ways—programs with user interfaces to mask and map some of the complexity related to logging in, making queries (usually Boolean in syntax), and displaying results. Still, matching is too often based on exact occurrences of index terms or text words. Although word root truncation and thesauri of synonyms help to a limited extent, what is really required is a way of mapping these words into concepts located in semantic networks so that items that fail to match exactly can still be located within a small neighborhood of nearby concepts. Information systems should enable the learner to define the radius of generality, specificity, and/or relatedness for a concept, as well as to set the level of importance in the overall combination of concepts used in the description. ("Corruption" should probably include "bribery" and "political favors" and correlate inversely with "honesty"; "corruption" is probably more important than "lead poisoning" in identifying similar situations.)

Using examples, the learner should be able to define "interest neighborhoods" by locating each attribute of the example in the concept index and moving, narrowing, or expanding the focus of the concept. This approach is similar to that used in the Rabbit system (Tou 82; Williams 84)—query by reformulation, where the user refines a query by explaining what's wrong with an example. Alternatively, the learner might deal entirely with a collection of examples, giving feedback such as "Good," "OK," or "Bad" for each example as a whole without detailing why—marking individual sentences, paragraphs, or articles as good examples of what the learner is interested in (Stanfill 86). If explanations of reasoning to the learner are a hallmark of AI systems, then we should intuitively expect the reverse—that examples and explanations the learner gives to the system could be used to demonstrate and debug the learner's intelligent behavior.

Beyond Browsing and Memex

Traditional information systems often impose a sense of tunnel vision—like you get when you access books in a library through card catalog and order form: You must guess at how a concept is described and, when you look at the results of a search, it's often unclear what else of relevance you might have missed. Hypertext systems now coming into use hold the promise of letting us look at the library shelves to perceive neighborhoods of information and many interesting connections within and between subject areas (for example, cross-references between encyclopedia articles or bibliographic references to books). Initially, the ability to see the relationships between many nuggets of knowledge is appealing (alternate paper title: "Knowledge McNuggets: Fast Food for Thought"). However, many problems must be overcome.

Without help, browsing through everything in an information system can be as ineffective as searching blindly, creating a higher level of "information gridlock"—through electronics, we have access to much more information than was available to earlier generations, especially with technologies like CD-ROM storage and fiber optic networks. A large number of interesting associations between pieces of information will be available (and an overwhelming number of perhaps less interesting connections from the cosmic view that "everything is connected to everything else"). Browsing through this universe of information directly, without intelligent filtering to create smaller neighborhoods or guidance to prioritize trail selection, will be frustrating.

Although much leverage can be gained by thinking of on-line information systems as "books" or "libraries," this metaphor can overshadow the dynamic nature of the information and its uses. We may think of the system more as pages to peruse rather than as a tutor to converse with or as a laboratory for conducting experiments. To prevent "dusty-tome syndrome" (a loss of interest in or distaste for paperlike presentations), electronic "books" must become nonbooks in both function and name. Knowledge is not static—to be user-oriented and malleable, information should be adaptable to the learner's preferences. In these directions, Weyer and Borning (1985) have proposed a model-tour-filter-guide metaphor.

Instead of thinking of an information system as containing information, think of it as an environment for communication, descriptions, and programs. Clearly, this is one way to embed simulations. Notecards (Halasz 87) is embedded in a general-purpose programming environment (Interlisp-D). Boxer (diSessa 86) is an object-oriented programming environment that can be used as a hypertext document system. CYC (Lenat 86) is a knowledge environment in which articles are described in terms of slots, constraints, and relationships. And Vivarium, a long-term Apple research project guided by Alan Kay, is as an "information grotto" or "knowledge playground" populated and explored by assistants (perhaps portrayed by animated creatures) that the learner imbues with behavior, plans, and limited intelligence for creating, filtering, and manipulating knowledge.

Instead of thinking of an information system as a passive entity on which the author performs neural surgery to add new components and connections, think of it as an active partner. Hyperknowledge systems should be able to

- Generate new content via rules.

- Look for inconsistencies.

- Form hypotheses about pedagogy and understanding from the learner's actions.

- Explain their own actions.

- Participate in the authoring process by classifying and critiquing annotations and revisions and refereeing debates by a community of learners (both human and artificial).

How much of a difference should be maintained between author and reader, teacher and learner, system and human? As knowledge accumulates and ferments (and is later distilled) in the system, should it all be treated equally? If the learner believes that knowledge that is heavily editorialized and filtered is better for his or her purposes than, say, electronic-mail discussions or political advertisements, then that value judgment should be an explicitly represented bias in the source selection.

All links are not created equal—they should depend on what you have seen before, on your current goals, your confidence in the sources, and on the author's guesses about what is most important for which of these contexts and purposes. Link types will probably be important, but we need good taxonomies and convenient authoring tools for creating and indexing. Links must be constantly annotated—why you find the information useful, why you think someone else might be interested, why the system suggested it to you. The learner must communicate intentions so that the system can highlight and prioritize what's important and hide connections and details considered unimportant. (The learner could always reveal more and ask why some things were revealed and not others.)

Guiding

Although work on search intermediaries and browsing and hypertext techniques may improve searching and browsing in information systems, fundamental change is more likely to arise from trying to create intelligent assistants that know not only more about what we want to find but also why we want to find it. Natural language understanding has reached a similar barrier: Progress in understanding is likely to come not from further work in syntax and semantics but from emerging theories of discourse. Discourse includes not only a history of the conversation (most current natural language systems, both research and commercial, are impressive only on single utterances or in very narrow domains) but also the speaker's intentions and listener's expectations (Winograd 86). Natural language itself could provide much of the required richness of dialog between learner and guide/assistant. Even if the user interface is not based on natural language, however, theories of discourse should influence the interface's design.

Intelligence in an agent will not be synonymous with omniscience, even assuming that learners can articulate what they're interested in finding and understanding. Although the correlation between an accurate description and relevant retrieved results can be high, the relationship is, by the nature of communicating about information, an imperfect match. There is a surprising discrepancy of views among human indexers about the appropriate terms to classify a document, although perhaps agreement can be improved with appropriate tools (Lenat 86). The correct phrasing of a query does not happen correctly the first time, except in trivial cases—refinement and clarification are a natural part of the process. A resulting interest neighborhood will not contain all the relevant items, and it will include ir-relevant ones as well (that is, the system will not exhibit perfect "recall" and "precision," in information jargon). Exploration, expanding, narrowing, highlighting, and rejecting of information should be expected. In trying to make our assistant emulate expert human behavior, we must realize that this seeming imperfection in communication is normal and, indeed, essential in modeling learning.

Conclusion

The powerful vision typified by Memex can be made even more compelling by transforming information into knowledge, by elevating the needs and importance of the learner, and by evolving a flexible tool in the direction of becoming an adaptive partner. Multimedia techniques are important not only to convey detail, motion, and emotional content of knowledge but also to create new organization and navigation interfaces to access this knowledge. Even if we regard our "hyperknowledge assistant" as only an information system, the preceding tour should lead us at least to new ways of thinking about searching and browsing. If we additionally consider the system as an exploratory and guided learning environment, the learner's needs and questions must become the focus.

What are the next steps? We need more research in highly interconnected hypermedia systems; intelligent tutoring systems; knowledge organizations; programming and authoring environments; conceptual and example-based description; natural language discourse and understanding systems; and models of user intentions, understanding, and behavior. Integrating these pieces will be a major conceptual, as well as software-engineering, task. A great deal of progress, much of it recent, has occurred in the past 40 years. It is my hope that the vision I have attempted to present here can be elaborated and made practical before another 40 years elapse.

REFERENCES

Bush, V. As we may think. *Atlantic Monthly* 176: 101-108; July 1945. Also pp. 3-20 in Lambert, S., and Ropiequet, S. (Eds.) *CD-Rom: The New Papyrus,* Microsoft Press, Redmond, WA; 1986.

Conklin, J. Hypertext: An introduction and survey. *Computer* 20(9):17-41; Sept. 1987.

CSCW '86. *Proceedings of the Conference on Computer-Supported Cooperative Work.* MCC and ACM, Austin, TX; Dec. 3-5, 1986.

Dervin, B. Information as a user construct: The relevance of perceived information needs to synthesis and interpretation. Pp. 153-183 in Ward, S.A., and Reed, L. J. (Eds.) *Knowledge Structure and Use: Implications for Synthesis and Interpretation.* Temple University Press, Philadelphia, PA; 1983.

diSessa, A., and Abelson, H. Boxer: A reconstructable computational medium. *Comm. ACM* 29(9):859-868; Sept. 1986.

Fischer, G. Enhancing incremental learning processes with knowledge-based systems. In Mandl, H., and Lesgold, A. (Eds.) *Learning Issues for Intelligent Tutoring Systems.* Springer-Verlag, New York; 1986.

Halasz, F., Moran, T., and Trigg, R. NoteCards in a nutshell. In *Proceedings of the ACM Conference on Computer-Human Interaction* (CHI+GI '87), Toronto, Ontario; April 1987.

Hypertext '87. *Proceedings of Hypertext '87 Workshop.* University of North Carolina, Chapel Hill; Nov. 13-15, 1987.

Lenat, D., Prakash, M., and Shepherd, M. CYC: Using common-sense knowledge to overcome brittleness and knowledge-acquisition bottlenecks. *AI Magazine* 6(4): 65–85; Winter 1986.

Lenat, D., Borning, A., McDonald, D., Taylor, C., and Weyer, S. Knoesphere: Building expert systems with encyclopedic knowledge. Pp. 167–169 in *Proceedings of the 8th International Joint Conference on Artificial Intelligence.* Karlsruhe, West Germany; 1983.

Stanfill, C., and Kahle, B. Parallel free-text search on the Connection Machine system. *Comm. ACM* 29(12):1229-1239; Dec. 1986.

Stefik, M. The next knowledge medium. *AI Magazine* 7(1): 34–46; Spring 1986.

Tou, F., Williams, M., Fikes, R., Henderson, D.A., and Malone, T. RABBIT: An intelligent database assistant. Pp. 314-318 in *Proceedings of the American Association for Artificial Intelligence.* Pittsburgh; August 16–20, 1982.

Weyer, S. A. The design of a dynamic book for information search. *International Journal of Man Machine Studies* 17(1):87-107; July 1982.

Weyer, S. A., and Borning, A. H. A prototype electronic encyclopedia. *ACM Transactions on Office Information Systems* 3(1):63-88; Jan. 1985.

Williams, M. What makes Rabbit run? *International Journal of Man Machine Studies* 21:333-352; 1984.

Winograd, T., and Flores, F. *Understanding Computers and Cognition: A New Foundation for Design.* Ablex Publishing Corp., Norwood, NJ; 1986.

Yankelovich, N., Meyrowitz, N., and van Dam, A. Reading and writing the electronic book. *Computer* 18(10):15-30; October 1985.

NoteCards:
A Multimedia
Idea Processing
Environment

Frank G. Halasz

FRANK G. HALASZ

Frank Halasz received his Ph.D. in Cognitive Psychology from Stanford University in 1983. His thesis research explored the role of mental models in learning to use complex machines. In 1983, he joined the Intelligent Systems Laboratory at Xerox PARC, where he developed NoteCards (a hypermedia-based idea-processing system) and investigated the use of such systems to support authoring and argumentation. In 1986, he joined the Software Technology Program at the Microelectronics and Computer Technology Corporation (MCC) in Austin, Texas, where he continues his research in human-computer interaction, specifically the design of computer-based tools to support intellectual work. He is currently building the ultimate hypermedia system, and exploring its use by teams of designers in the early, decision-making phases of large software projects.

NoteCards is a computer environment designed to help people work with ideas. Its users are authors, researchers, designers, and other intellectual laborers engaged in analyzing information, constructing models, formulating arguments, designing artifacts, and generally processing ideas. NoteCards provides these users with a rich and extensible set of tools that support a variety of specific activities ranging from sketching on the back of an envelope through formally representing knowledge. Together, these tools provide an environment for capturing, representing, interrelating, managing, and communicating ideas. In this environment, users can develop their ideas, transforming informal and unstructured jottings into formal analyses and structured presentations.

NoteCards is a hypermedia system. Its basic framework is a semantic network of electronic notecards connected by arbitrarily typed links. This network serves both as a medium in which the user can represent collections of interconnected ideas, and as a structure for organizing, storing, and retrieving information. NoteCards provides the user with tools for displaying, modifying, manipulating, and navigating through the network. It also includes a set of well-defined methods and protocols for programmatically manipulating the network. These basic components constitute the core for NoteCards's extensible environment for idea processing.

There are four basic constructs in NoteCards: notecards, links, browsers, and fileboxes. Each notecard contains an arbitrary amount of information embodied in text, graphics, images, voice, or any other editable or presentable substance. On the screen, a notecard is usually displayed in its own editor window. Links are used to represent binary connections or relationships between cards. Each link is represented by an "active" link icon located at an anchor point in the link's source card. Clicking in the link icon with the mouse traverses the link; that is, retrieves the destination card of the link and displays it on the screen ready to be read or edited. Browsers are cards that contain editable node-link diagrams showing the structure of some portion of the network. Fileboxes are cards that provide the user with a hierarchical filing structure for organizing collections of cards into topics or categories.

NoteCards was developed and runs within the Xerox LISP environment on the Xerox 1100 series workstation. The system includes a well-documented programmer's interface that provides programmatic access to all of the system's functionality. This interface can be used to tailor the system to particular tasks or users. In addition, NoteCards can be integrated with other systems running in the LISP environment such as mail systems, data bases, and rule-based expert systems.

NoteCards's multimedia characteristics derive from its type mechanism, which allows users to add facilities for handling arbitrary new types of notecards to the system. The basic system handles text, graphics, and images, with the ability to integrate all these media into a single notecard. Users of notecards have created several dozen additional card types, including animation cards, voice cards, video cards, and action cards. Many of these new card types stretch the notion of "displaying" a notecard. The video cards control a videodisc player that plays a designated video segment on a separate screen when the card is displayed. Action cards contain a short program describing an action that is carried out when the card is displayed.

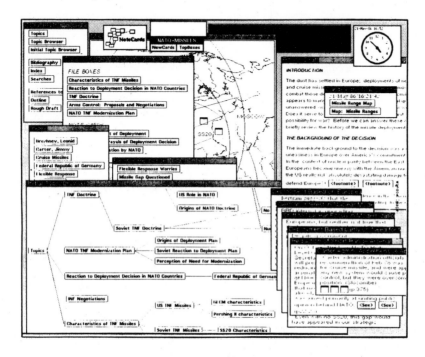

Although it is an experimental system, NoteCards is currently being used for a wide range of applications. The majority of these applications center around the creation, management, and analysis of loosely or irregularly structured information. Examples of such applications include researching and writing complex legal briefs, analyzing the arguments presented in scientific and public policy articles, and managing the general personal and project information for small group research projects. In all of these applications, the use of NoteCards focuses on authoring and structuring a network of notecards, with subsequent access to this network primarily by the original authors.

A significant minority of NoteCards applications focus on the presentation of nonlinear multimedia "documents." For example, NoteCards has been used as the basis for a number of interactive, nonlinear tutorial and reference manuals. More important, NoteCards has been used for the design, development, and delivery of interactive computer-assisted training for copier repair technicians. This application includes interactive video as well as interactive graphics simulations within the NoteCards framework. One important feature of this application is that the same system was used for both course design/development and for course presentation.

Observation of NoteCards in use has shown that much of its power derives from the fact that it presents a uniform, spatial, direct-manipulation interface to a wide variety of different kinds of information represented in a variety of different media. The same access operation (following a link) can bring up a text file to be edited, start a running animation, carry out a data-base search, play a video sequence, or execute an action. All of these "pieces of information" are uniformly represented as notecards and can be integrated into a NoteCards network for access and organizational purposes. Moreover, NoteCards provides the ability to easily view and edit not only these pieces of information, but also the organizational structure into which they are placed.

Observation on NoteCards in use has also shown several limitations inherent in the system. NoteCards (and hypermedia systems in general) rely too exclusively on navigational access to information. A significant improvement in functionality would accrue if navigational access were augmented by search mechanisms that allow query-based access to both the content and structure of the hypermedia network. NoteCards is also limited in its facilities for supporting collaborative work within a single network. It is not uncommon for one user to get lost in the web of information created by another user, since NoteCards makes no effort to enforce a (as yet undiscovered) rhetoric of hypermedia. These and other limitations form the basis of our ongoing research into the next generation of hypermedia systems.

References

Halasz, F.G., Moran, T.P., & Trigg, R.H. "NoteCards in a nutshell." To appear in the *Proceedings of the ACM/SIGCHI Conference on Human Factors in Computing Systems (CHI+GI 1987),* Toronto, Canada, April 1987.

Trigg, R.H., Suchman. L.A., & Halasz, F.G., "Supporting collaboration in NoteCards." *Proceedings of the Conference on Computer-Supported Cooperative Work (CSCW '86),* Austin, Texas, December 1986.

An emphasis on educational uses of multimedia systems was articulated by the educators at the Conference, in the context of solving specific problems they had encountered in their work which were amenable to the incorporation of multimedia systems. **Larry Friedlander**, for example, deals with teaching college students Shakespeare as theater rather than as literature. He acknowledges that texts alone, or even occasional theatrical experiences on a small scale when logistically possible, simply do not allow students to understand Shakespeare's contributions or to develop any "feel" for the performance aspects of theater. More important, he finds that the components of theatrical presentations that are controlled by directors and actors are invisible to typical audiences; analysis of these techniques by beginners is stifled at the onset. Multimedia presentations—particularly using videodiscs for presentations of movies of "great performances" and graphical simulations that can be manipulated by students for explorations of techniques of the theater ("The Theater-Game")—let Friedlander address these problems. They provide a beginning for solving the problem of communicating to students what Friedlander knows as a professional; they provide a way to combine what is accessible in texts and what requires more visual and kinesthetic experiences. The presentations give Friedlander the basis for tools for student manipulation of these "types of media" so that students can begin to understand what the study of Shakespeare requires and the issues that performers who present Shakespeare's works must address.

Bernard Frischer has run into similar issues in trying to make the Classics "come alive" for his college students, and is trying to use multimedia tools to provide "an everyday view" of ancient civilizations. Once he can get students to think about the people who populated the plazas—the kinds of shoes they wore, the arguments they had, the views from their bedrooms—he can begin to provide these students with analyses of those people's activities. He can discuss the literature of the era, as well as the politics, in context. He can provide students with tools to wander around ancient cultures much as they do vacation centers, picking up information about these cultures quite easily and comfortably. And then he can give them guided tours to make the points made by the theorists of those eras.

At a high school level, **Pat Hanlon** and **Bob Campbell** have found that they, too, have been lacking tools to provide their students with contexts in which to address particular topics. Similarly they have found few available resources which have been integrated to provide teachers with the means for creating these contexts day in and day out. As an example, to understand *The Grapes of Wrath*, they find it important that students know a bit about the Depression (which many don't). Also, they have found that to understand the deliberate structure of a novel such as this, it is important that students understand a bit about the author of the novel and about alternative media forms such as magazines, movies, and filmstrips available for the communication of similar messages. Of course, Hanlon, Campbell, and other teachers have known this for a long time. And curriculum developers and librarians have been working to provide materials that can assist teachers and students in gathering together these critical perspectives. What multimedia tools can provide is a sensible, integrated scheme for doing this: to take advantage of existing sources by indexing them and putting them in one place (a task well suited to Campbell's library background), to integrate audio-visual and text experiences in classrooms and labs, and finally, to make everything neat and compact by putting it in "one box" (or at least a small number of boxes functionally connected with a computer).

The Shakespeare
Project

Larry Friedlander

LARRY FRIEDLANDER

Larry Friedlander has been a professor of Shakespeare in the Stanford University English department since 1965, and has a background in both literary criticism and practical theater. He has worked as an actor and director in many companies on the West Coast, including the Shakespeare Festivals at San Diego (the Old Globe), California, and at Ashland, Oregon. He has long been interested in the problem of integrating traditional Shakespeare education with performance theory and practice. As a graduate student at Harvard, he created an experimental course combining criticism and performance of theater. He has since taught similar courses not only at Stanford, but at the Free University of Berlin, and to professional actors at the London Academy of Music and the Dramatic Arts. Professor Friedlander has a longstanding interest in student theater and theater education. He founded one of Stanford's oldest and largest undergraduate performing groups, The Company, in 1966, and teaches acting and directing for the Drama and English departments. He also has written on the teaching of drama in the university.

ABSTRACT

The Problem

A broad spectrum of important subjects cannot be successfully taught within the constraints of the traditional classroom. The creative arts, for example, are notoriously resistant to standard teaching practices. As a result, many of our culture's richest and most vital traditions, such as theater, become tame and impoverished in the classroom: unidimensional.

What Is To Be Done

The extraordinary development of technology in recent years allows educators a dramatic new possibility: how, at last, to teach those complex, elusive subjects like the creative arts. The Shakespeare Project—the most comprehensive effort to date linking the arts and humanities to both the power of the computer and the flexibility of the videodisc—offers educators a radically new way to teach not only Shakespeare and theater, but also those disciplines like psychology, sociology, and communications, which depend upon the observation of complex, visually "dense" and hard-to-record events.

Through its innovative interactive videodisc computer program, the Shakespeare Project grants students options never before possible, bringing even novice students into intimate contact with the entire process of theatrical creation. Using the Shakespeare Project, students go beyond a mere reading of the text: they *see* a performance, study it in detail, interact with it, isolate and analyze its components, simulate its processes, and make the play's world their own. The Shakespeare Project freshens students' perceptive powers—opening them to the marvelous richness not only of theater, but of all human interactions. By offering a new form of learning, the Shakespeare Project will thus create a new type of learner.

Who Will Do It

The Academic Computing and Information Systems of Stanford University is sponsoring the Shakespeare Project. Stanford Professor Larry Friedlander, who has been teaching Shakespeare and acting for more than 25 years, will direct the project. Staff from Stanford Instructional Television Network (SITN) and Instructional Research and Information Systems (IRIS) will implement the project, assisted by a panel of distinguished advisors especially assembled for this project.

PROJECT SUMMARY

"Educators should reconceptualize the good student, not as one who sits, listens, agrees, cooperates, and regurgitates, but as one who is critically aware, curious, questioning, and active but sensitive in critical disputation."
(Jarvis, Lifelong Learning)

The Problem

A broad spectrum of important subjects cannot be successfully taught in the traditional classroom. It has often been argued that fields like the creative arts can be "learned but not taught"—that creativity does not lend itself to the standard teaching practices so prevalent in disciplines such as math or biology.

Theater, for example, has proved itself particularly elusive in the academic setting because of its complex, "mixed" nature—the way it daringly combines elements of painting, music, literature, dance, psychology, and even anthropology. Like the novel, theater is a narrative with a relatively stable but "dense" text. Like dance or music, theater also moves forward in time in ways that don't easily allow the viewer to stop or study the "text." As a social spectacle, theater also recalls the complexity of public ritual, while its concern with interior motivation and role-playing connect theater to the intricacies of psychology and philosophy.

One can understand how difficult (if not impossible) it is to convey the complex, elusive qualities of such a mixed form in the traditional classroom, where a great, complicated play such as *Hamlet* is usually taught merely as a "text," as a branch of literature—an approach that robs the play of much of its creative essence. All too often in the academic setting, theater—one of our culture's oldest and most vital traditions—becomes tame: unidimensional.

The Solution

The extraordinary development of technology in recent years allows educators a dramatic new possibility: to teach complex, elusive subjects that have hitherto resisted the academic setting. The Shakespeare Project is the most comprehensive effort to date linking the creative arts to the power of the computer and the flexibility of the videodisc. It offers educators a radically new way to teach Shakespeare and theater (or any complex, hard-to-record live event, be it an intense session between psychologist and patient, or a complicated maneuver among players on the football field).

Through its innovative interactive videodisc computer program, the Shakespeare Project grants students options never before possible in the traditional classroom. Using the project, students can:

- "Attend" rehearsals with directors and performers.

- "Discuss" a play's key issues with interviewed actors.

- View and instantly compare several intriguingly different versions of a particular scene.

- Design their own "versions" of a crucial scene on a computerized, digital stage.

- Peruse an "archive" of hundreds of historical photographs documenting the rich array of sets, costumes, and props.

- Browse through an "electronic" wardrobe and prop room, choosing costumes that suit their own interpretation of a play.

- Create their own "case study" of a character's motivation and psychology.

- Skip through the expanse of a play almost instantaneously, making comparisons that reveal the large, embracing structure of the play.

- "Read" a staged performance with the ease and freedom with which we now read a text—stopping, starting, viewing, re-viewing, and selecting segments for detailed study.

In short, the Shakespeare Project allows expert or novice students to study, design, and enjoy theater. The project familiarizes students with the entire process of theatrical creation—from finding an interpretation and a guiding concept, to choosing appropriate designs, to actually envisioning and executing the details of performance. Using the Shakespeare Project, students go beyond a mere reading of the text: they *see* a performance, study it in detail, interact with it, isolate and analyze its components, trace its processes, and make the play's world their own.

Innovatively allowing students to move from theory to practice, from discussion of critical problems to the testing of those problems in performance, the Shakespeare Project freshens students' perceptive powers—it opens students to the marvelous richness not only of theater, but of all human interactions. Students gain a rare learning experience: how to deal with creative situations in which there are no "right" or "wrong" answers. Students who, sadly, have been trained to confuse timidity with "correctness" learn the importance of "letting go"—of allowing their imaginations free play. Exposing students to problems that have no fixed or single solutions, the Shakespeare Project provides students with a greater tolerance for complexity, for what the great Romantic poet Keats praised as "negative capability," the ability to exist "in uncertainties, mysteries, doubts." In short, students using the Shakespeare Project can move closer to being the flexible, open, responsive, and self-confident adults that our culture needs.

The Background

The Shakespeare Project grew from a longstanding concern with the teaching of the creative arts. To enhance a student's understanding of an artist like Shakespeare, educators have long looked for ways to supplement ordinary curricula (which tend to emphasize only the plays' texts) with a wider, richer view of the entire theatrical process.

In 1984, Stanford University funded development of an animated theater simulation. In 1985, IBM, impressed with the initial results, contributed additional funding for a feasibility study to develop videodisc-based theater lessons and tools. During the preliminary stages of this feasibility study, it became clear that the advantages of the technology being considered applied to a wide spectrum of disciplines. Stanford professors from psychology, anthropology, athletics, and the arts gathered to discuss how interactive video could help express the rich and complex human interactions that form the basis of study in their fields.

It was agreed during this preliminary stage that the Shakespeare Project, already under way, would serve as a model for development of similar systems in other disciplines, and that the tools and lessons of the Shakespeare Project would be designed to be as transferable as possible. It was also agreed that the purpose of the feasibility study was this: to test whether, in fact, a complex theater concept could be taught through videodisc and computer technology.

We designed and built a prototype, not to be used as a kernel for future development, but to test our basic assumptions. The prototype consisted of three basic programs:

- A videodisc-based "tutorial" called Page to Stage that taught how a performance is created by interpreting the text.

- An annotated visual data base of theater and art history on videodisc, called The Browser.

- A computer animation program, The TheaterGame, that allowed students to simulate design and staging choices, and to create an actual scene on the computer screen.

The two videodisc-based components were programmed on two computers, an Apple Macintosh and an IBM Vision attached to a videodisc player. The students worked at a keyboard, facing a screen that displayed film, graphics, text, instructions, and student responses. Students controlled the pace and direction of their learning by touching the screen to select items from menus or displays.

Page to Stage included four videodisc-based lessons: text, subtext, beats, and blocking—about three hours of instruction in all. These lessons showed two-minute segments of *Hamlet*, with three versions of the same scene. Students analyzed the way the scene was "built up" from a text and investigated how and why performers arrived at certain interpretations of a scene (see Figure 1).

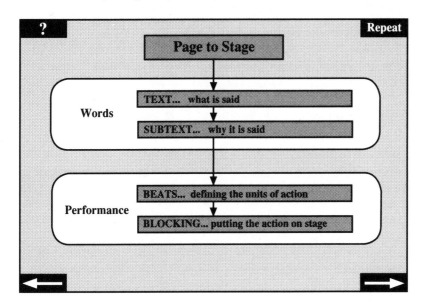

Figure 1. *A computer screen from Page to Stage showing the structure of the lesson.*

The lessons showed that differences in performance sprang from different readings of the same text. Performers work by first analyzing the text, then developing a psychological "script" for the scene, which is called a *subtext*. They then transform this interpretative material into a performance.

For example, Jean Simmons, playing Ophelia against Olivier's Hamlet, has decided that Ophelia is terrified of Hamlet, but also deeply in love with him. She must convey this interpretation to the audience by the way she speaks her lines. Her first line in the nunnery scene is, "Good my Lord, how does your honor for this many a day?" As she begins she does not look at Hamlet, but stonily recites the first three words almost to herself, in embarrassment and fear. Then, feeling his gaze upon her, she glances at him, melts in affectionate tenderness, and sighs in a completely different tone, "How does your honor for this many a day?" The actress has translated her psychological interpretation, her subtext, into performance choices, or *beats*. Students then imitated the performers' procedures and, working with a new text, built up a full performance, ending by staging the scene on our TheaterGame, which will be described later.

The Browser. The prototype's second component consisted of a data base of approximately 1,000 images and 200 pages of text on Shakespeare—his life, productions of his plays—and the history of theater from the ancient world to the present. As students looked at an image, they could touch the screen to read an explanatory text. The text also suggested other related sequences of images that students might explore. For example, if students looked at a picture of a court scene in *Hamlet*, they might be directed to pictures showing Elizabethan court life.

TheaterGame. The prototype's third component involved a staging simulation on the Macintosh computer. Using the TheaterGame, students could select stages, props, and characters in various costumes. They could create a computer "movie" with the actors and actresses moving through a scene according to the text and the students' subtext. The TheaterGame was not tied to any one scene or play, and worked equally well for Shakespeare, Ibsen, or one's own work.

At Stanford, we used Page to Stage and The Browser with students from two small under-graduate classes, "Shakespeare Through Performance" and "History of Theater Design," and from a large survey course, "Art and Literature in Western Culture." We tested the Theater-Game at Stanford, at San Francisco State University in a special graduate program in directing in the drama department, in an English class at San Francisco's Lowell High School, and at Bank Street School (an experimental elementary school in New York) with a group of 10-year-olds who used it to create stories.

Researchers observed students working on the tutorial, and interviewed them after each session. Researchers found that the tutorial's most immediate strength was that the students tremendously enjoyed using it. Students were fascinated by the chance to see different versions of a scene, they liked looking at and really noticing the details of an actor's performance, they liked having a library of examples with which to play, and they appreci-ated the expert comments on the scenes. In general, they felt a privileged and intimate connection with the material, as though they had been invited backstage by Olivier himself.

Part of their delight was in the sense of freedom and adventure they gained from watching the widely differing versions of a scene. This experience of the freedom possible, indeed necessary, in interpretation acted as a kind of personal permission for them to explore on their own—permission to think wildly and boldly. This new sense was reflected in students' class work, in a willingness to make risky choices and to appreciate the daring and outra-geousness of Shakespeare's own imagination.

Slowing down to work through a text or a scene, instead of floating through the experience vaguely accumulating impressions, forced the students to pay careful attention to the significance of each moment, each detail, and to come to a precise decision about each moment of choice. As one student said, "(I learned) to be simple, taking analysis line by line (moment by moment) rather than in general."

What most struck them were those elements they had never previously considered when thinking of theater: the significance of an actor's pause, the use of space and timing to create emotion, and the way these details affected their reactions as spectators. "I think the only way to understand beats is to watch them. You cannot learn about beats simply from the text," remarked a student.

Working on the character's motivations and interior monologues, they saw that theater represents the actions of real human beings, operating out of concrete circumstances and needs. Another student commented, "I analyze too complicatedly (sic). The computer's analysis was always simpler and more emotionally concrete than mine. I should get simpler and more 'basic' about feelings—that is, away from 'why' someone is behaving a certain way and more about what the behavior actually is."

The quality of the workmanship and creative skill now visible to the students was an impressive learning experience in itself. Again, a student remarks, "(there are) endless possibilities and nuances of interpretation . . . these are not flat characters, but characters with a whole history and network of feelings and motivations."

Instead of valuing Shakespeare for some vaguely felt quality of "seriousness" or "depth," students glimpsed the exquisite care and precision of the text and of the performers' interpretive labor. They were able to see how difficult the performer's task is, and thus were able to acquire some standards with which to measure the accomplishment. "I learned . . . how actors and actresses, without saying anything, can express a great deal."

Students enjoyed simulating and participating in the creative work, collaborating with the performers, comparing their responses with the experts', and making something of their own. It was important to the students that their activities and responses mattered. For example, students enjoyed having a record of their own reactions and of their work; it made their feelings seem significant.

In short, the prototype was a considerable success: "I think this is a great program—very enjoyable. It entertains and intrigues while it educates."

The Next Step

Benefiting from its exploratory work on the prototype, the Shakespeare Project has expanded and refined its design in the creation of **On Stage. On Stage** adds new lessons and capabilities, as it integrates the three components of the prototype into one simple work space.

On Stage will consist of three programs:

- A **Scholar's Kit**, which allows students to analyze a scene and a play in great detail.

- A **Director's Kit**, which allows students to design a scene creatively.

- A **Director's Notebook**, which supplies a simplified version of the first two programs for use at home on a personal computer.

The programs will run on a computer that controls a videodisc player. The performances and still images will be recorded on two videodiscs.

Using the Scholar's Kit, students select a text or performance for study, and are given a "menu of procedures" they can use, in any order, to analyze the work. Each procedure allows them to work closely with one aspect of the play, the language, the psychological motives and constraints, the performance techniques, the sources and uses of the design, the structure of conflict and resolution, and so forth (see Figure 2).

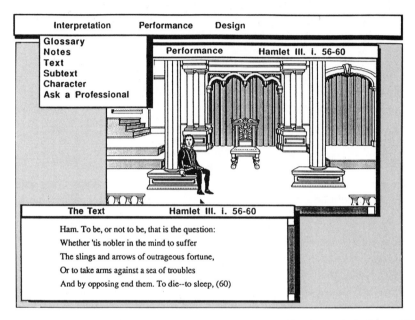

Figure 2. *The Scholar's Kit. The screen shows the choices available, along with the Text and Performance windows. The student has chosen Interpretation and has selected a text, which is shown in the lower part of the screen. The controls at the right side and bottom of the windows scroll the text and control the playback of the video.*

The Director's Kit lets students choose the cast, costumes, and stage design for their interpretation of a scene and then make an animated "movie" or record of their work. The students are directors and designers. They make theater, discovering the process–the chain of choices–that leads to opening night (see Figure 3).

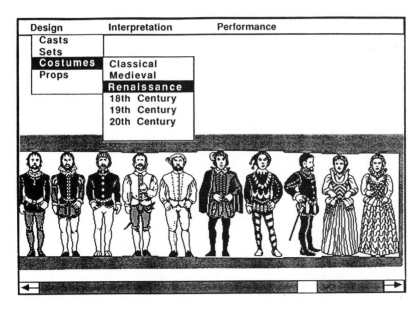

Figure 3. *The Director's Kit. Students start by choosing from the menus. Here the student has chosen to examine Renaissance costumes.*

An archive of hundreds of costumed actors and props can be viewed on the videodisc. The students browse through this electronic wardrobe and prop room, make selections that suit their interpretations, and place all these elements on a staging space, where they will, in fact, work out the scene. Students move characters across the stage to create blocking patterns, which are recorded and can be played back (see Figure 4).

The Director's Notebook stores the students' work together with portable versions of some of On Stage's lessons, so that the work can be saved and used at home or school.

In On Stage, students do not follow a rigid tutorial format, but choose activities as they need them. If they are unfamiliar with a particular concept, they can request a "mini-tutorial," and can also go to a library of annotated examples where they can practice at their own pace.

Figure 4. The Director's Kit. The student has chosen the desired costume and will transfer it to the stage area. When all the design elements are selected, the student can animate the scene.

The sequence of activities is determined by the students' goal, whether it be to interpret a scene, to describe a character, or to design a performance. The resulting work is arranged and recorded for them on disc or tape, and can be used for further study. In Tasks and Methods (Section 5), we will describe the multiplicity of activities available in these three programs, but we may now pause to mention three representative ones.

Watching a scene and comparing different versions. On Stage allows a close, comparative viewing of several versions of a scene. Viewing different productions of Hamlet one after another, for example, changes the way that students perceive theater.

Consider the nunnery scene in *Hamlet*. Hamlet seems very angry with Ophelia, tells her he does not love her, and accuses all women of infidelity and treachery. At the same time, however, he expresses his longing and love for her and accuses himself of unworthiness. What is going on? What is happening in Hamlet's mind? Does Hamlet love Ophelia, or does he hate her? How can students make sense of all these contradictory bits of information?

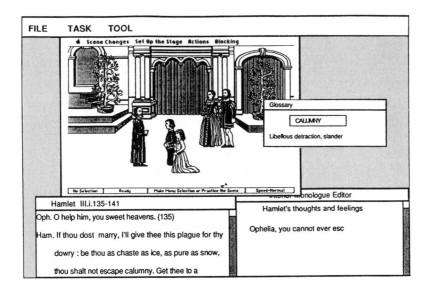

FILE   TASK   TOOL

Scene Changes   Set Up the Stage   Actions   Blocking

Glossary

CALUMNY

Libellous detraction, slander

No Selection | Ready | Make Menu Selection or Practice the Scene | Speed-Normal

Interior Monologue Editor

Hamlet III.i.135-141

Oph. O help him, you sweet heavens. (135)

Ham. If thou dost marry, I'll give thee this plague for thy

dowry : be thou as chaste as ice, as pure as snow,

thou shalt not escape calumny. Get thee to a

Hamlet's thoughts and feelings

Ophelia, you cannot ever esc

Figure 5. The Director's Notebook. The screen shows a text from Hamlet, *with the corresponding interior monologue, glossary, and animated stage. The student is in the process of developing a subtext for the scene.*

On Stage allows students to address questions like these by viewing several versions of the same scene. For example, in one version with Nicol Williamson, Hamlet is rather seedy and lascivious. Here the performers have solved the illogicalities in Hamlet's language by imagining that Hamlet is playing with Ophelia's feelings because he wants to seduce her.

In contrast, in the Russian version a tortured, handsome Hamlet is discovered brooding under the stairway in a dark hallway by a fragile Ophelia, whom he proceeds to humiliate and terrify. This Hamlet's illogical behavior is portrayed as stemming not from sexual teasing, but from the repressed violence and paranoia of a man who both loves Ophelia and suspects her of treachery, and who resents the attraction he feels toward her.

Notice that both versions present appropriate, compelling solutions to the same puzzle; yet they are utterly different. The entire meaning of the scene has changed—the very story, events, and emotions.

As students articulate and evaluate different interpretations "they are more likely to realize that interpretation is an art rather than a science," and they are emotionally freed from the tyranny of the "right" answer. They develop their own standards of judgment and taste and are encouraged to undertake a bold investigation of the possibilities of theatrical interpretation.

Creating a subtext. On Stage also allows students to master one of the central concepts in theater, the subtext. Actors create an inner life for their characters by imagining the characters' basic assumptions, their goals and intentions, their feelings about the situation they are in and the people they are with. These decisions about the characters' inner life form the subtext of the interpretation, the level of feeling and motive operating beneath the text.

As students using On Stage observe a character, they try to imagine what that character is thinking as he or she acts. For example, as Hamlet says "Are you honest?" he may be thinking "I don't trust you" or conversely "I love you." Students type this "interior monologue" on the keyboard, and it appears as a subtitle on the screen. Working with this monologue, students formulate the character's general motives and needs, what obstacles face the character as he attempts to get what he wants, and what strategies he employs to overcome the obstacles.

In order to create a subtext, students have to become active and engaged viewers, to "slow down" and carefully watch and judge. They must observe the actor closely, and by empathizing with the character, imagine the character's psychological state and the precise flow of his motives and thoughts. They also have to notice how thoughts spring from motives and self-interest; and how motives in turn flow from deep assumptions people have about their lives. They thus make visible the constant and fascinating tension between what people want and think, and what they actually do.

Analyzing relationships between characters. Plays are long and complicated events. One way to grasp the overall shape and movement of the work is to follow major characters through the course of the action and note the ways they change and develop. For example, students using On Stage may be reading the text of the nunnery scene from Hamlet and want to examine the relationship between characters. They can select any two characters (see Figure 6).

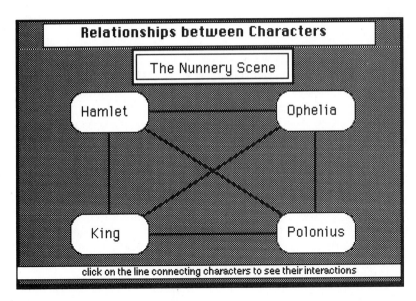

Figure 6. *Choosing the characters. The screen displays the characters from the nunnery scene with lines connecting them. Students indicate a line to choose the pair they want to study.*

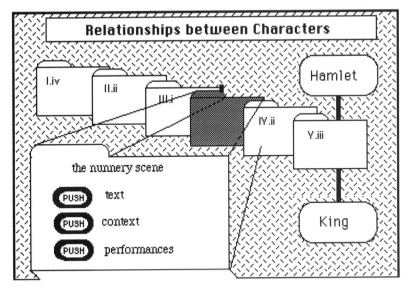

Figure 7. *Choosing the scene. Examining the relationship between Hamlet and the king, the student has selected the nunnery scene and will work with the text, the context, and the performances.*

The program then offers the students a selection of the most important scenes between the two (see Figure 7).

The student's goal in On Stage is to construct a full portrait of the characters by analyzing each scene for the evidence it contains about the characters' lives, emotions, thoughts, and beliefs. They can examine the language for information and clues, and then assess how this evidence has been interpreted and presented by the different performances. Of course, each performance will have interpreted the evidence differently. Students can accept a particular interpretation or come to their own decisions.

They assemble this evidence in a character portfolio—trying to reconstruct a complete history, description, and analysis of the character, including information that is missing from the text. They then plot how the character changes and develops. Students use the portfolio to argue a case, citing sources, and advancing interpretations of specific moments in scenes. They can include evidence from performances by "clipping" images and segments of scenes and "pasting" them in the portfolio, thus creating a kind of multimedia essay.

Students learn how to discover and assess evidence, to evaluate choices, and to see the interconnections among characters. They can take the portfolio that they have created and use it at home or in class, to further analyze the play.

The Summary

On Stage does not overwhelm the students with technology, nor imprison them in narrowly conceived learning paths. It offers a simple, open space for study and creation.

With On Stage, students control the pace, sequence, and goals of their learning. However, they are also guided and supported at every turn by tutorial and example; and are supplied with the information, concepts, and tools they need. Working through the lessons, they have the satisfaction of completing many intriguing tasks. At the end of their work, they see their efforts in the product they take away with them.

Instructors will remain in control of the teaching and the content matter. On Stage does not reflect any specific approach to Shakespeare, but simply provides tools and the basic materials for study. Teachers can easily rearrange these materials by linking film segments and images with text, animations, and graphics, and in effect, design completely new lessons. By substituting a new videodisc with materials from another play, On Stage can be directly adapted for use with a dramatic work by any playwright.

On Stage is extremely flexible. It can be used by one student or by groups of students; at home, in a classroom, or in a rehearsal hall; by beginning students or professionals; as a one-time resource or as the basis for an entire course.

Finally, as we will describe in the next section, On Stage's programs can be adapted for use in other disciplines that also focus on events that are difficult to present in the classroom.

SIGNIFICANCE

> This project is on the cutting edge of computer animation and creates a whole new class of "electronic marionette" applications for teaching that can be generalized to nontheatrical applications.
> (Barbara Bowen, Manager, External Research, Apple Computer, Inc.)

The invention of books revolutionized our study of the spoken word. Language was taken "out of time," so to speak; readers could move at their own pace through the work, without regard for chronological order. Details could be examined at leisure, comparisons made with other pieces of speech, and wholly new utterances could be created by selecting and combining unrelated parts. These wondrous capabilities have remained the foundation of our methods of learning for many centuries.

Advances in technology now promise an analogous transformation of our study of live events. All the pieces are in place, and solutions are appearing rapidly. On Stage can contribute a significant part to this transformation through programs that permit film to be handled like text, taken out of time, examined, annotated, recombined. While On Stage's immediate goal is a change in the way we can teach theater, On Stage will also contribute to a widely based change in education as a whole.

Current Status of Teaching Shakespeare

Inadequacies of current approaches. Shakespeare occupies a unique place in our schools and in our culture. No other figure is held in such high esteem by both the critics and the public. The fascination with Shakespeare is endless and deep: festivals flourish, new popular works based on the plays appear regularly, and he is studied throughout the land, from the lowest to the highest levels of our schools.

The plays were written for the mass audiences of Shakespeare's time, and they still can enthrall the widest range of viewers or readers. Yet a considerable group of students never overcome the initial obscurity of the language and the unfamiliarity of the theatrical conventions.

Film and television offer students competing models of performance and participation that do not prepare them for the kind of concentrated effort required by the plays, whose visual and sensual impact is lost in a traditional classroom.

On Stage is designed to supplement the strengths of traditional methods of teaching, and to remedy their inadequacies. There are three ways Shakespeare's plays are currently taught: by reading the text, by watching a performance, and by working on a production. Each way provides something irreplaceable, and each has its limitations.

Approach Through Text. Shakespeare wrote plays, not books. As David Riggs, eminent historian of Elizabethan stage, writes,

> We forget that when Shakespeare died in 1616, half of his plays, including masterpieces like *Twelfth Night*, *Macbeth*, *Antony and Cleopatra*, and *The Tempest*, had not been published and had little chance of ever finding a reading audience; Shakespeare regarded them as the property of his acting company, the King's Men. Perhaps the greatest single frustration of teaching a Shakespeare lecture course today is the prospect of spending an entire quarter teaching students texts that were never meant to be read.

Even when we consider the text not as a replacement for the play, but as a record of a performance, problems remain. The text gives only a partial record of the performance. To complete a reading of the text, students must imagine the play being performed. But to ask students to create a performance in their minds is to demand of them what is difficult even for the most experienced professional, for the text does not clearly describe the performance. Rather, the text suggests a pattern of possible choices to be made by a group of workers within the context of a specific performing situation. It is only as these decisions accumulate ("I will pause here; I will turn there; I will design blue costumes or metal furniture") that the "meaning" of the production slowly emerges. Any one production of *Hamlet* is a unique creation arising from the one-time collaboration of playwright, designer, director, and performers.

In fact, there can be no final, "correct" version of the text. Diametrically opposed interpretations may be equally powerful and legitimate. When the only experience students have is the text, it is hard for them to understand how different choices could be equally valid. Are there not rules that control interpretation? How can one actor be "better" than another if they both are following the same script? Only by teaching students to regard the text as a set of suggestions for a performance can students grasp the standards of judgment that govern theater.

We need to help students imagine a performance from the text, by giving them extensive and intimate contact with performance. This is true in other fields: notation in dance, musical scores, diagrams of a football play, transcripts of a therapy session, a doctor's written diagnosis of an illness, missals in a church; all these are poor records if students lack extensive experience of the events to which they refer.

Approach Through Watching a Performance. Watching the play on stage or on film obviously solves one major problem. Students see the event. However, there are other problems:

- Students watching a performance tend to assume that they are seeing the authoritative version. Any performance, however, is merely one possible realization of the script. Students need to develop standards of taste in order to compare and evaluate different performing versions.

- On film, the world of process, creation, and choice is invisible. In order to judge the performance, students need to understand what choices were made in the course of the production.

- A performance must be studied slowly and carefully, for it is so densely packed with detail and implication that even the best students can only absorb a fraction of the experience.

Compared to text, film is an inflexible medium. We can "flip" through a book, isolate passages, read and reread, quickly compare widely separated passages. We are in firm control; our interests, rhythms, habits, and needs determine the study process. We make decisions, we select, underline, omit, review; in fact, we imagine a world. We need a comparably flexible and interactive way to work with film.

In brief, students need to know what to watch in a performance and how to evaluate what they see.

Approach Through Participating in a Performance. Students' actual participation in performance provides a powerful supplement to reading text and viewing film. Students vividly experience the complex unfolding of the interpretive event as they enter into the social, sensual, and theatrical worlds of the play. However, as a general and embracing method of teaching drama, it, too, has problems:

- Students need to experience a fully realized, excellent production, because the full range, daring, and power of theater are revealed only in professional work. Often neither teachers nor students have enough experience to produce an exemplary version of a play.

- Practical theatrical people are rarely trained to think abstractly about their work or to help students to articulate and generalize broader implications. Students worrying about cues and lights usually do not ponder large questions and meaning.

- Theater is extremely costly. Most schools cannot offer theatrical opportunities to all students.

In summary, students need to see, study, and participate in theater. On Stage offers students the chance to do all three in an integrated manner.

The Teachers

The criticism of Shakespeare in our century, starting with the work of such great pioneers as Granville-Barker and Chambers, has greatly benefited from approaches that combine traditional literary scholarship with a deep knowledge of the world of theater. On Stage allows these kinds of insights to be demonstrated in the classroom.

On Stage will appeal to teachers as a chance to incorporate their feeling for theater directly into the classroom. Professor Ron Rebholz, a distinguished teacher of Shakespeare at Stanford, described exactly that desire in his letter of support for On Stage:

> I have been following, on the sidelines but with great interest, the development of your Shakespeare Project.
>
> Obviously Shakespeare wrote his plays to be performed. Without slighting the attention they deserve as great literary texts, I know we agree that they should, first and foremost, be taught and studied as texts to be created and re-created on the stage or in comparable media, like film or videotape.
>
> As a teacher of Shakespeare for 25 years at Stanford, I have been frustrated by the limited opportunities to teach the plays and get my students to study the plays as works for and in performance. Simply to get them to see the plays I once, several years ago, organized a year-long Shakespeare film festival; and the possibilities of seeing the plays have been enhanced by the advent of videotape versions, especially the BBC-PBS series. But seeing and studying are two different things. I have since incorporated in my courses staged readings, directed and performed by the students, of scenes from the plays we study, but the quality of the scenes is not high and the experience benefits mainly those who do the readings. If I understand the thrust of your project, it will offer a completely new and exciting possibility of *all* my students *studying* the plays as they have been and might be performed.
>
> I don't have to tell you the extraordinary educational value of the experience offered by your project. It will show students the many possible ways of staging scenes and playing characters and the implications of the actual choices for the interpretation of the whole play. Most important, it will make them grasp the point that I have been trying for years to make them grasp in my fumbling ways: Shakespeare wrote *plays,* there are virtually limitless ways of performing them, and some ways are better than others in capturing the "spirit" of the text and in affecting the audience.
>
> I know many teachers of Shakespeare throughout this country and in Britain, and I am confident that they will all greet your project as a genuine and welcome revolution in their teaching of his plays.

Response to news of our project has been gratifying. Professor Rebholz's sentiments are echoed in the more than 50 letters of inquiry and support we have received from all over the country. Professionals whose work is introducing technology into the curriculum have been particularly excited by the prospect of such a new system. We have been invited to participate in conferences in Prague and Brussels on art and technology, and our programs have been written about in many papers and magazines. Both the BBC and the SFB in Berlin will feature the TheaterGame on television programs next winter.

We are particularly proud of the list of internationally prominent scholars, editors, and artistic directors who have consented to work on our advisory board. We feel this interest flows from the recognition that On Stage is a new solution to a critically important educational problem.

The Students

On Stage is designed to enhance the educational experience of the average college student and to extend the world of Shakespeare to the nontraditional learner.

Courses on Shakespeare. On Stage, because of its emphasis on student design and collaboration, should lead to a more fluid and open environment for both students and faculty, freeing the teacher from the restraints of a lecture format, and allowing students considerable independence.

In lectures, the professor could demonstrate basic ideas about staging and interpretation, or could show variant scenes, or do sample stagings on the simulation program. Students could also work privately on workstations, following their own interests, or could do research for papers or student productions. If teachers wished to provide a special focus for their classes, they could author new lessons that reflected their own interests.

Teaching Shakespeare demands that instructors deal with issues from intellectual history, psychology, history of art, and poetry. Instructors necessarily focus on one or more of these approaches, and often do not have much time to devote to teaching theatrical form. On Stage could be used as a weekly activity to supplement lectures. Discussion groups might focus on student assignments done at home or experimental staging exercises in the class itself.

Survey Courses. Many universities require all students to take courses that offer some Shakespeare. In such a large survey course, On Stage could be used in discussion sections and demonstrations in class.

Lecturers in such courses often have little foundation in theater and little time to spend on any one subject. With On Stage, students could quickly learn enough about theater to guide them through the readings; they could study on their own at home or in a computer lab, and then do a written assignment.

Special Courses on Shakespeare in Theater. On Stage could form the nucleus of an entirely new kind of class, which integrates the criticism and practice of an art form. Last spring, Professor Friedlander, the principal investigator of the Shakespeare Project, experimented with the creation of such a course, called "Shakespeare in Performance," using components of the prototype system.

The students were of all ages, backgrounds, and majors, and did not generally have previous theatrical or artistic experience. Students read plays and criticism, discussed dramatic theory, and applied performance methods to solve problems of interpretation. Students used the prototype for assignments, demonstrated the results in class, then actually performed scenes.

The result was a fluid interchange between kinds of learning—theoretical and practical. The goal was to let students grasp the translations from one domain to another, to understand how criticism aids performance, how performance choices solve interpretive issues, and how concepts translate into design choices.

The course created an environment in which students felt free to make daring choices, and to support and inspire one another. Students with no special talent for theater actually did very nice work—much to their surprise. They learned to watch others and themselves critically, to evaluate creative choices, to find complex standards to measure their own and others' work. They also learned to play, to improvise, to have fun; they discovered that relaxation, curiosity, and joy are powerful aids to creativity.

This kind of course demands teachers who have interest and expertise in both criticism and performance. It is somewhat expensive, since the class cannot be very large, but it provides a powerful environment for expanding students' thinking about art and their own experience.

Increased Access for Nontraditional Learners. Often, students who resist literary and analytic approaches can be caught by the power of visual experience. And once caught and engaged, students can move faster and further than they would have imagined. Because On Stage allows so many levels of approaches, students have opportunities to fulfill many goals, receiving immediate rewards for their efforts.

On Stage provides students with all the instruction they need to use its programs. On Stage can thus reach out to students who, because of poor verbal skills or lack of formal education, are effectively deprived of nourishing contact with classic theater. With no preparation or background, students could watch different versions of scenes; spend time in our practice libraries, looking at annotated segments of scenes and reading explanatory background comments; browse through archives, picking costumes and cast; and move characters around a stage.

On Stage would also appeal to the numerous "lay" people who love Shakespeare—who take their families for weekends to the major festivals, but who lack formal training in theater. The many institutions that provide nontraditional learning, such as community

On Stage would also appeal to the numerous "lay" people who love Shakespeare—who take their families for weekends to the major festivals, but who lack formal training in theater. The many institutions that provide nontraditional learning, such as community colleges, public libraries, and the educational arms of major theaters and festivals, could integrate On Stage into their programs, granting people a rare chance to learn what happens "behind the scenes," thus deepening their enjoyment of live performance.

Finally, it would not be difficult for a teacher of English, possessed of a love for Shakespeare but with no background in theater, to learn enough from On Stage to include teaching about drama in class; or in fact, to create a new course offering on theater. In this way, many small or poor schools could afford to add theater to their curricula.

In summary, On Stage would significantly expand the public's access to theater and theater education by inspiring the creation of new classes, by reaching out to learners alienated from traditional education, and by enlarging the repertoire of public extension courses.

A Model for Teaching Art, Not Science

On Stage provides a model for instruction in the arts in general. Theater is not science or math, but an art form; and we need to teach it in ways appropriate to its nature. The form of a work of art is complex, and not easily analyzed. What we say about a poem is less rich than the poem itself. Teaching art, we need to convey a correspondingly rich, complex, and multiple view of the art object.

Our goal is to guide the student to full comprehension of the work without reducing its complexity and power. We need to find a correct balance between mastery of the field (information and history), and developing the student's ability to respond to the experience. We believe that students are capable of enlarging and deepening their insight into the field even if they are not trained or talented in theater.

The center of our instructional technique is not a series of right or wrong answers, but a series of concepts about theater and art. Students see how great performers solve problems, and they read what experts say about those performances. They then imitate the procedures both through working out interpretations and by designing theater. In the process, they develop a tolerance for the uncertainty and multiple possibilities inherent in all forms of art.

Traditionally in the arts, teaching information, while important, is not central. Instead, students learn by exposure to great works, and by acquiring techniques of observation and description. In poetry, for example, students are asked to read many poems, then they learn to analyze the language, and finally they read criticism, as models of the analytic or inter-pretative process. In short, they sharpen their taste and perception by sustained contact with the works and with high examples of critical response.

On Stage provides similar instruction: students watch many performances, learn analytic concepts and procedures, see many examples of expert analysis and response, and then design a performance themselves.

Our Approach to Learning. Social learning theory (Bandura, 1977) supports the major premises of our instructional design. Bandura's research has found that people learn a great deal through direct observation of events, even when the events are dramatized or portrayed in media such as film or television (Bandura, Ross, and Ross, 1963). Vicariously, viewers construct internal models of behavior that they can later translate into action.

This theory reminds one of the complex transformations that are so central to theater. The actor translates his internal motivations and cognitive processes into behavior, action, and speech. In order for spectators to appreciate the event, they, too, must grasp these relationships, internalize them, understand them in a unified way, and finally respond.

Bandura emphasizes that this complex process is sustained by the excitement of completing "proximal" goals, which are short-range and easily fulfilled. In On Stage, students learn in short sequences, and can easily manage to complete any one cycle of observation, description, and production.

Bandura's model further emphasizes the importance to learning of self-regulating, self-directing, and self-reflecting qualities. Because the environment is swiftly changing, people must continually remain open to new models of experience that they can absorb, internalize, and use.

By moving from study to design, students can externalize and explore their own learning. Guided instruction takes students through the tasks in an orderly and nonthreatening way, which permits students with no particular talent for theater to extend their capabilities. On Stage offers students multiple pathways to multiple solutions, allowing them to create at their own level, inspired by the highest examples.

A Model for Applications in Other Disciplines

While On Stage's programs have been developed for use with a theater videodisc, they can be applied with relative ease to visual materials from other disciplines.

Background. At Stanford, a group of faculty began discussing such applications in the spring of 1985. The initial planning meeting was attended by representatives from the departments of Humanities, Geology, Athletics, Drama, Computer Science, Communications, French, and Italian, and by the director of Stanford's Audio-visual Laboratory. Other faculty members have since indicated their interest in working toward a widespread introduction of videodisc-based instruction into the classroom. The group decided to create a portfolio of applications that could use the programs developed for On Stage.

Applications. Faculty interest in these applications is reflected in the letters they have written describing their initial ideas for applying On Stage to their disciplines. Kris Samuelson of Communications says that the introduction of such programs would be "like opening new windows to learning." Elizabeth Larkham of Dance remarks, "This tool would make dance choreography, technique, and production come alive for the student in ways that might surpass experience of a live performance."

Other instructors are equally eloquent about the effect of having students interact with these complex events. Professor Zimbardo of Psychology writes: "The wonderful thing about this new methodology is its energizing of the learner's involvement with the text, the scene, the decisions to be made, and the predictions of outcomes of various interventions. Then in an instant, the response options materialize, then can be reviewed until the fundamentals are mastered at the student's own pace."

Zimbardo especially welcomed the power of the program to convey the nuances of behavior, and to teach students how to observe with precision: "I could definitely use the technology so well developed by your team to help students better realize certain fundamental principles in social psychology, such as the significance of alternative 'construals' of the same environmental situation by different actors and observers. I can think of no better way to aid me in the teaching of the subtle dynamics involved: (a) in dyadic interactions, (b) in nonverbal communication displays, (c) in cross-cultural behavioral differences, (d) in the ways gender roles bias or filter the perceptions of reality, and more."

Professor Zelditch of Sociology emphasized how important visual materials are in his field: "I teach a course called American Society in Film and Literature. Students taking this course read one novel or play each week and see one film each week. The focus is entirely on sociology—that is, not on aesthetic methods or values. Literature and film are used as a method of increasing insight into the society that produces and is portrayed by it." One advantage of using On Stage he cites is in the possible financial savings: "I also foresee a long-run reduction in costs. It costs me about the price of a teaching assistant to rent films through the Meyer Film Service each year. The initial costs of videodisc would be greater, but after that the costs should decrease substantially."

Instructors such as Zelditch and Samuelson already depend on film and video and could "move up" to interactive video, using both On Stage's programs and its workstations. Another professor in sociology, Henry Walker, foresees this technology's increased role within his discipline:

> Professor Bernard P. Cohen and I have just received a generous grant, which will permit us to fully computerize our laboratory facilities during the upcoming year. It is my understanding that the technology you are developing permits interfacing microcomputers with videodisc equipment. If our department had access to such technology, we could replace much of current instructional and research materials (which are on videotape) with

videodiscs. Since it is easier and simpler to locate and play back information on videodisc than videotaped material, I am sure that those of us who presently use videotape would increase our instructional use of video materials. In addition, I suspect that some of my colleagues who do not presently use videotape as a teaching aid would be enticed to do so.

Professor Walker also reiterates Professor Zimbardo's excitement at the opportunities for research offered by On Stage:

The most exciting prospect for us would be the capability of using the technology in our undergraduate courses which have a strong research emphasis. Several of our courses require students to observe social interaction that has been recorded on videotape, and to simultaneously record what they are observing. By using videodisc equipment interfaced with our system of microcomputers and one of the available "window" programs, we could carry out these activities more efficiently—and at the same time record and store the data students are generating.

Summary. The future development of this project at Stanford will be designed to crystallize a range of ongoing efforts in a range of disciplines at the University. For it will provide a technological context into which a range of individuals—teachers and learners—can supply their favorite "if I only had the capability to..." scenario. Theater will become an alive and accessible field as will many others that are currently "alive only for the moment."

REFERENCES

Bandura, A. (1977). *Social Learning Theory.* Englewood Cliffs, New Jersey: Prentice-Hall.

Bandura, A., Ross, D. and S.A. Ross. (1963). "Imitation of Film Mediated Aggressive Models." *Journal of Abnormal and Social Psychology*, vol. 66.

Cicero

A Framework for Multimedia Projects for Classics

Bernard Frischer

BERNARD FRISCHER

Bernard Frischer received his B.A. in Classics from Wesleyan University in 1971. He entered the Ph.D. program in Classics at the University of Heidelberg, wrote his dissertation on a new theory of literary hermeneutics applied to Virgil's pastoral poetry, and received his doctorate in 1975. As a Rome Prize Fellow in Classics at the American Academy in Rome, he expanded his horizons to include Roman art, archaeology, and topography. Since 1976, he has been teaching classics at UCLA; for the past two years, he has been chairman of the Classics Department. Dr. Frischer's last book, The Sculpted Word, is about how the Epicurean school recruited new students by using sculpted portraits of their leaders as publicity. Currently, he is writing a book about how Horace's Art of Poetry parodies neoclassicism in the arts during the Augustan Age. In 1982, Dr. Frischer bought his first personal computer. He sees the commercialization of the personal computer in the 1980s and the development of multimedia technologies as a great boon for those who believe in studying mankind from integrated, interdisciplinary perspectives.

BACKGROUND

Thanks largely to the efforts of Theodore Brunner of U.C. Irvine, Classics is now one of the most computerized fields in the humanities. Since 1972, Professor Brunner has overseen the Thesaurus Linguae Graecae, a project to digitize all surviving Greek literature from Homer to 600 A.D. The work is largely complete, and a computerized corpus of some 2,900 authors and 50 million words has been released to the scholarly public.[1]

To date, use of this immense data base has been limited to string searches, which may be either global or limited to a subset of texts and authors. Two different systems have been developed to perform these searches on minicomputers. The first, called IBYCUS, was developed by David Packard in the 1970s to run on Hewlett-Packard equipment. The second, created from 1982 to 1984 by Gregory Crane at Harvard, can be used on any computer that runs UNIX.

In typical configurations of the Harvard system—such as the one David Blank and I designed for use at UCLA and the Getty Center for the History of Art and the Humanities— Macintosh computers are used as smart terminals linked to a VAX 750 or 780 by modems and asynchronous line drivers. In the last few months, both the Packard and Crane systems have been experimentally ported to microcomputers with optical disk drives in order to exploit the reformatting of the data base onto CD-ROM. Meanwhile, a project creating a data base for Latin has been started this year at Yale University under the direction of George Goold.

---

[1] See L. Berkowitz and K.A. Squitier, *Thesaurus Linguae Graecae. Canon of Greek Authors and Works*, second edition (Oxford 1986) xi–xii.

MULTIMEDIA PROJECTS AND
FIFTH-GENERATION COMPUTER SYSTEMS

Strengths and Weaknesses of Existing Classics Software

The capabilities of the Packard and Crane systems are truly astonishing. Within a few seconds, one can search the entire works of an author or even all of Greek literature to find every instance of a certain string; and one can telephone from home and read any text in the entire library of Greek literature. This ability has helped researchers to do things never before possible. For example, the concordance (an alphabetical listing of every word in a text with one line of context) is now a virtually defunct genre of Greek scholarship.

On the other hand, as a scholar and educator, I must confess that, for a variety of reasons, I am dissatisfied with existing computer applications for my field. First, there are no instructional uses of the data base, for the simple reason that current software presumes a fairly high level of fluency in ancient Greek. Second, the available search programs leave much to be desired, both in their user friendliness and in their power to manage and manipulate the data base. Boolean operators are not yet available, nor have the resources of the Macintosh been tapped to any degree. Finally, the preoccupation with string searching, while understandable, has given many classicists the mistaken impression that the primary use of the data base is as an electronic library or concordance. There are many other potential uses for this wonderful data base.

UCLA's Plans for New Classics Computer Applications

At UCLA, we have been encouraged by the central administration during the past academic year to develop a three-year plan for use of the computer in research and instruction. In our department, we began by envisioning an ideal multimedia expert system for Greek, Latin, and Classical Civilization. We proceeded on the assumption that our vision could be realized in the next ten to fifteen years, when fifth-generation computer systems[2] and massive textual and visual data bases will have been created and made commercially available. Our three-year plan was thus understood to be a step in the direction of a definable goal.

The Basis of Planning: A Vision of the Year 2000

Before describing our short-term plan (the focus of this paper), let me sketch my vision of where we will be in 10 or 15 years. By that time, we should have created a Classics Expert System that will serve everyone from the beginning student to the most advanced scholar. At the heart of this system will be vast visual and textual data bases of the primary materials

---

[2]See T. Moto-Oka (ed.), Fifth Generation Computer Systems. Proceedings of the International Conference on Fifth Generation Computer Systems, Tokyo, Japan, October 19–22, 1981 (Amsterdam, New York, Oxford 1982).

of the field—manuscripts[3], inscriptions, archaeological sites, art, architecture, and other artifacts—as well as the major reference works and about 25 percent of the secondary literature that is used 80 to 90 percent of the time[4]. Communication with the system will be almost entirely by voice.

Voice recognition and synthesis and the natural-language processing of Greek and Latin will have progressed far enough to permit computer-managed instruction in the ancient languages, starting from the elementary level. Machine translation[5] will permit students of Classical Civilization—that is, those who study antiquity through English translations—to access the same textual data base used by students and scholars of Greek and Latin. Instruction and research will emphasize interdisciplinary approaches, since much of the expertise of the ancillary specialties of the field will have been incorporated into the expert system.

For instruction, this means that learning will take place in environments in which a linguistic signifier is encountered with immediate visualization of—and, when possible, dramatized interaction with—the corresponding referent. For scholarship, this means that quantification and statistical analysis will become increasingly important, as will the methodologies of economics, psychology, and sociology, which facilitate the analysis of cultural artifacts of different periods, proveniences, and types. In this ideal world, students will learn faster and better, and for the first time in centuries[6], will even be able to speak Greek and Latin. Scholars will be freed from much, if not all, of the drudgery presently involved in data collection, and will have more time to develop and discipline their informed historical imaginations. The advent of the Classics Expert System will thus make this central field of the humanities less mechanical—more accessible and vital.

---

[3]The Thesaurus Linguae Graecae project gives us ancient Greek literature through modern scholarly editions; the ideal Classics Expert System will include a data base of the actual manuscripts and papyri on which the modern editions are based, along with a collation program for automatically representing the ancient, medieval, and modern evidence for the text.

[4]Using a library data base program such as UCLA's ORION, it should be easy to determine the most frequently consulted books and journals within a certain range of call numbers. It is my undocumented suspicion that a very small percentage of books accounts for a very high percentage of what readers actually use in a field.

[5]See H. Tanaka, et al., "Intelligent Man-Machine Interface," in T. Moto-Oka, op cit, 147–155.

[6]This feature of CALI (Computer-Assisted Language Instruction) in Latin and Greek cannot be overemphasized, since it will enable classicists to benefit from "modern language" techniques of interactive oral instruction. Thus, while CAI has been found to have only modest effectiveness in general (see J.A. Kulik, C.-L.C. Kulik, P.A. Cohen, "Effectiveness of Computer-based College Teaching: A Meta-analysis of Findings," *Review of Educational Research* 50 (1980) 525–544; K. Ahmad, et al., op cit, 119–122), it is reasonable to expect that CAI will have a high level of effectiveness in Greek and Latin instruction. Significantly increased effectiveness via videodisc-based instruction is reported by A.M. Abdulla, L.O. Watkins, and J.S. Henke, "The Use of Natural Language Entry and Laser Videodisk Technology in CAI," *Journal of Medical Education* 59 (1984) 739–745. The advantages of the videodisc for foreign language instruction are discussed by S.E.K. Otto, "Videodisk Image Retrieval for Language Teaching," *System* 11 (1983) 47–52.

MULTIMEDIA PROJECTS FOR THE NEXT THREE YEARS AND THE EDUCATIONAL NEEDS THEY ADDRESS

Our goal in the next three years is to take some small but important steps toward the Classics Expert System, by showing that a multimedia computer system can be built today that will help solve pressing problems confronting us in teaching Greek, Latin, and Ancient Civilization to our students.

Immediate Problems to be Addressed: Booming Enrollment, Stable Faculty Size

What are these problems? First, there are the welcome problems stemming from soaring enrollment in Classics. The following table shows the steady growth in the number of undergraduate and graduate enrollments in Classics at UCLA from 1977–78 to 1985–86:

Table: Total UCLA Classics Enrollment, 1977–1986

Year	Enrollment
1977–78	1,117
1979–80	1,278
1981–82	1,489
1983–84	1,547
1984–85	2,181
1985–86	2,995

Some of the factors responsible for this trend are local: for example, the number of undergraduates at UCLA grew by nearly 10 percent during this period; and in the fall of 1983, the Classics department initiated a new major in Classical Civilization, in which the study of Greek and Latin is recommended but not required. Local factors cannot, however, explain the entire rise, since many colleagues around the country report similar trends at their institutions.

Perhaps the most pressing problem caused by the near trebling of enrollment at UCLA during the past 10 years results from the simple fact that our faculty size has remained constant. Thus, our student/faculty ratio has worsened, and we need to find some remedy other than increasing the size of the faculty to ensure that we can maintain the quality of our instruction.

This problem is especially noticeable in the large lecture courses on Greek and Roman civilization that satisfy "general education" requirements at UCLA. In these courses—often the student's only exposure to the humanities in college—the average enrollment has grown from about 100 to more than 400 in the past ten years. As a result, education has become quite impersonal for both instructor and student, and the humanities have had to be presented in a nonhumanistic way. Opportunities for class discussion have diminished, as have the odds that a student will ever visit the professor during office hours to pursue discussion of some topic that aroused the student's curiosity. Multiple-choice examinations have become more frequent and have, indeed, all but replaced essays and research papers as the basis of grading.

Curricular Problems

The second set of problems we need to address is curricular. I suppose that one reason Classics is booming across the country is that it is a field that was able to attract many bright new assistant professors during the past 20 years, even during the depressed academic job market of the 1970s. These new faculty recruits brought vitality and energy to the field. Now entering their most productive years as teachers and scholars, many professors in this generation have been great believers in interdisciplinary approaches to Classics. As such, they have faced great frustrations in operating within a curriculum that is unidisciplinary at most universities, and they have been thwarted in their attempts to infuse even traditional courses with interdisciplinary perspectives by the absence of suitable textbooks.

For example, I teach a course called Roman Civilization to about 400 students each year. Although there are acceptable texts for political and military history, customs, and the arts, there is no single text that adequately synthesizes these major facets of the civilization, relating developments in one area of the culture to what is happening in other areas. In the courses in which Greek and Latin literature is read in the original, the situation is still worse: the older commentaries are going out of print faster than new ones are being published to replace them, and only rarely do these commentaries—old or new—treat nonlinguistic or nonliterary matters.

Traditional humanistic education is quite labor-intensive. Ideally, students study individually or in very small groups with senior tutors. If this approach were ever appropriate and feasible in a large American research university, it isn't any longer. Although our enrollment has trebled, I would be pleasantly surprised if our faculty is allowed to grow by more than 15 percent (the equivalent of two new faculty positions) in the next few years. Some other solution to the problem of our worsening faculty/student ratio is needed.

We think that a major component of any solution has to involve greater use of the computer in instruction. We also think that the computer, used creatively, can help solve many of the curricular problems we face. Since both kinds of problems are most acute in our civilization courses, it is there—specifically in Roman Civilization—that we propose to begin implementing our multimedia computer project. We will also be trying to apply the same approach to our intermediate Latin courses, in which enrollments have also been considerably higher in recent years.

Multimedia Solutions: Data Bases, Utilities, Applications

The great challenge during the next three years is to create a flexible framework for software design that will last through years of innovation in technology and educational theory. The framework that we have developed for our project has three parts: a core of multimedia data bases; around the core, an inner ring of scholarly utilities for using and modifying the data bases; and an outer ring of pedagogical applications, which use the scholarly utilities and the data bases.

The nature of the core and inner ring is fairly clear and requires more funding than imagination to create. The core includes data bases for Greek and Latin texts, morphologies, dictionaries, and syntax; images of archaeological artifacts of all kinds, from coins and lamps to statues and buildings; and an encyclopedia and bibliography.[7] The inner ring includes search programs with Boolean operators for data collection from the data bases; and parsers for morphology, syntax, rhetoric, and meter. The character of the outer ring—the interface with the student on all levels—has taken over a year to sketch out through the collaboration of subject experts and specialists in instructional-media development. I will summarize our plans for the student interface in a moment, after a word about our pedagogical assumptions.

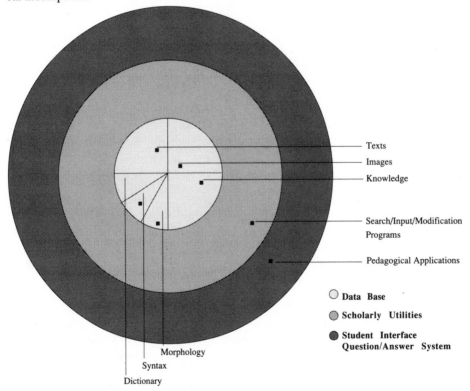

Texts
Images
Knowledge

Search/Input/Modification
Programs

Pedagogical Applications

○ **Data Base**
◉ **Scholarly Utilities**
● **Student Interface**
Question/Answer System

Morphology
Syntax
Dictionary

---

[7]Many of these data bases are already being created; for example, the American Philological Association is digitizing the standard Classics bibliographical annual; the J.Paul Getty Museum is creating a videodisc for Greek iconography; and our department is digitizing the Greek-English lexicon.

Pedagogical Theory: Curiosity Arousal

Whereas the structure of the core and inner ring reflect that of the field of Classics itself, that of the outer ring must be dependent both on this field and on a theory of knowledge acquisition. The theory I have devised is a hybrid based on the key notions of student involvement in learning[8] and the arousal of the student's curiosity.[9] The theory of interaction holds that students learn best when they become actively involved in their own education; the theory of curiosity (or "effectance") arousal explains how we become motivated to learn in proportion to the confusion and challenge we experience in a new environment. Russ, Gold, and Stone have recently shown that when students are exposed to extremely foreign material and asked to learn it, they tend to turn for help to "dissimilar others," that is, "experts" perceived to be more oriented to the new knowledge than were the students themselves. Russ and his colleagues have also shown that this kind of experience significantly increases student curiosity.[10]

It seems to me that these two theories of learning are complementary—one stresses the need for the student to be curious, the other tells us how to make people curious.

---

[8]The importance of active student involvement in learning has been emphasized in two recent reports on American education; see M.J. Adler, *The Paideia Program* (New York 1984), especially pp.167–179; and Involvement in Learning (National Institute of Education, October 1984), especially pp.17–19. On strategies for increasing student involvement, see V. Roadrangka and R.H. Yeany, "A Study of the Relationship among Type and Quality of Implementation of Science Teaching Strategy, Student Formal Reasoning Ability, and Student Engagement," *Journal of Research in Science Teaching* 22 (1985) 743–60.

[9]See R.W. White, "Motivation Reconsidered: The Concept of Competence," *Psychological Review* 66 (1959) 297–333; R.C. Russ, J.A. Gold, and W.F. Stone, "Attraction to a Dissimilar Stranger as a Function of Level of Effectance Arousal," *Journal of Experimental Social Psychology* 15 (1979) 481–91.

[10]Ibid., 489

How can the computer help us implement these two theories? One of the potential strengths of CAI is its highly interactive nature—however rare interactivity may be in existing courseware.[11] As for curiosity arousal, the computer with multimedia programming is an ideal tool for creating an imaginary world that is at the same time challenging and intriguing to the student, and for providing the student with a friendly guide (a "dissimilar other") for successfully navigating through that world. This guide I will call "Cicero," after the Italian word (*cicerone*) for a tour guide.[12]

Cicero: The Student Interface
With this background, I can now describe our proposed structure for the outer shell, the student interface for Roman Civilization and Intermediate Latin.

In the Museo della Civilita' Romana in Rome, there is a model of the city at its height of development in 315 A.D., when the population had reached about 1 million and the urban fabric covered some 30 square kilometers. The model is extremely accurate because our archaeological knowledge of the city is quite precise, and we even have an enormous ancient map of the ground plan of every building in the year 211 A.D. at a scale of 1:250. Added to this visual material are hundreds of pages of literary and epigraphical sources, making Rome the best-documented city from antiquity. The model in the museum is itself quite impressive—it is over 60 feet in diameter and reflects the state of the scholarship in Roman topography.

Classics is the study of every aspect of ancient civilization, including literature, religion, art, science, and even clothing and footwear. What better way to study Classics than by return-ing to a cultural center like Rome, learning about the city and its civilization, and discover-ing how to survive with the help of a friendly guide? We intend to use techniques of macrophotography developed for contemporary city planning by Donald Appleyard of U.C.

---

[11]See K. Ahmad, et al., *Computers, Language Learning and Language Teaching* (Cambridge 1985) passim, especially p.4: "the computer can offer interactive learning. This means that it can conduct a two-way learning session with the student. It is much more than a mere programmed textbook, whose powers of interaction are virtually limited to an ability to reveal the correct answer: the computer can 'assess' the student's response. It can also display messages, take the student through subsequent attempts at a question, and even take the student to a different section of the package, depending on the nature of the response. The computer can do all this very quickly—its response is practically instantaneous. If the computer is impersonal and literal-minded, it is also unfailingly accurate and precise. It does not tire, and its attention does not falter. It can repeat an activity with none of the errors which easily arise from repetition by humans, and it is as impartial and unbiased as the linguistic material which is typed into it. It can handle a very large volume of interaction and can deliver to the student feedback of some subtlety, at more frequent intervals than would be possible for a human teacher in all but individual tuition sessions. And it is flexible in a number of significant ways...." On the importance of eliciting student interaction in language learning, see J.H. Schumann, "Second Language Acquisition: The Pidginization Hypothesis," *Language Learning* 26,2 (1976) 391–408, at p.403.

[12]"Cicero" is also the name of a CAI authoring system used at the Open University in Great Britain; see A. Jones and T. O'Shea, "Barriers to the Use of Computer Assisted Learning," *British Journal of Educational Technology* 13 (1982) 207–217, at p.207.

Berkeley to photograph the model of Rome at street level. We will transfer thousands of photos of the model to a videodisc or CD-ROM, thereby enabling us to simulate visits to the city at the high point of its development.[13] There, students of Classical Civilization and of Latin will take guided tours emphasizing different aspects of the culture, such as religion, economics, or politics. On each tour, the student will be able to print the screen, thereby collecting evidence, visual ("snapshots") or literary ("quotations"), to be used as documentation for an essay.

Figure 1. *Detail of the city center in the model of ancient Rome.*

Cicero: A Sample Session

For example, in the lesson on entertainment, students will be asked to plan their weekly tours through the city to investigate the varieties of public entertainment and recreation available to the average citizen. The student will also be asked to study one type of entertainment or recreation (for example, parks, baths, or theater) in some detail.

---

[13]For a comparable (if much more modest) project, cf the "Montevidisco" CALI package for students of Spanish, as described by E.W. Schneider and J.L. Bennion, "Veni, vidi, vici via videodisc: A Simulator for Instructional Conversations," *System* 11 (1983) 41–46.

In a sample session, a student would log in, select the tour of the week, and find displayed on the screen the twenty or so places in the city related in some way to entertainment. The student would be asked to explore at least five of the places and then to link them by some original observation or idea in an essay. As the student moves into the model at street level to approach the first place, he or she will find various resources that will be helpful on the tour: a group of guides (personified along the borders of the screen by actual polychrome portraits from the Roman period and given names by which they may be invoked), a glossary of technical terms, a bibliography with leads for further research in the University Research Library, and a small reference library, including key ancient and modern texts about the sites.

The student might begin with very little idea of how to approach the assignment. He or she might therefore consult a guide, asking for advice on how to proceed. The guide will teach socratically whenever possible, answering a question with a question, in order to force students to think through their problems themselves.

A student choosing to study the theater might notice and comment on the concentration of the three main theaters (Pompey's, Marcellus's, and Balbu's) in a "theater district" in the western Campus Martius; or the dedication of the theaters to famous politicians; or the freestanding design of the structures, differentiating them from their Greek prototypes, which were generally built into hillsides; or the presence of large public peristyles behind the stage.

Wondering why one theater (Pompey's) has a temple atop the seating section, the student would search for an explanation. He or she might, for example, consult the technical glossary on "theaters" under "building types," and there would note that temples are not, in fact, common enough appendages to be listed and illustrated in the axonometric drawing of the typical Greek and Roman theater. The student might then look for a particular historical explanation, perhaps by requesting biographical information about Pompey from the reference library. There he or she would find the famous story about how Pompey could build Rome's first permanent theater only by pretending to be erecting a temple with a large "staircase" in front.

The student might then look in the bibliography for an entry such as "theater-temples" and there would find a reference to J.A Hansen's monograph on the subject,[14] which he or she might then consult in the University Research Library. (We consider use of the library crucial, by the way, if the system is to be an aid to the student's intellectual development and not a crutch, since students still need to be prepared to function in a world in which the printed book will continue, for quite some time, to be the dominant medium.) The point of the weekly essay might well be to note features in common to all the theaters in the city of Rome (location, peristyle, dedication to a political figure) and to explain why Pompey's theater differs in one important respect (by having a temple to Venus grafted onto it).

---

[14]*Roman Theater-temples, Princeton Monographs in Art and Archaeology* 33 (Princeton 1959).

Cicero: Other Uses and Future Enhancements

Equally exciting is the prospect of adapting Cicero to our Intermediate Latin (and perhaps Greek) sequence. The main purpose of the sequence is to review basic grammar and vocabulary while teaching students how to read such authors as Virgil, Plautus, Cicero, and Caesar. Since the literature in the reference library is, of course, written in Greek and Latin, we will have our language students read in the original these sources for the topography and history of the city. By supplying such utilities as a morphological and syntactic parser, a dictionary, and a rudimentary commentary, we should be able to let Cicero totally replace the traditional schoolboy commentaries used at this level. And right from the first moment they can read Latin or Greek, students will be involved in the kind of exciting research projects that have customarily been reserved for graduate students. The tedium of in-class recitation and translation will be replaced by students' reports on what they have learned while wandering through Rome investigating the weekly topic.

CONCLUSION

The advantages of using the city itself as the framework for the student interface in these civilization and language courses should be clear: like the field of Classics, the city contains all of ancient life, and so all aspects of the study of Classics naturally arise during a visit to Rome. Secondly, the city—and the model of the city—is vast and impressive, fascinating and foreign enough to arouse the students' curiosity. The city is filled with helpful guides who are ready to help students experience the challenges of everyday life in a foreign environment. Thus, through the simulation afforded by the videodisc, computer-assisted language instruction can move beyond the structuralist approach used all too often in the past and can be based on the concept of communicative interaction[15]. Moreover, the setting of individualized instruction at a computerized multimedia workstation allows for the development of the students' intrinsic motivation and minimizes extrinsic (and often counterproductive) motivators such as grading[16]. The weekly writing assignment will replace objective testing or translation, and will add an important dimension to the students' educational experience in the course.

Finally, this project should help us solve our department's major problems. Cicero provides a powerful tool for increasing faculty productivity and for providing the student with the kind of experience hitherto possible only to the handful of students who could afford a tutor and an extended stay in Rome. Cicero creates a multimedia and interdisciplinary environment for learning. And, Cicero enhances students' involvement in learning by placing them in a fascinating simulated world in which their curiosity and creativity can blossom and flourish. The city is as infinitely rich as life itself. As such, it offers us a comprehensive framework for integrating new scholarly discoveries and methodologies, as well as innovations in hardware and software. Moreover, if our pilot projects are successful, the city can continue to set the scene for many of our other language and civilization courses by a simple expansion of the various multimedia data bases.

---

[15]See D. Sanders and R. Kenner, "Whither CAI? The Need for Communicative Courseware," *System* 11 (1983) 33–39, especially pp. 34–36, stressing the need for graphics and games. On the communicative, as opposed to structural, approach to language learning, see T.D. Terrell, "A Natural Approach to Second Language Acquisition and Learning," *The Modern Language Journal* 41 (1977).

[16]On intrinsic motivation, see E.L. Deci, *Intrinsic Motivation* (New York 1975); on the theory that challenging tasks are preferred to simple ones, see S. Harter, "Effectance Motivation Reconsidered," *Human Development* 21 (1978) 34–64.

Grapevine

An Excursion into Steinbeck Country

Robert Campbell
Patricia Hanlon

ROBERT CAMPBELL

Robert Campbell, a librarian at Lowell High School, San Francisco, has also worked at writing educational proposals and as a high school English teacher. He actually remembers the Depression, or so he claims.

PATRICIA HANLON

Patricia Hanlon, an English teacher at Lowell High School, San Francisco, has also taught in junior high and is a fellow and member of the advisory council of the Bay Area Writing Project.

WHAT IS IT?

A high school teacher and a librarian are collecting and analyzing material in every medium for teaching John Steinbeck's *The Grapes of Wrath*, including the political and social history of the 1930s—altogether some 33 topic headings touched upon in the novel and in about 54 related works: books, films, television documentaries, still photographs, record albums and sound tapes, filmstrips, magazine and newspaper articles, and more. These are being linked and indexed by topic to provide an extensive and interesting educational resource and an interactive teaching tool. In this project, we are provided with the perspectives of a classroom teacher teaching the novel (Hanlon), a high school librarian (Campbell), and an education/technology theorist (Kristina Hooper from Apple Computer, Inc.). Our sense is that the fruitful collaboration will produce great juice—if not wine.

WHAT NEED IS BEING MET?

An English teacher working with *The Grapes of Wrath* may be aware of the many ramifications of the novel in terms of American institutions and history but lack the specialized knowledge and the time required to locate the related films, books, and other materials that would help most to make the connections between literature and the world his or her students live in. The teacher of social studies, on the other hand, may hesitate to encroach on the world of literature, or be unaware of how relevant a novel like this one can be to social and political matters.

Even the most conscientious and informed teacher is hard-pressed to assemble large collections of teaching materials in many media and to make them accessible to students. School librarians typically gather a modest number of such materials at a teacher's special request or compile a subject bibliography, but the materials are soon returned to their arbitrary decimal-numbered slots, and even annotated bibliographies suggest little about the fascinating and complex relationships between the works.

The Grapes of Wrath is about the Dust Bowl, "Okies," the exodus to the promised land of California, and the desperate plight of migrant workers such as the Joad family. But it is also about the American family and about our economic system, about the love of land and its care, about government programs, folk beliefs and folk music, about the thirties, the New Deal, prejudice, brotherhood, violence, and the idea of a utopia out west. To extract all the juice from these grapes, and to help students see connections to their own lives and experiences, a teacher deals with a novel not as an isolated piece of literature, but as one reflecting the times, the issues, and the author and other writers, artists, thinkers, and survivors.

When it is completed, Grapevine will provide the teacher with the following:

- An extensive selected body of teaching material in the form of text, still and moving pictures, and sound.

- Easy access to that material in a large data base linked by topic.

- A method by which the teacher can modify, add, edit, and rearrange text, still and moving pictures, and sound.

- A system for skimming through the material, browsing, searching, or studying it thoroughly.

- Extensive annotations, suggested activities, and questions on command at critical points.

- Information on sources for all quotations, citations, and graphics on command.

- In its ultimate stage of development, a powerful system that will allow the user to manipulate and integrate text, still and moving images, and sound in order to create multimedia documents.

COLLOQUY AMONG SOME REAL
AND HYPOTHETICAL TEACHERS

[The following conversation never took place, because five of the participants are fictitious. Yet we imagine that they represent some of the viewpoints and questions of real teachers. The relatively real people—Campbell and Hanlon—speak with one voice, that of "reply."]

Mrs. Blue: What are all these topics you mention? What was it? 33 works and 54 topics? Or...

Mr. Gold: I believe it was the other way around, Mrs. Blue. They said 33 topics and 54...

Reply: ...works. That's it. 54 works, with others being added from time to...

Ms. Green: What works are those? Where did you find them?

Reply: We use the term "work" to mean each of our sources, not only books, such as *Factories in the Field*, but also TV documentaries, films, magazine articles, and recorded interviews. By "topics" we mean ideas or subjects from *The Grapes of Wrath*, for example California, migrant workers, and economics, which are touched upon in other works, such as *Hard Times* or the Farm Security Administration photographs. Some were in the school library from the beginning—but not connected directly with *The Grapes of Wrath*. Others we had to search for, or we came across, or they just happened.

Mr. Gray: You say 33 topics? What are the others?

Reply: Glad you asked. Here's the list of all 33 topics:

Alien Labor	Government	New Deal
Arts	Programs	1930s
California	Growers	Okies
Camps	History	Photos
Criticism	Influence (of	Prejudice
Depression	Steinbeck's	Reaction
Dust Bowl	Work)	Philosophy & Religion
Economics	Land Ownership	Social History
Ethics & Morals	Land Use	Steinbeck
Family	Love of Land	Unions
Farmers	Migrant Workers	Utopia
Folklore	Music	Violence

We needed them, because teachers want not merely stacks of books, articles, videotapes, and the rest, but a wealth of material like that *connected* logically, *linked* to form paths that lead the student to intriguing byways and illuminating vista points. Teachers want conceptual organization in order to present materials to students in effective and meaningful ways.

Ms. Green: How do these topics connect to all those works? Every work doesn't deal with every subject, does it?

Reply: No, you're right—some topics are touched on in only a few works. And some works are related to only one topic, or a few topics only.

Here's part of a matrix, or "web," we drew to show the relationships:

STEINBECK PROJECT WEB (SECTION)

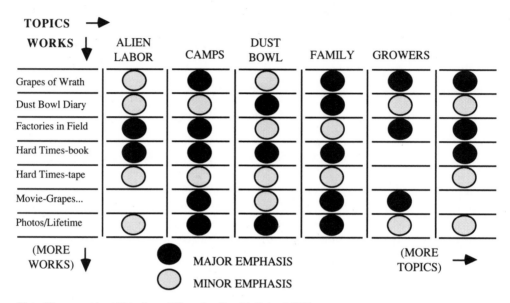

(Note: There are at least 33 topics and 54 works. Possible links=1,836.)

You see that this is only a sample showing how seven works connect to six topics, for 42 possible combinations. The full 54 works times 33 topics...

Mr. Gold: Your arithmetic is correct—1,836 possible links. Have you explored all those?

Reply: No, that's part of the total program, but we haven't developed all of it yet.

Mr. Gold: I'm not an English teacher. Math and science are my fields. But seeing you go to all this trouble with a novel, I have to ask, what is it you English teachers think you need?

Reply: The text of a novel is only where we begin in literature. I want to be able to look at a question, to do a data search of the text of *The Grapes of Wrath*, to search related books. What is the role of the grower, as elaborated on in *Factories in the Field*, compared to the way Steinbeck views the grower? Are there any other works about growers in California in the 1930s? How do these materials compare with Steinbeck's work? I want to look at the styles of the other writers—the conclusions they drew. Did others see the same world Steinbeck saw? The asking, the searching, and the answering will provide pleasure to the student and the teacher. It will make the student a more critical thinker and involve him or her in ideas. The teacher and the student can become collaborators and partners, asking and answering important questions about literature and ideas.

Mrs. Blue: What started you two on this project?

Reply: Well, Pat was teaching a unit on *The Grapes of Wrath*. Bob was rummaging around in his card catalog and his memory for related material, but the conventional library tools and techniques—though they led to some obviously useful things, such as a filmstrip *"The Grapes of Wrath* and the Thirties"—were not adequate to the task, as is often the case. For example, there was no subject heading for "Dust Bowl." The closest was "Droughts—U.S." Some of the best information was buried here and there as chapters in books, such as one on "The Okies Forty Years Later" in a book titled *Unknown California*.

Mrs. Blue: Then it wasn't simply a shortage of material that was your problem?

Reply: No, but many of the links were supplied by us, groping in our memories for names like Studs Terkel, Woody Guthrie, and Dorothea Lange. Without these links, students couldn't find, or overlooked, materials that proved fascinating and useful. After a worthwhile set of materials is found and used, it must then be disassembled, returned, and scattered. The next teacher must repeat the whole procedure.

Mr. Gray: Isn't even redoing all that a pretty healthy research process?

Reply: In some ways. But well-motivated and able students can learn the whole array of research skills with no difficulty. When they don't succeed, it's generally out of frustration, because the system of cataloging doesn't go deep enough to help them find all the scattered appropriate materials. Using three-by-five cards is a pretty crude technique in the age of electronic data processing.

Mr. Gold: Aha! So now the computer enters the scene. Is that it?

Reply: Yes, but not as the hero coming to our rescue, exactly. More as a possible tool. We three represent a teacher with a need for materials, a librarian with a limited supply of the materials and a not wholly satisfactory system for delivering them, and a computer technology theorist with some ideas for bridging the gap.

Ms. Green: So you decided to computerize Steinbeck?

Reply: No, we didn't start by thinking of a computer and then asking, "What can the machine do for us?" We started with *The Grapes of Wrath* and began a process of assemblage: searching, annotating, labeling, looking for links to works of any kind that might shed light on the novel, the issues it raised, the author, and the times. Only after we were under way making links did the need for a computer data base with some special features become very apparent.

Mrs. Blue: All this about how you proceeded in the work is very well, but it isn't telling me what the program *does* for me or my students. What happens when we follow one of your links?

Reply: Well, let's visualize the program when it's operational in one possible form, including moving images and sounds that can be edited.

We'll assume that you want to see a presentation first, so we'll see what a **Presentation** screen *might* look like.

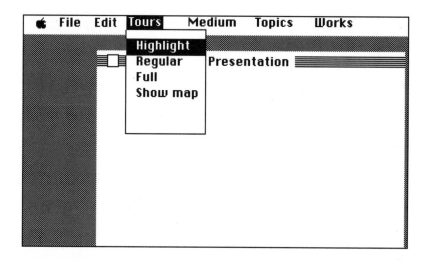

Now, in the role of researcher, or reporter, or time-traveling tourist, your first choice is to decide on a brief Highlight Tour, a longer Regular Tour, or the Full Tour. In this example, we have chosen **Highlight Tour**.

As to the medium—whether **Images**, **Sound**, or **Text**—we will choose all of these, and **Regular** speed.

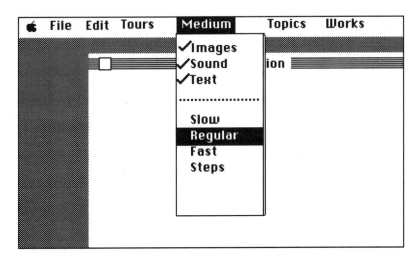

Since the tours are by topic or work, you give the computer that information by clicking on one of the topics or works in the menus.

Your menu supplies a list of all 33 topics—though in this abridged example only a few topics are listed—and **History** is highlighted.

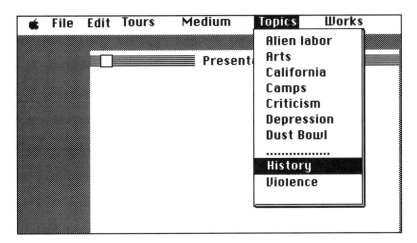

You also have a choice among works, and here all types of works would be brought up because of the check in front of **All**.

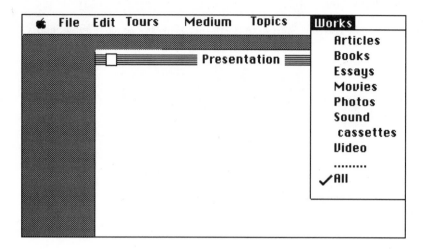

Your Highlight Tour of the topic History begins. First, you might decide to click on **Show Map**; if so, you would be shown something like this:

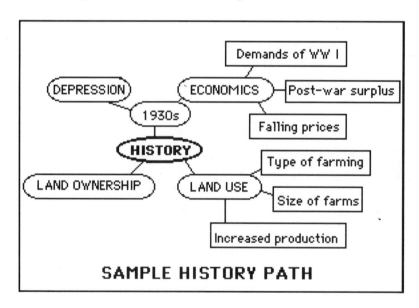

You notice that History is highlighted, and you may take time to study some of the paths, links, and loops. A very brief Highlight Tour might consist of displays of text, sound, moving and still pictures, including material like the following examples.

BLACK AND WHITE PRINT ("Dust" by Mervin Jules, from *Graphic Works of the American Thirties,* **plate 61)**

Text (from *The Grapes of Wrath,* **p. 313)**

> "And the little farmers who owned no canneries lost their farms, and they were taken by the great owners, the banks, and the companies who also owned the canneries. As time went on, there were fewer farms. The little farmers moved into town for a while and exhausted their credit, exhausted their friends, their relatives. And then they too went on the high- ways. And the roads were crowded with men ravenous for work, murderous for work."

DOCUMENTARY FILM CLIP
(from "The Plow That Broke the Plains")

PICTURES

Newspaper headline: "WAR NEWS TUMBLES SECURITIES...WHEAT PRICES SOAR"

Tractors moving through fields of wheat, cultivator blades cutting into the earth.

Scenes of World War I bombardment in Europe. Tractors and tanks, military parades.

Huge combines moving abreast through fields of wheat.

Poster: "SERVICE MEN! FREE LAND! GOVERNMENT HOMESTEADS IN THE PLAINS!"

Stock ticker tape running faster and faster, wheat pouring ever faster—then the stock ticker falls and smashes.

Scenes of arid farms, abandoned machinery. Sand blowing. Dead cattle. Wind rising to storm level. Dust storms. Farmers loading up to leave.

NARRATION

"Wheat will win the war! Fast wheat. Wheat for the boys over there... Wheat for the Allies... Wheat at any price!"

"Then we reaped the golden harvest. Then we really plowed the plains! We turned under millions of new acres for war wheat. We had the manpower. We invented new machinery. The world was our marble."

"Once again the rains held off and the sun baked the earth....This time millions of acres of plowed land lay open to the sun."

"Blown out, baked out, and broke."

TEXT (from Herbert Hoover. "The Challenge to Liberty" in *Problems in American Civilization,* p. 65)

> "The farmer is the most tragic figure in our present situation. From the collapse of war inflation, from boom, from 'displacement of work animals by mechanization,' from the breakdown of foreign markets, from the financial debacle of Europe, and from drought, he has suffered almost beyond human endurance."

AUDIOTAPE (interview with Oscar Heline, Iowa farmer, from Hard Times audiotape)

> "Grain was being burned. It was cheaper than coal. Corn was being burned. A county just east of here, they burned corn in their courthouse all winter, '32, '33. You couldn't hardly buy groceries for corn. It couldn't pay the transportation. In South Dakota the county elevator listed corn as minus three cents. Minus three cents a bushel. If you wanted to sell 'em a bushel of corn, you had to bring in three cents…

> "We had a lot of trouble on the highway. People were determined to withhold produce from the market—livestock, cream, butter, eggs, whatnot. If they would dump the produce, they would force the market to a higher level. The farmers would man the highways, and cream cans were emptied in ditches and eggs dumped out…

> "The rank-and-file people of this state—who were brought up as conservatives, which most of us were—would never act like this. Except in desperation."

TEXT (from *The Grapes of Wrath,* p. 383)

> "The men who work in the fields, the owners of the little orchards, watch and calculate.
> "And the first cherries ripen. Cent and a half a pound. Hell, we can't pick 'em for that…And on the ground the seeds drop and dry with black threads hanging from them.

> "The purple prunes soften and sweeten. My God, we can't pick them and dry and sulphur them. We can't pay wages no matter what wages…. The meat turns dark and the crop shrivels on the ground."

COLOR ILLUSTRATIONS (from *American Heritage*, April, 1977, pp. 88-93)

California fruit box labels: brightly colored and highly romanticized views of western animals, mountains, produce, señoritas, cowboys, Indians, and other fantasies.

PHOTOGRAPH, BLACK AND WHITE (from *This Fabulous Century*, v. 4, pp. 14–15)

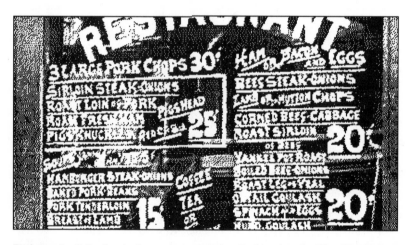

Photograph of the front of a restaurant and a barber shop in New York's Bowery in 1935.

TEXT (Ibid, p. 24)

"Annual Earnings: 1932 to 1934," a table of average annual income of workers in 37 occupations. Examples: dentist, $2,391; hired farmhand, $216; steelworker, $422.87.

Mr. Gray: That music and those pictures really had a wallop. And when we came to that image of the stock ticker falling over, I wanted to get some prices right then on some actual commodities.

Reply: You could do just that, Mr. Gray. At that point you could give a **Pause** command. Then you could click **Show Tour Map**. You would get a map not just of the Highlight Tour, but of branches, including one to your **Falling Farm Prices** side road. If you clicked on that branch you could detour and return to the main Highlight Tour later—or not, as you wished.

Mr. Gray: Excuse me, but I have to find out how much flexibility is allowed in a program like Grapevine. I mean, if I want to play down the sentiment when I teach Steinbeck and concentrate on technique or philosophy or economics, can I do that?

Reply: Certainly. The very wealth of material that the technology is going to make available ensures that any kind of emphasis will be possible. No one will be able to cover it all—or want to. If you or your students want to pursue the legislation, the history of land ownership in California, the climatology—a lot of factual material of that kind will be included, and still more pointed to.

Ms. Green: Speaking of that, you showed quite a lot of text in your example. Are you including just quotations from books and articles, or whole chapters or more? And is reading so much on a screen a good idea?

Reply: We've thought a lot about that, and we have some guidelines for ourselves that we think make sense. First, if you can have a book or an article on paper for anyone who needs it, that is obviously best—so having a computer program is not a substitute for a book or a set of books if you can get them. On the other hand, there are *never* enough books. It appears that technology is going to give us enormous storage capability, so *why not* include as much relevant text as possible? Text on the screen can be used for browsing and selecting. When needed, you can print out longer text selections. Some materials are absolutely essential yet not easily available, like Benson's "To Tom Who Lived It" article. In addition, a great deal of text needs to be in the program as junction points for linking to everything else. We can't emphasize too strongly that Grapevine is not just a lot of stuff—it's a lot of intricately *connected* stuff.

Mrs. Blue: And the reason that Mr. Gold and I were invited to sit in on this panel is that someday there will be similar linked programs for us to use in social studies and in mathematics and science? Is that right?

Reply: Yes, we hope so. Since the computer can store so much text and sound, and so many pictures, connect them, and allow users to follow or change those connections and manipulate the stored material in *any* subject, the applications have no limits. In the case of social studies, though, it will be possible to create from Grapevine itself a unit on the Depression and the 1930s from the social studies point of view as readily as from the literary.

Mr. Gray: Your Grapevine seems to be an impressive package. But will it really be different from any other collection of articles, books, pictures, sound, and so forth?

Reply: Yes, not only because of the interconnections and links that are included (and which you can expand), but also because you will be able to tailor it to your classes.

Mr. Gray: Explain to me what "tailoring" the program to my classes means.

Reply: We envision at least three levels of interactivity and "modifiability."

The first level of interactivity is a scratchpad, perhaps on the data disk—a place where the teacher or another user can make comments and additions. Next would be the capability of writing, pasting, or deleting directly within the program. The ultimate stage, available to both teacher and student, is a built-in media processor analogous to a word processor but capable of editing and manipulating moving and still pictures and sound as well as text.

Mrs. Blue: Do you mean pasting in film scenes?

Ms. Green: Oh, I'd want to do more than just paste them in. I'd want to be able to direct—or edit, at least—and have zooms and dissolves and all that.

Reply: Again, just pasting in a film scene or recording a "voice-over" or "music over" track would be simplest—and useful. But we have no doubt that complete authoring/editing power over all media will be possible eventually. That's why we listed some pretty sophisticated techniques on this **Production** application menu.

Mr. Gold: Do you really need to give an elaborate authoring system like that to students?

Reply: We believe there is no reason to provide a power to the teacher that is not also available to the learner. Currently, learners and teachers, too, are primarily *consumers* of media, subject to media's power to persuade and convince. Students and teachers need the skills to use all of these tools for their own purposes and in their own styles. The world speaks to our young people not only with words but with color, motion, music, all shaped with dazzling virtuosity. We think that all students should learn to communicate with the world using this new language.

Mrs. Blue: You're not forgetting, are you, that teachers and students *do* make videotapes, and audiotapes, and slide shows?

Reply: True, but you have probably experienced, as we have, the fact that a teacher can put together a multimedia presentation with about the same degree of ease as a medieval monk producing an illuminated manuscript. Computers ought to be able to help.

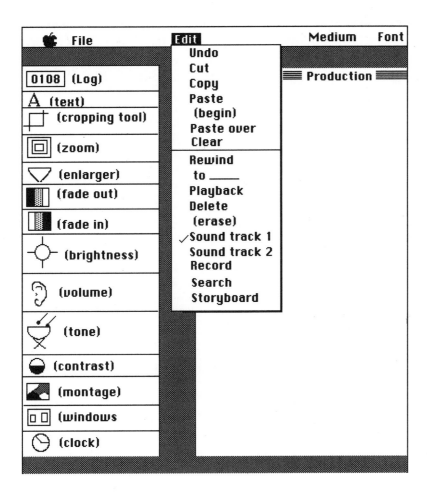

Mr. Gold: Let's get back to the essential question of how a teacher could use a program like Grapevine. For instance, do you see it used only as a supplement for individual students? Or could it be used with the class as a whole? If so, how?

Reply: Obviously, more computers are going to be available to more and more students. Still, we can't assume that overnight every student is going to have a personal workstation. And even were that the case, there would always be a need for class discussion, teacher instruction, and other activities. We have developed the Hanlon-Campbell law of program design, which states: Given more than one attractive alternative, choose them all. We see Grapevine today as eminently applicable to individual, small group, or large group learning, whichever is appropriate at the time—the only limitation being that of logistics and hardware: how big the class, how large the available screen.

Mr. Gray: Do you know what you're asking? These things don't just happen, and when they do, they won't come cheap.

Reply: All the more reason to make clear to computer engineers now what our needs are. And should we make the erroneous assumption that the technology we need will *always* be beyond our means?

Mr. Gold: I have a question about the role of the individual user. Is he or she a gamester, a tourist, a reporter, a researcher, or what?

Reply: Perhaps any or all of those roles might be appropriate at various times. We believe the teacher, not the program, will have the greatest influence in determining the user's role.

Mrs. Blue: I hope so. If a student of mine tried to be a *passive* tourist in a program, she wouldn't get by in my class. The student would have to assume a role like a reporter and investigate and solve problems.

Mr. Gold: I have a question about being able to modify the program. Do you have in mind that a class may add or subtract questions, think of new follow-up activities, make new links, or even new paths?

Reply: Yes.

Mrs. Blue: Then how will you preserve the integrity of the program? And how could I decide what was worth passing along and what to discard?

Reply: Of course you could always maintain a master copy of the program. Then you would be free to make your own judgments concerning changes and act on those, or…

Ms. Green: …or you might want to set up a student review board in your class, or have the whole class review the changes as a culminating activity in the unit.

Mr. Gold: One of you is a librarian—I don't remember which one—but do you see this kind of linking up of books and other media as something that relates to a library?

Reply: Definitely, in school libraries, at least. If a library is to be something more than a room where books are standing up instead of lying down as they are in the textbook room, then it is a place where connections—paths leading from one thing to another—can be discovered and pursued. The catalog and indexes let learners follow these leads now, in a rudimentary way, but the computer will expand that power beyond our ability to imagine it. Until now, libraries have hung together like a wired-together skeleton of a brontosaurus. They are about to start acquiring a nervous system.

Ah…pardon me, Mr. Silver, but I can't help noticing that you haven't had a single word to say in this whole session. May I ask why?

Mr. Silver: That should be obvious. I'm merely a hypothetical teacher, not a real one. Look, there's straw sticking out of my shirt! How do you expect a hypothetical character to ask the really tough questions?

Reply: You have a point. But haven't you heard of fictional characters who took on a will and a life of their own? Like Pygmalion with...with…

Mr. Silver: ...with Galatea?

Reply: Right. Why don't you give it a try? Go ahead, ask the toughest question you can think of.

Mr. Silver: (after a pause) All right, here it is. Schools today are preoccupied with the problem of accountability. More and more the effectiveness of teachers is based on student performance on standardized tests. In a climate like this, why create a program with such broad goals as Grapevine seems to have, one that will be very difficult to evaluate?

Mr. Gray: Whew! Was that a question or a lecture?

Reply: It's a fair question, all right, and a tough one indeed. A short answer is this. Accountability we teachers cannot shirk, nor do we want to. We must be able to defend and prove the effectiveness of what we do. Where there are valid measures of skills and knowledge, and when student performance falls short, we should be held responsible and be required to obtain better results.

Still, this doesn't mean that we may therefore shirk the obligation or miss the opportunity to teach as richly and complexly as we can. The instruments available to tell us whether we are teaching well still remain crude in comparison to the complexity of human interaction and insensitive to the whole range of insights that literature, history, science, and other disciplines entail. While we refine these instruments, should we be content to teach only what can easily be measured and quantified? Of course not.

While computers can be used in the service of any educational philosophy, some think that they lend themselves most readily to what is most rigorous, austere, and authoritarian. We believe that this is not necessarily so. Without computers we would teach *The Grapes of Wrath* or the history, the culture, the economics of the 1930s in as *organic* a style and as intellectually nourishing a context as we could manage. We look forward to teaching with the help of the computer in that style with that philosophy simply because the computer will allow us to do that better.

ALL: We wholeheartedly agree with you!

Reply: How remarkable...and how gratifying. Thank you all.

When the Grapevine project is completed, it will clearly be the work of a fairly large corps of experts in curriculum, literature, educational technology, and computer programming—all of them having spent dozens or hundreds of hours at the task. In contrast, what exists of the project today reflects the after-hours efforts of a teacher, a librarian, and an education technologist.

For this project to go forward, we three need the following: some refinements in technology that we believe are on the way; more time; financial and technical support; and help in resolving issues of copyright and ownership.

The technology to make any large, linked repository of multimedia materials easily available to teachers is not yet in place, but most of the pieces are there, and there is no doubt that they will soon be combined and engineered into a tool of unprecedented power for teaching. But for teaching what? That is a question for which we think Grapevine provides an answer.

As for technology needs, we don't yet have a data base program that allows us to make the many links we want from one piece of information—one picture, sound track, film clip, paragraph—to another. We need a data base that creates an index we can use to search, browse, manipulate, format, and print our data, and that accommodates unlimited text.

We need an interface with CD-ROM to include all the text necessary so that we can browse and search and print out with ease.

We need an authoring system, if not identical with the one we have described, then at least one that would give the user the capability to add, change, and link materials and to set up his or her own path.

When we receive funding which will buy us time, what will we do with it? We need to construct a prototype of Grapevine, a videodisc with still and motion pictures connected to the text in our data base and a clear, easy-to-follow program with which to make these links. In this way, we would set up a path, a tour through the materials for the user. And such a tour would provide a template for the teacher's lesson plans.

Projects like Grapevine will be a necessary test of the doctrine of "fair use" of information in all its forms. Flexible and fair compromises will have to be worked out. For us, an important ameliorating factor is that projects like Grapevine will not supplant the books, films, videocassettes, and the like from which sample materials are used, but rather give them greater attention and in the long run, stimulate sales and so increase royalties.

Only when we have secured additional support, bought more time, tapped many more resources, and engaged more technical help will we be able to proceed with the task: processing all the material; that is, additional research and writing, analyzing and linking the material, finding, selecting, storing, and indexing still frames and moving footage as well as audio interviews and music....

We know that teachers would like to get their hands on the kind of teaching instrument Grapevine will be. Grapevine is not yet a completed product, but an idea for a product, and a beginning. What we need now is the support of foundations, publishers, or others who also will see the possibilities of this project as a prototype for a whole new series of exciting applications of technology to education.

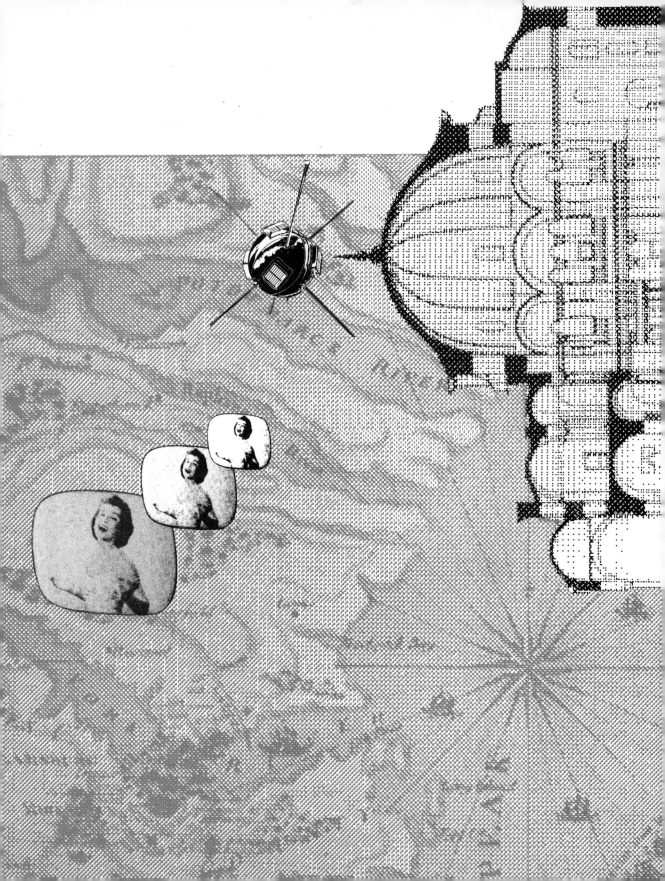

A prominent example of a media tool that has a pervasive influence in our culture is television. Early visions of this tool in the field of education were not dissimilar to those currently discussed in the context of computers and optical media. The educational opportunity provided by television is to bring "real places" and "real people" into the classrooms, bringing life to materials that might be considered dry or boring by making them relevant to personal experience. The opportunities provided with computer control are interactivity and explicit personalization, as well as reuse of existing materials in a number of contexts.

Sam Gibbon brings his perspective as a children's television producer to the task of multimedia development. In The Voyage of the MIMI program he has chosen to use linear video as a major structural element in an educational experience, because he knows how to use this medium to tell sensitive and engaging stories to children. It is through the use of other materials—computer modules, print exercises, and videodisc displays—that students can directly and personally manipulate concepts introduced to them and made relevant in the linear television materials. So Gibbon succeeds in doing what most artists attempt: using each medium available for what it is best suited. In this context, computer-driven multimedia experiences complement, rather than replace, existing media.

In his work at WNET, **Tom Anderson** has a slightly different perspective on the use of television in a computer multimedia context. His goal is to make use of existing television in a different way in order to effectively provide learning environments for adults. Specifically, he wants to use optical media and computers to enhance the effectiveness of explanations that are already quite effective in linear television. Optical media can make excellent programs available for individual viewing at the individual's convenience rather than in the broadcaster's time frame (in much the same way as videotape). Computer control of these optical media can assist the viewer in understanding what is presented—by simple methods such as interrupting and elaborating, and in more complex ways such as resequencing and relating to other materials. In the same way Friedlander's tools are designed to help students manipulate and understand visual displays of Shakespeare, Anderson's proposed tools of reexamination and use can help learners to understand explanations of principles of physics at their own rate. Anderson's idea is that direct involvement and control of presentations enhance conceptualization, a notion well supported by modern-day cognitive psychological theories.

The Voyage
of the MIMI

Sam Gibbon with Kristina Hooper

SAMUEL Y. GIBBON, JR.

Samuel Y. Gibbon, Jr., is the executive director and executive producer of multimedia projects at the Bank Street College of Education in New York. Mr. Gibbon has extensive experience in television production for children, having been creative advisor at the Children's Television Workshop, and executive producer of projects at CTW, including "3-2-1-Contact" and "The Electric Company." In addition to teaching at the Harvard University Graduate School of Education, Mr. Gibbon has consulted for the Office of Technology Assessment of the U.S. Congress, SRI International, the National Science Foundation, and the Smithsonian Institution, among others. Mr. Gibbon earned his B.A. at Princeton University and was a Fulbright Fellow at London University.

Sam's presentation at the Conference was direct and clear. I have summarized the basic issues Sam raised, and I have then commented on the implications of each of these. As a member of the Voyage of the Mimi advisory committee, I have tried to make explicit some of the reasoning behind different design approaches so that they are made obvious. Not so clearly, my comments reflect my own opinions, but the hope is that juxtaposed with the basic description of this project they will provide the reader with a sensible approach to Sam's perspective, much of which currently is reflected in the Voyage of the MIMI project at Bank Street College. (kh)

General Description of the Project

The Voyage of the MIMI is a major educational project housed at Bank Street College, in New York City. It is directed toward the development of extensive television, computer software, videodisc, and print materials for use in science and mathematics education for students in grades 5–7.

Bank Street College provides an excellent setting for this kind of innovative program. It is one of the few academic institutions with the technological and video sophistication required for an effort on this scale, and it also has an in-house elementary school, an in-house teacher-training facility, and the talent to do extensive testing of new materials.

This project is funded by the Department of Education; materials are distributed through Holt, Rinehart, and Winston Publishers.

This project arose as a response to a Request for Proposal (RFP) from the Department of Education in 1982 to combine a range of media—particularly TV, videodisc, and computer software—in the teaching of science and mathematics. This RFP was crucial historically in focusing national attention on the potential of this multimedia approach, as well as indicating a commitment at a national level to fund such a large-scale project.

The first series of the Voyage of the MIMI has been completed and has been available to schools for the last year. The materials include a 13-part dramatic TV series, which portrays a scientific investigation of whaling on the East Coast on a ship called the *MIMI*; in this series, research scientists and a very young crew note patterns of whale migration, using a number of scientific approaches, and they encounter a number of exciting adventures. In addition, there are 13 TV documentary-style visits to different "real" scientific establishments, which complement this dramatic series (using some of the dramatic series actors as hosts).

These TV materials are accompanied by a teacher guide as well as a book that describes the TV series. There are also four computer programs that complement the TV series, providing students with hands-on experience with the topics investigated by the MIMI scientists.

The integration of these materials happens in the classroom and in the students' minds. It is not a technological integration, then, but the combination of a range of single-purpose media, each of which enhances the others. Central to this project is the TV dramatic series; it focuses kids' attention on the excitement of "doing science" and on the people involved in this endeavor. Sam's excellent talents in storytelling on TV for children are then put to very good use; the stories lay out the basic principles and provide motivation for students to pursue different topics in the other materials.

The TV documentaries extend the notion of "hands-on science," showing how people work in the world on a range of related topics. Making good use of the characters established in the dramatic series—particularly a young boy named CT, who is about the same age as the student audience—these documentaries help students see how science might be relevant to their lives, and possibly a focus for their own development.

The computer software for this project is designed to work like that used in the scientific community. One module focuses on ecosystem development and population growth patterns; it is based on similar simulations used by scientists. A navigation game provides students with experiences not unlike those of a ship's captain, engaging computational and mathematics reasoning skills. A set of computer-based tools lets the young student try out a range of measurement experiments tried in the dramatic series, as well as extend experiments beyond this context.

A second series—*Voyage of the MIMI II*—is currently in production. It extends the route of the *MIMI* to the Yucatán to investigate Mayan ruins. This series also focuses on mathematics and science, though the scientific context is anthropology rather than marine biology.

Lessons Learned: The Story

The project team and students learned a number of things from the production of the first Voyage of the MIMI series.

For one, the project team learned that the dramatic story had an immense value to students. It served as an excellent motivator for introducing students to mathematics and science, areas that are typically of little interest to most students. In addition, a number of the characters served as excellent role models for the students, making it clear to many of them that these topics were well within their own reach.

Students also indicated an appreciation of science and human values after experience with the program materials, seeing how the "dull and dry" pursuit of science is actually quite lively and human oriented.

It seemed, then, that these materials served a viable role in letting scientific and mathematical information be housed in a credible context that could be brought into the classroom.

Most of these outcomes were not simply "happy coincidences," but represented the success-ful implementation of design strategies brought to the project. For example, the characters in the drama were carefully chosen and consciously developed as approachable to the students as well as compelling in the drama. The choice of a woman scientist to head the expedition and a Chicano to be her main assistant helped set the tone of this scientific inves-tigation; stodgy stereotypes and white lab jackets were left on shore. The inclusion in the young crew of a Black boy from New York City as well as an affluent female suburbanite also extended students' ability to relate to the presentation and to move beyond expected stereotypes. The deaf crew member made the day-to-day aspect of this handicap as well as topics related to sound transmission easily approachable and understandable. And, the choice of an endearing boy about the age of the students, who was the grandson of the MIMI's captain, brought notions of family conflicts directly into the show.

The choice of whales as the topic of investigation also enhanced student engagement in the series, of both girls and boys. Similarly, the adventure stories—including a classic ship-wreck and test of survival—added to student involvement with the story.

Lessons Learned: Teacher Response

Teachers have had a range of responses to the materials, finding them both exciting and innovative as well as somewhat difficult to fit into their traditional classroom contexts. Some of the teachers have had difficulty dealing with the emotions raised by the stories portrayed in the dramatic episode; they are simply unaccustomed to addressing human issues in their investigations of mathematics and science. They also seem unaccustomed to saying "I don't know" to a question raised by students who have seen the MIMI presenta-tions. It is difficult for many teachers to move from the role of the "all-knowing" director of teaching activities to the role of collaborator with the students.

For many teachers, these materials offer a welcome relief to most materials available to them; many have chosen to base an entire curriculum year around the series, relating the materials to topics that were not initially anticipated.

As with anything new, it is important to consider what will be required for adoption in schools. The Bank Street team has now initiated a number of teacher-training programs to encourage teachers to integrate the MIMI materials into their classrooms. It will be interest-ing over time to see just how these rich materials are used, and whether they will provide a template for how classrooms might work differently. Instead of being a great program that doesn't quite fit into standard classrooms (though adapted by many exceptional class-rooms), it just might be the first of a class of programs that set new directives for the nature of thinking and learning.

Lessons Learned: Resources

The production of these materials was extremely expensive, relative to most educational materials. This resulted often in large uncertainties in terms of available funding extensions, as well as in the omission of intended developments.

This effort clearly required federal support, as it was too big and too risky for publishers to undertake. Also, issues of pricing and costs of bringing materials to market make the delivery of these materials over the long run quite uncertain; it is still a question, for example, if the second series on the Mayas will come to market.

Having watched this project develop over the last five years or so, I am impressed with Bank Street's perseverance in dealing directly with the financial implications and problems of this product. Very few organizations would commit the resources for fundraising that have been required for this venture, nor would they dare deal with the commercial worlds that are central to the eventual release and distribution of this product. And the fights are long from finished.

At some level, this is quite discouraging, for one would hope that high-quality materials would "sell themselves" and that there would be funding available for grand experiments such as this one. Yet the Voyage of the MIMI materials have been quite successful in spite of all these difficulties; perhaps they will lay the framework for other similar activities in the future.

Final Comments

There are a number of aspects of this project that, in my opinion, are noteworthy. As mentioned earlier, the development of materials relevant to students is extremely impressive. Whales and young scientists who are very human are very good entries into the field of science.

The portrayal of science as an activity, not as a set of facts, is also a critical contribution of this project. Complex scientific ideas have been taken from dull textbook accounts to direct human experiences and questions about the world. The integration of computers into this scientific enterprise is natural for this approach, thereby making clear to students how the very same devices they have in classrooms work as well for scientists in their endeavors.

The integration of the media is handled well in this project, with each class of media working well in its own right and playing a critical role in amplifying the effectiveness of other media. The use of the computers on board the ship in the drama makes their use viable in the classroom, for example. Similarly, the shipwreck adventure makes accessible issues related to population biology shown in one of the computer modules. The use of the same actors in the dramatic and documentary series also enhances the unification of the materials, and the integration of the concepts by the students.

The print materials developed are central to the effective use of these materials in the classroom, as are the teacher-training programs that have been initiated. The Bank Street team has acknowledged the importance of "standard materials" and "normal teachers" for integrating programs such as these into a wide range of American classrooms.

Finally, the impact of the dramatic episodes cannot be underestimated. These noninteractive, linear presentations demonstrate the power of television at its best—to motivate, to explore general topics, to "bring the world into the classroom." They make clear just how "standard media" have been used to serve particular purposes very well, and suggest that we keep all the advantages of each of these as we attempt to extend our media capabilities and develop our expertise as communicators.

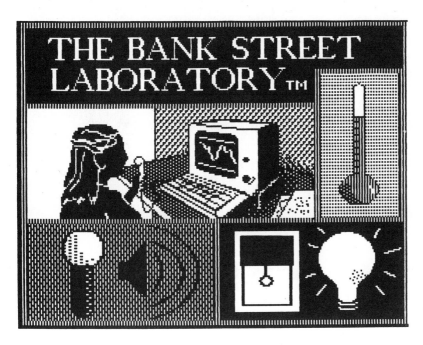

Figure 1. This software package involves students as "scientists" very naturally in measurement and data analysis activities; the computer serves as an analysis and presentation tool, while the various probes attached to the computer (for detecting light, sound, temperature, etc.) provide measurements of "real world phenomena".

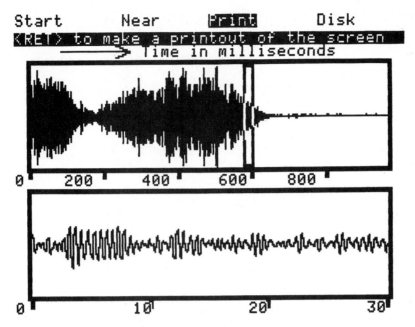

Figure 2. This printout from the Bank Street Laboratory provides students with an analysis of a sound from their environment. "Seeing" the sound in this form while hearing it provides students with an understanding of the nature of sound typically unavailable to children of this age.

Figure 3. Set in the context of a survival game, this software lets students work with an ecosystem model like the ones used by scientists; it lets them "see" how changes made in one population affect other populations in often unexpected ways.

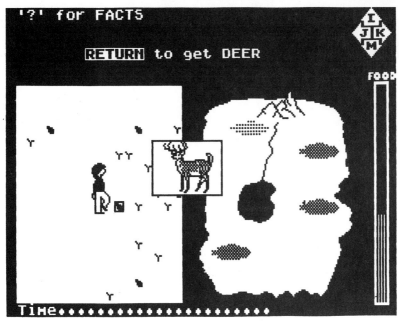

Figure 4. *(a pair) Animations provide students with a feeling of "being there" on an island; map-views provide them with the tools for analyzing the impacts of their activities on the island ecosystem.*

The centerpiece of the Voyage of the MIMI materials is a dramatic episode; it depicts a scientific whaling voyage and the adventures of its captain and youthful crew.

Beyond Einstein

A Case Study in Interactive Television

Thomas Anderson

THOMAS G. ANDERSON

Thomas G. Anderson is a Principal with the Boston consulting firm of Commonwealth Strategies, Inc. He has specialized in the fields of publishing and broadcasting, particularly as they deal with education. He has worked since early 1984 with WNET in New York on strategies for interactive media and in developing the prototype "Beyond Einstein."

Earlier, Anderson was the Vice President for Business Planning and Development at Ginn and Company, then part of the Xerox Publishing Group. He was also General Manager of Ginn Press, and of Ginn Electronic Products. In addition, he managed the Technical Seeding Program, which transferred technology from Xerox Palo Alto Research Center to Ginn. He worked with John Seely Brown and others to develop advanced interactive learning materials and to investigate the possibility of transforming the publishing process through the application of new computing capabilities and expert systems.

Before joining Xerox, Tom Anderson was Editorial Director and head of language arts curriculum at Open Court Publishing Company. He was educated at Canadian schools and colleges in the days before cognitive science was born, and had to settle for Classics and English.

THE IDEA OF A LEARNING LABORATORY

The best educational television programs are hopelessly overengineered. In a sense, they can never earn an adequate cognitive return on the assets they employ. An example of this is the recent PBS show, "Creation of the Universe," written by Tim Ferris and produced and directed by Geoffrey Haines-Stiles. This program made extensive use of computer graphics, costing $4,000 per second to produce. The graphics embodied, in the most intelligent and conscientious way, a virtual textbook on modern particle physics: every detail, down to the smallest and almost imperceptible, signified something real about the particles, the quantum forces, and the structure and behavior of the atom or of the virtual particles that well up out of the vacuum and disappear before the laws of conservation of energy can catch up with them.

While the script valiantly struggles to get the points across, the graphics march across the screen even faster, and are gone.

I would bet that not a hundredth of what is built into this extraordinary material is really perceptible, much less learnable, within the medium, though it serves to tantalize and provoke the viewer. It simply cries out for viewer control of the pace, and for interactivity. And those wonderful computer graphics are there, equally available for use in another medium.

WNET Channel 13 in New York, the premier producer of prime-time programming for PBS, has been aware of this lost opportunity, not just with "Creation of the Universe" but with a large percentage of its broadcasting. Because of this some years ago the station began thinking about setting up a "learning laboratory" where we could conduct research and development on how to design and produce interactive media products related to broad-cast series.

Before we could justify such an undertaking, we had to be sure we had thought about our educational and business goals as carefully as we could. We knew that, after we had done our homework, we would have to produce a demonstration of what we had in mind. This paper is about what we learned and how it shaped our demonstration of interactive media, "Beyond Einstein," based on "Creation of the Universe."

The central questions were these:

- In what sense did we want our products to be educational? How was that different from the sense in which our television productions are educational?

- What made us think interactivity was educational?

- Even if we understood what we meant by education and interactivity, how would we translate these ideas into products?

- Why would people want products like these? Why would they be better than other software?

- Even if it made educational sense to develop interactive programs from or in parallel with television series, would it make production and economic sense?

Where Did We Stand on Education and Learning?

One of the first decisions we made concerned audience. We thought about what WNET is expert at—producing information-packed entertainment for a prime-time audience of adults—and what we knew less about—teaching children either formally or informally—and concluded that we should start with the audience we knew best.

Even though WNET has been the presenting station for "Sesame Street" and other history-making children's programming, the real producer of "Sesame Street" was the Children's Television Workshop, which has shown plenty of interest in extending its ideas into interactive formats. Similarly, Bank Street College of Education, Harvard's Educational Technology Center, and several other highly qualified groups were working on educational computing for children.

However, we knew of no group engaged in the development of principled learning materials for adults from about the age of high school juniors on up. Since these are the people for whom we produce most of our television programming, they seemed the right people for whom to develop interactive programs.

There is a startling implication to the idea of producing "principled learning materials for adults" within the context of a PBS producing station. It is that education for us means *self-education*—learning, not teaching. And if learning materials are to be principled, they have to be based on a model of learning, not one of tutoring or teaching. As it turns out, this means they have to be based on what is now being called cognitive science, rather than on more traditional educational psychology.

It also turns out that interactivity demands much more explicitness about why we design programs one way and not another than producing television does. Television production demands great creativity and subject-matter knowledge, but every interactive program also entails a theory of education. The final structure and feel of the program depend on the choice of theory.

The learning theories being codified in modern cognitive science make interactivity seem almost indispensable to effective learning products. However, the kind of interactivity they suggest is often different from what designers of educational programs have accustomed us to, as I'll try to show in due course. Hence, the choice of cognitive science rather than competing educational or behavioral theories leads to innovation. "Beyond Einstein" took us beyond convention and into unexplored zones.

A Digression on Cognitive Science

It is a cliché for which there is plenty of evidence that television, movies, and many other media require very little effort or engagement from their consumers. We all understand intuitively that this means that these media don't provide much intellectual growth—"no pain, no gain."

Our intuition has, of course, a solid underpinning in modern cognitive psychology. This is not the place to go into a detailed examination of all cognitive science has to say on the subject, but some of the arguments for interactivity are most powerfully stated in cognitive terms. Therefore, at the risk of insulting the psychologically sophisticated, I will recap a few of the high points that helped us to shape "Beyond Einstein," and that we think are generalizable to the design and production of any interactive media.

Cognitive psychology is about how we acquire knowledge and how we remember and use it. It is concerned with what is called "knowledge representation," and how this differs among novices and experts in a given field. Knowledge representation is, in brief, our way of mentally "looking at" what we know. Together with knowledge acquisition, it raises a number of issues that are relevant to the informational value of interactivity.

Cognitive psychology has mainly focused on two big topics. The first is how we organize and interrelate information in our minds, and how what we already know helps us learn new information that in turn modifies and restructures our previous knowledge. This topic is basically about knowledge—cognition—itself.

The second topic is not as obvious, but it is critical to self-education. It is called "metacognition," and it has to do with the conscious processes by which we come to understand, remember, and use what we learn. Metacognition deals with a person's awareness of how he or she learns or knows, as well as with the strategies that make learning and remembering more efficient and secure. Obviously, a learner who can assess his or her own understanding effectively and take just the right steps to fill the gaps and remember information will learn more than someone with less self-awareness and fewer "metacognitive" skills.

Knowledge is not facts. Cognitive science suggests that our minds make huge collections of interconnections and categorizations among the facts we learn. We cannot be said to "know" anything until the mind breaks it down and labels it, on the one hand, and cross-relates it to the maximum number of other things we know, on the other. In fact, the difference between an expert on a subject and the rest of us is in part that the expert breaks down new information into more relevant chunks than we do and has more knowledge to connect it to.

In cognitive jargon, the breaking-down process is "schematization," something we might get better at with conscious practice. A somewhat trivial example of a "schema" might be our idea of "car." How could we break that down? Here are some of the ways we all use:

- Make
- Model
- Year
- Engine (4, 6, or 9 cylinders, horsepower, displacement)
- Number of doors (2 or 4)
- Number of seats
- Full-size, intermediate, compact, or subcompact
- Power or manual steering

The list can go on for a long time, because we are all experts on cars in this sense. We know the right questions to ask, and we can judge when the answers make sense. Not many of us have as good a schema for particle physics! Still, if we were skillful learners, we would know that we should be working toward one, and that it would be a set of labels to help us direct and monitor our learning.

The other point, about the advantage of connecting new information in webs or maps of relations with every other relevant piece of knowledge in our minds, is even more critical to learning.

More is more. The more we know, the more we understand about new information. The more connections we make among the data in our minds, and the more patterns we form from them, the more secure the information becomes and the easier it is for us to remember in a variety of contexts. The more we know, the better we understand what questions to ask ourselves in seeking or absorbing new information, thus ensuring that we "represent" it to ourselves more fully and expertly.

However, just knowing information is not enough when we are approaching a complex and unfamiliar subject; we also need to know where to begin to make attachments with what we already know. A successful learning program will therefore suggest ways to hook the new knowledge to existing information maps in our minds.

Implied by all this is that it takes time for anyone to build up a large body of well-rounded information. "More is more" has implications for the design of the information bases for interactive learning products, and also for the kinds of interactivity we build into them. What cognitive science has to say about metacognition has implications for how we design browsers and interfaces to operate on the information bases in our products.

Three more findings of cognitive science particularly bear on interactivity and suggest how it may be connected to the kind of user-controlled programs that a place like WNET, with its television broadcasting background, should develop.

1. Visual learning. People find it easier to learn when they are able to represent knowledge to themselves in mental images that the mind can "scan" and that serve to pull ideas together. (Hardly a startling idea; the wisdom of the ages states that "one picture is worth a thousand words.") This is especially true when, as they learn, they construct in their minds models or networks of interrrelated knowledge, in accordance with the cognitive principles already discussed.

2. Visual memory. Memory for information represented visually is greater than for verbal information. (There are hints from the exceptional size of our visual cortexes relative to those of other mammals that the ability to organize concepts by spatial relationships, rather than, say, by smell, may be "hard wired" in the human brain. Of course, speech is unique to human beings; maybe information taken in and internally represented in words is less accessible because speech takes place over time, and we cannot keep many words in mind simultaneously as we can the parts of a visual image.) This encourages us to use visual representation of abstract (hence difficult to learn) concepts and their interrelationships, even when the visual analogies we use are inexact and have to be "debugged" at a later date.

3. Active engagement. Deep, long-term understanding requires active, prolonged engagement and construction of meaning. Passive engagement may allow for short-term memory; long-term memory is most effectively developed by a learner's actively reaching out for and manipulating information.

These cognitive propositions seem almost to have been formulated to justify the kind of interactivity that can be achieved on advanced graphics-oriented computers (combined with videodisc technology, in our case), perhaps especially by producers of inherently visual programming, such as those who have had experience with television. In the next section, I will describe some of the ways in which we have tried to bring theory to life and practicality in our demonstration project, "Beyond Einstein."

Beyond Theory: "Beyond Einstein"

The core team to work on "Beyond Einstein" was very small. It consisted of myself as director and Hugh Osborn as associate director and media integrator, Lauren Resnick and Alan Lesgold (both from the Learning Research and Development Center at the University of Pittsburgh) as cognitive scientists and participants in the design process, Neil Patterson as science editor, Gary Zamchick as art director, and Christopher Pino as programmer. Geoffrey Haines-Stiles served as advisor and provided a television series treatment based on a content outline drawn up for us by Paul Davies, the eminent English physicist and writer. Finally, Steven Weinberg (Nobel laureate in physics) and Abraham Pais gave us counsel on the science.

Before going further, I must say that in the end it was Hugh and I who determined the contents and shape of the program. The others named above can only be held responsible for what is right with it, not for its errors in either science or psychology.

In planning for the WNET Learning Lab, we established several criteria—even before the "Beyond Einstein" team came on board—for what would be appropriate subject matter for the first few research and development projects. It would have to be important socially, intellectually, and educationally, and it would have to be difficult to understand and learn.

Why set the barriers so high? This was to be a research activity. We wouldn't be able to learn much if we set the barriers so low that we could clear them on blind luck. If our approach was right, it would do a better job in giving motivated adults access to really challenging intellectual content than past methods had.

How did we decide on quantum mechanics as the subject? It had everything: To put it simply, quantum mechanics says that all physical reality consists of subatomic particles of various kinds that operate on one another through forces conveyed by yet more particles; that individually all these particles behave in random and unpredictable ways; and that there are strict limits to the amount of information we could have about them at any given time, even if we had perfect measuring instruments, because when we observe them, we change them.

Quantum mechanics is central to the rest of the twentieth-century hard sciences: our most characteristic late-century technologies depend on it; it raises really shocking philosophical questions; and it has the romance of being the rock on which one of its principal architects, Einstein, ran aground.

"Creation of the Universe" is not primarily about quantum mechanics, but about a related topic: the "Big Bang" at the beginning of time. However, the show was wide-ranging, and it contained enough material on the history and concepts of quantum mechanics that, for a demonstration at least, we could reedit large portions of it and supplement them with new material and an information architecture (more on this in a moment) that would allow us to show and test our idea of interactive media.

How to get this material across to nonscientists? The challenge is twofold: technical and psychological. Very often in the past, the technical problems and solutions have driven design, so that learners had to make do with well-engineered but basically opaque programs. We wanted to try it the other way around—to think out what an intelligent, motivated, uninformed adult might want to know and how he or she might be able to come to terms with the subject matter, and then to "reverse-engineer" a program to meet these needs.

Following the cognitive principles outlined above, "Beyond Einstein" would have to intrigue learners enough to give them the motivation to start and to go on; somehow it would have to suggest what the contents were without overwhelming absolute novices, and to show how they could find hooks into what they already knew. It would have to provide a means of orienting them to the most important ways of looking at the subject. At all times, it would have to give hints about good questions the learner could work on next and how to find the information to answer them. It would have to be entertaining rather than didactic, and it would have to help users make appropriate "schemas" and "maps," just as experts do, to support their understanding and memory. Since the program was going to be interactive, it had to stay fascinating and helpful through many reuses, which meant that it would have to be adaptable to different users' level of knowledge about the subject. It also needed to take into account the fact that the individual users would learn from it, and hence, want increasingly sophisticated information from it as they went along. Holy Toledo!

Sensible people might have quit right there. Instead, the design team members bashed their heads against the issues for quite a long time. We made a lot of false starts that led us back to conventional learning software that seemed all right for school settings where students have to use it, but all wrong for adults who can choose how to invest their leisure and hobby time. "What happened to the *weirdness* of this stuff? Why would people want to interact with a simulation like this?" Gradually, we made progress.

Everyone eventually agreed that there are certain ways of looking at any fact in science that the whole world would find familiar and helpful:

- The science itself—facts about the physical world, the names and actions of the various particles, models of how they work (such as the conventional model of the atom), and so forth.

- The scientists, and the labs and apparatus they used for experiments.

- The issues the science raises, such as "Does God play dice?" and "If the atom is too small to see, how can we learn if there's anything inside it?"

- The applications and uses of science, such as the television tube or the computer, or the nuclear weapon and nuclear power.

In addition, there is another organizing principle everyone uses and understands: time. Time enables us to order things, it helps us ask about whether earlier things caused later ones, and it helps us to ask what else, either in our own histories or in the world at large, happened at the same time, earlier or later.

These five ways of looking at science can all be made to work at once, so that, if we know one fact, we can immediately fill in the rest of the information by asking the right questions and looking efficiently for the answers. In other words, we had devised a *schema* that even a layperson could use for learning quantum mechanics.

An example: Suppose you learn that the electron was the first subatomic particle discovered. Using this schema, you would be in a position to begin looking for answers to other questions in the schematic framework.

When was it discovered? By whom? Where? What kind of apparatus did the discoverer use? How did he or she arrive at that method? Did this discovery raise any important issues about previous scientific knowledge and models? Did it raise philosophical—or even religious—questions? What applications did it lead to? How did those change the way we live? Did the discovery of the electron come before or after the discovery of the quantum? How are the two things connected? (And so on.)

Laying things out this way also supports another basic cognitive principle: that learners need to take an active and questing role in building knowledge, rather than having it packaged for them, however logically.

In practice, our schema told us how to lay out the data base of "Beyond Einstein." This means that, since we were going to encourage learners to pose and answer questions as we've discussed, we had to put the information into the program in the same way.

I should stress here that "information" in this context does not mean only text. It mostly means short pieces of video, audio, and computer data, backed or supported by text only secondarily. The video and audio were to be on videodisc, along with some of the still graphics and facsimile text materials; the rest was to be in a computer software program that would also control the videodisc.

The best way to visualize how we organized the information is to think of a spreadsheet. Along the top, imagine a timeline from 1895 to the present. Down the left-hand side, imagine four headings:

- Physics
- People
- Issues
- Uses

(In practice, we used subheads under each of these in the data base, but that's a detail.) To make the task easier for ourselves and to make sure that all the members of the team were operating from the same model, we festooned my office with butcher paper all around the walls and set up the spreadsheet framework there.

Then we began making 3-by-5-inch file cards; on each one, we wrote a single fact from the history of subatomic physics. Free association helps here. Examples: Nucleus; Rutherford; Cavendish Laboratory; Niels Bohr; Quantum jump; Max Planck; Einstein; Photon.

Take the first card and place it on the spreadsheet. The nucleus is a piece of physics, so it goes in the Physics row. Its discovery was announced in 1911, so it goes under that year in the timeline column. Now Rutherford. He is associated with a number of important advances in atomic physics, but he is credited with the discovery of the atomic nucleus, so he goes in People, directly below Nucleus, at year 1911. Cavendish Laboratory, the lab at Cambridge University where so much of the early work on the structure of the atom was done, was under the direction of Joseph John Thomson when he discovered the electron in 1897, so we can put it with Thomson in the People row (Places is a subhead) below 1897 in the timeline column. That reminds us to put Electron in the Physics line.

And so on. Now imagine that the entire matrix of spreadsheet is filled out, to some arbitrary level of detail. Each item of data (remember, it might be a video clip, a still photo, a piece of voice-over, a page of text) can now be given a unique address in the data base, and we can begin writing a computer program to get at it as appropriate.

There are some interesting technical challenges here, but the most fascinating ones concern what learners would want to be able to do. These boil down to two things: to get some initial orientation to themes in quantum physics through what amount to television shows, and to then move about freely through the information.

The structure of the data base allowed us to create both of these capabilities. If we think of the information spreadsheet as a map, then we can package "tours" simply by specifying which places (data cells) are to be visited in what order. For each such tour, we can create an advance organizer that previews what the tour is about and where it goes. Then we can create a voice-over that ties the individual pieces of media together into a coherent whole. This is what we did for the orientation tours.

We made sure the tours available subtly reinforced the five ways of looking at the science information that we've discussed, since these could be used as learning aids when users began to browse freely through the information map later.

I've already mentioned advance organizers. We decided (it became a joke, in fact, because of the rigor with which it was enforced) that "Beyond Einstein" would not have any menus in the usual sense. We felt that menus are a price users have to pay for getting where they really want to be. However, users have to have some way of finding out what is available and how to get to it, no matter whether it's called a menu or something else. The "choice screens" would have to be entertaining and educational in themselves. Why not make them information maps, with voice-overs to let viewers know what they were looking at and how to use it?

In addition, we could make the maps browsable—that is, merely resting the cursor on a choice for a moment would bring up a voice-over preview of that topic that also, almost subliminally, told how it was related to the other topics on the map. So menus, too, could become real cognitive devices and entertainment in themselves, rather than mere gatekeepers. When the user made a final choice, a simple click of the mouse would take him or her directly to it.

We've looked at the basic information architecture and the way a user gets started in "Beyond Einstein." What happens then? How does one navigate? How does one interact with the system? These two questions turn out to have the same answers in this program. The answers were determined by a combination of the cognitive science that we made a design principle and of a more general concern for what users would want from an informal education product from a source like WNET.

In the end, we defined five kinds of interactivity and navigation in "Beyond Einstein." Most of them are served by more than one feature in the program. I'll list them:

1. Touring. Already mentioned. It serves to orient, suggest ways of looking at the subject matter, motivate, and set people up for later browsing.

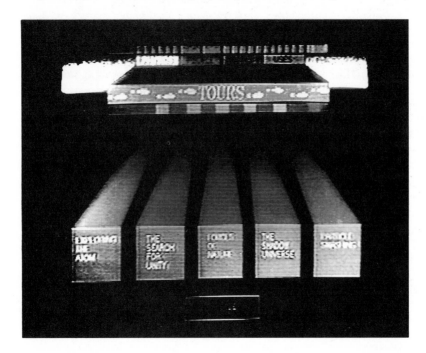

2. Browsing. Also mentioned. When users understand the architecture of the information (the fivefold structure discussed above), they are in a position, especially with the help of the Choice and Topic screens with their advance organizer feature, to begin simply exploring the subject on their own.

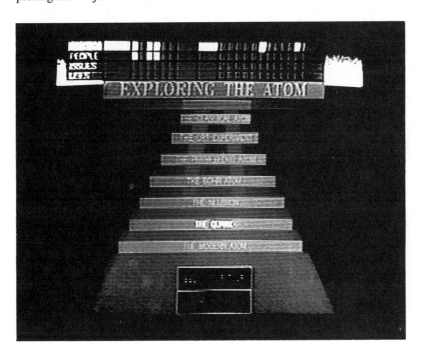

3. Connecting. We wanted, everywhere in "Beyond Einstein," to help learners create the kinds of cognitive maps or networks that seem to be so critical for memory and comprehension. The voice-over previews are one example of how we tried to support mapmaking. Another is the feature we called *semantic nets*. (The term derives from work by Quillian and Collins and others on memory.)

Cognitive scientists distinguish between two levels of memory: short-term, or working, memory, and long-term, or semantic, memory. Short-term memory is like a small "buffer" in the mind; we can keep a small number of things in mind for as long as we are working with them. For the longer term, they have to be anchored "semantically" if we are to retain them and be able to recover them at will.

The semantic nets in "Beyond Einstein" occur at the ends of major topic sections. They are patterns of words arrayed around the topic word, color coded as to whether the terms refer to science itself, people or places, issues, or uses of science—in other words, to reinforce and make use of our fivefold schema. They are interconnected by lines that represent precedence, cause, or authorship. They serve as a method of pulling together what was in that section of the program and other material elsewhere in the program, and as a review mechanism. They are also active: clicking on any term in the semantic net takes the user there directly. Thus "connecting" in our sense also means something like "orderly free-associating." Almost every part of the program can be directly addressed from a Choice screen, a Tour screen, or a semantic net.

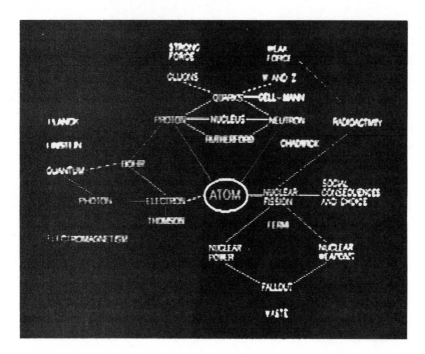

4. "Question asking." I started this paper by saying that "Creation of the Universe" cried out for user control of the pace, and for interactivity. The most obvious kind of interactivity for a program like this is the ability to question it. Being able to stop the show and ask "What was that word again? What did it mean? What did I just see?" would alone transform television into something much more rewarding.

Therefore, we built into "Beyond Einstein" four features to support active questing and adaptivity to individual users. We called them *script, glossary, magnifying glass,* and motion pause.

Because the narrative portions of the program inevitably bring up unfamiliar terms that most listeners couldn't even spell, we built in the capability to stop the action and display in text the script of the narrative. In the script, technical terms are highlighted in color. Pointing to one and clicking brings up an entry from the glossary, defining it in multiple media (for example, print and video).

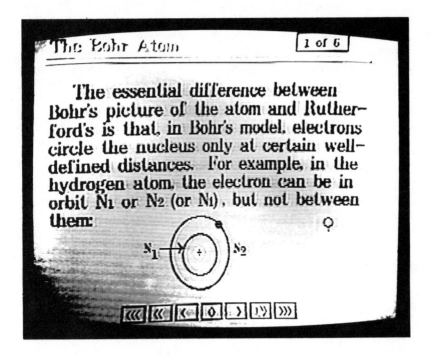

The magnifying glass is displayed as an icon at the bottom of the screen whenever (which is often) there are additional levels of information available on the material being treated. Clicking on it first brings up a somewhat expanded version of information, perhaps with a formula written out rather than in mathematical notation, a labeled diagram of experimental apparatus, or a longer selection of text. Going down further would take the user to a level perhaps roughly appropriate for an undergraduate taking a course on the subject. This level might bring up a simulation or the full mathematical representation of the topic.

Finally, the motion pause stops the action and draws boxes around the objects on the screen for which labeling and other information are available. Pointing to a box and clicking brings up a full screen of information, while retaining the box of video in the same position it occupied before the click.

5. "Condition changing." Sometimes the only way to understand what is being said is to set up a model and tinker with it. This we call "condition changing"; it is better known as simulating. "Beyond Einstein" treats simulations as cells of information that can be brought up as appropriate from a variety of different parts of the program. To take one example: the simulation of Niels Bohr's 1913 model of the atom can be reached by taking a tour (on the history of our concepts of the atom), directly from a Choice screen (by clicking "Bohr atom") or from a semantic net; the Bohr atom would appear on several nets. On arrival at the segment on Bohr's concept of the atom and definition of the quantum jump, the simulation would be lying in wait below a magnifying glass. The voice-over would suggest going down to look at it.

If "Beyond Einstein" sounds like a complex design, that's not surprising—it's very complicated. What *is* surprising is that the program is not at all complicated to use. The actual command structure, from the user's point of view, is among the simplest we have ever seen—and deliberately so.

At all times, the screen looks like a television screen, not a computer screen. This is because, in our opinion, most people who are interested in interacting with a program like "Beyond Einstein" have no interest in becoming computer operators. We think they want television to do a better job of helping them learn and remember some of the big subjects. If our program were regarded simply as a more successful form of television or publication, we would be very flattered.

MAXIMIZING RETURN ON
PROGRAM INVESTMENT

One of the unhappiest facts about public broadcasting is that the enormous expense involved in producing high-quality programming brings such a small audience reach for its producers and underwriters. We are not thinking here primarily of financial return (though heaven knows that it's important, too), but of the fact that most programs are seen two or three times, then disappear, taking their investments with them.

By planning interactive products in advance with the producers of related television series, we could not only anticipate reuse of important and expensive video and audio segments, but also plan additional shooting on location, where crews are already needed for the television production. With advance planning, we need add very little to the cost of broadcast programming. We would become producers of interactive material that reuses television programming effectively, because the television was planned with this in mind, and the extra material was produced at low cost, since it involves virtually no new expense in travel and setup.

The skills we develop for making interactive multimedia products—in animation, graphics, and audio, to name a few—have potential future benefit for the broadcast organization as well, especially with stereo and multichannel broadcasting just over the horizon.

WHATEVER BECAME OF "BEYOND EINSTEIN"?

Good question. "Beyond Einstein" is first and foremost a demonstration project. It is finished only on the demo tape. In reality, while there is more on the videodisc than we were able to show on tape, there is less computer programming than is needed for a viable product.

As I said at the beginning, the program is put together from bits of material gathered from several sources. Our plan for an interactive modern physics curriculum for older students and adults, and for a corresponding telecourse, has always been to build from the ground up. The function of the tape is to show what our concept might look like if funded and implemented.

The present demonstration was made on a shoestring. We had a small grant from the Corporation for Public Broadcasting for the development and another from the Hyde-Watson Foundation for equipment. If the core team members had not invested a great deal of "sweat equity" in the project, it could not have been accomplished for the budget. The kind of product that is needed will cost something like $2 million to develop, test, and refine, even with the amount of design already done. WNET is a nonprofit educational television station and production center. Clearly, the funds would have to be raised elsewhere. The question is whether the possibilities demonstrated in "Beyond Einstein" seem worth the investment.

But, as often happens, that is part of the question we need money to answer. Our claim that this program embodies sophisticated ideas of learning, based on the latest cognitive theories, and that it will be more attractive to and effective with older learners than earlier materials, needs a thorough test. The kinds of cognitive outcomes we are suggesting could come from a program like this are very hard to measure. One of the reasons the ongoing research and development of "Beyond Einstein" is worth investing in, in our view, is that it will force an advance in the state of the art of cognitive testing.

In the meantime, "Beyond Einstein" is a set of design principles based on reasoning that can be captured and replicated. This paper does some of that capturing. The replicating is up to all of us.

The need to understand interactive media and develop principled learning products cannot be put off much longer. The time seems to be rapidly approaching when a viable interactive multimedia technology will penetrate consumer and education markets. It may well be based on the compact disc and knit together home audio and video systems. It may, in fact, prove to be the recently announced Compact Disc-Interactive (CD-I). Initially, CD-I will be unable to handle much motion video, and its access times may be slow, but it will be a powerful medium computer based on a very successful audio technology.

The extent to which interactive compact-disc players are overtly computers will be a matter of marketing experimentation on the part of hardware companies, and there may be enough different models to encompass several alternative product concepts: the CD-I player as home entertainment center; CD-I as computer peripheral; CD-I as media computer. We can probably expect CD-I to be around long enough to find its niche in the marketplace.

It is not my purpose to push a technological breakthrough. Whether CD-I succeeds or not, we are so close to the widespread market availability of a machine on which "Beyond Einstein" and its successors will play that it hardly matters exactly what its name will be. What is much more important is *why* it should be, and how we should put it to use in the service of an appropriate goal. The right goal, from the perspective of WNET, is information made transparent and attractive to users. Surely that's something we can all sign up for. "Beyond Einstein" is a start on our exploration of "information transparent and attractive."

BACKGROUND READING

For anyone interested in reading further on cognitive science as it might apply to the design of learning materials, I might recommend the following as a one-volume introduction:

Cognitive Psychology and Its Implications, by John R. Anderson, published by W.H. Freeman and Company, New York.

Anderson's book was published in 1980, and quite a lot of work has been done since. Nonetheless, it's a fine starting place.

Those feeling the need for strong medicine should begin by reading...

Mental Models: Towards a Cognitive Science of Language, Inference, and Consciousness, by P.H. Johnson-Laird, Harvard University Press, Cambridge, Mass.,1983.

For almost the whole world of cognitive science, go on to the catalogs of the Harvard Cognitive Science Series (of which Johnson-Laird's book is one) and the publications of Lawrence Erlbaum, Hillsdale, N.J. Erlbaum makes a speciality of publishing current work by the best-known cognitive scientists. Then follow the citations in the bibliographies of these books.

To the **Kings** *most excellent Majesty*

Most gracious Sovereign:

We your Majesty's faithful subjects of the colonies of New Hampshire, Massachusetts bay, Rhode island and Providence plantations, Connecticut, New-York, New Jersey, Pennsylvania, the counties of New Castle Kent and Sussex on Delaware, Maryland, Virginia, North carolina and South Carolina in behalf of ... and the inhabitants of these colonies, who ha... pointed us to represent them in general Congre... that your Majesty's gracious attention to this... humble petition.

The union between our Mother country ... colonies and the energy of mild and just gov... ment produced benefits so remarkably important, and afforded such an assurance of their permanency ... crease, that the wonder and envy of other nations ... ... while they beheld Great Britain rising to a ... power the most extraordinary the world had ever known.

Her rivals observing that there was no ... ...bability of this happy connection being broken

At the heart of the computer and multimedia revolution is a set of economic and business factors. At the moment, there is no scheme for the development, use, and distribution of multimedia computer-based materials. Many organizations are expressing interest in interactive experiences, including computer companies and optical media companies. In addition, a number of different organizations have decided to consider themselves information companies rather than media-specific distributors. Tom Anderson of WNET states eloquently, for example, that PBS stations are in the education business, not the television business, and that it is, therefore, most appropriate that they extend their offerings beyond television broadcast to books and "long distance" courses that complement their broadcasts (which WNET has already done), as well as to interactive materials that extend their video materials (as Tom is now proposing).

Peter Cook has provided Groliers with a similar message over the years, as he has assisted them in moving into electronic media in a systematic way. This means that in addition to producing leather-bound books called encyclopedias, Groliers is in the business of encyclopedic information. It is in the business of effectively portraying information, using whatever media are available, in addition to book production and organization. The skills involved in preparing encyclopedic information for printing seem to transfer to new media—though clearly, it is a slow and tedious transfer. Issues of how to index materials in electronic form are somewhat different from those for print delivery, for example. Yet Cook's perspective is to attempt the transfer and make appropriate changes. Grolier's intention is to lead in the electronic information business by setting up infrastructures for advertising, distributing, and pricing first versions of electronic media, thereby preparing for later, more sophisticated presentations.

The National Geographic Society also has made a serious commitment to avoid becoming "media bound," as described by **George Peterson.** This is not new to the National Geographic Society, for they have an almost one-hundred-year history in media innovation, beginning with the fundamental decision to include pictures in their magazine, and more recently evidenced by their decisions to produce filmstrips, topical books, and television materials that extend their offerings well beyond the pages of their magazine. This experience in non-media-specific development is now assisting the National Geographic Society in its work in computer software and optical media, areas that finally seem ready to engage the kinds of image presentations and quality of display for which this organization is known. This enables the society to continue to fulfill its nonprofit charter of delivering geographic information to American citizens; these new media complement its existing materials and expertise while providing new experiences for its audience.

Multimedia Technology

An Encylopedia Publisher's Perspective

Peter Cook

PETER COOK

Peter Cook is the Vice President for Creative Services for Grolier Electronic Publishing, Inc. After 10 years of international publishing experience in London, he came to the U.S. specifically to help develop the original print edition of the Academic American Encyclopedia. Since the printed edition was published in 1980, he has played a key role in the development of the various electronic editions of the encyclopedia (using on-line data base distribution, videodisc, and CD-ROM technology) and has recently returned to London to work on the development of a CD-I (compact disk interactive) version of the encyclopedia. As a trained graphic designer, he is particularly interested in the graphic representation of the knowledge structure of large data bases, and in the integration of text and graphics media.

Among the dozen or so companies, individuals, and educational organizations represented at Apple's "Multimedia in Education" seminar, Grolier occupied a unique position and—we believe—offered a unique perspective. Grolier is not a computer manufacturer, software developer, university research lab, or not-for-profit organization; it is a publicly traded international publisher that is very heavily involved in one particular information-delivery technology, a technology that has remained remarkably stable throughout its long history: the publishing of printed books. It is a technology that we know intimately in terms of the creative/editorial process, the production and manufacturing, and the marketing and distribution of the end products—products that meet a real need in a particular market or market segment.

Because print technology is so stable, and the market forces that create the demand for print products (particularly within the education market) are well defined, print publishers have little incentive to pursue ill-defined alternative delivery technologies, with all their associated risks and uncertainties. In fact, publishers who are used to working in product life cycles of 5, 10, and—in the case of encyclopedias—20 years or more, are often confused by the rapid and apparently helter-skelter development and introduction of new hardware devices and new software delivery media.

Given all of the above, perhaps this question should be asked: Why should an encyclopedia publisher such as Grolier—a representative of the most traditional, unchanging segment of print publishing—be interested in multimedia technology in the first place?

A simple answer would be that any information-delivery technology that is *viable* for Grolier's products and markets is viewed as a potential business opportunity, and as a possible threat to the company's current business. I could go on at great length outlining the nature of both the opportunities and the threats that face traditional print publishers, but I want to step back from that discussion and instead look at the impact of information technologies on society as a whole, so that Grolier's longer-term strategy, and its view of multimedia technology in particular, can be seen in a broader context.

Grolier has elected to ride the wave of technology because—from our publishing perspective—there is no other sensible alternative. We are in the information business, and the mode for disseminating information of all forms—data, text, audio, visual—is undergoing rapid change, in terms of both the media of dissemination and the relative importance of the various kinds of media.

Print publishers today must compete with other media for valuable time and resources, as we move from a predominantly paper-based to a screen-based society. In some areas of life, that transition is already accomplished: television is the medium of greatest influence on much of modern society—children in the U.S. are already exposed to a staggering 6–7 hours of TV viewing per day. Television is a seductive medium: the illusion of reality created by its images; the passive, relaxing nature of the viewing experience; the strengthening of family bonds through sharing the experience—no matter how slight; each of these factors is a powerful reinforcer of the dominance of television in our lives.

Computer technology (at least as viewed by the end user who has little understanding or interest in the underlying technology) is also screen based, but, because it cannot function without interaction, it is the antithesis of television, which is passive by nature. The value of the computer lies in its ability to manipulate many kinds of information under the control of the user, information that already exists as published software (from adventure games to physics simulations) and information that is entered directly by the user into a software tool (such as a word processor or a data-base manager). In an educational setting, it is the user's interaction with the content of a computer program, in particular the degree of personal control of the information exchange, that sets the computer apart. Interaction requires involvement, which in turn can enhance the learning experience.

Television, or more correctly, the video medium, is already all-pervasive in our society. Computers, particularly personal computers, have already changed many aspects of our working lives and will ultimately become as prevalent in schools and homes. The domains of television and computer technology are beginning to converge, and early examples of this convergence, such as interactive videodisc, demonstrate some of the potential of multimedia products. Such products allow the user to interact with video and audio information, selecting individual pathways through the program and controlling the pace of the information displayed.

Computer-controlled videodisc players are already being used to great effect in meeting the training requirements of large corporations, and a few educational programs have recently been introduced into schools (for example, the *Core Concepts in Science and Math* series, produced by Systems Impact, Inc.). But the videodisc/computer systems of the present are frequently hardware hybrids that do not effectively integrate the audiovisual materials with those generated by the computer. Future systems will combine all functions in a single hardware device, providing true multimedia capabilities.

But what are the potential advantages of such systems? We believe that multimedia products will break down the barriers that currently exist between the worlds of print publishing, film and television production, and computer technology, providing a hardware system and a delivery medium that can blend materials from all sources. If this potential is fully realized, multimedia delivery systems could provide us with exciting new tools for working, learning, and entertainment.

GROLIER'S STRATEGY FOR BUILDING A
MULTIMEDIA ENCYCLOPEDIA

Having outlined a somewhat seductive vision of the future potential for multimedia products—with the underlying promise of the business opportunities created by such products—I will now return to the present, and even refer to the past, as I outline Grolier's goals and the strategy for implementing those goals.

One of the company's longer-term objectives is the creation of a multimedia encyclopedia, an information tool for the 1990s and beyond. However, it is a product concept that cannot be delivered via current technology; nor, we believe, would the market be ready for it even if a truly viable delivery technology were available today. Our strategy, therefore, is to build toward that long-term goal through a series of product-development stages that are acceptable in strict business terms and that are providing the building blocks for our longer-term goal.

Because current technology cannot provide us with a viable delivery system for multimedia products, our development plan has two tracks—one for the *development of an encyclopedic text data base* and the other for the *development of of an audiovisual data base* —but it is our firm belief that both tracks will converge and eventually merge into one. It is not prudent for any company to base its business decisions on future events that it has little control over, but we believe that our step-by-step development plan minimizes the current business risk while still building toward the long-term goal.

Developing an Encyclopedia Text Data Base

The decision to develop and market an electronic edition of an encyclopedia was greatly facilitated by Grolier's acquisition of the Academic American Encyclopedia (AAE), a 20-volume, 9-million-word general reference set that was first published in 1980. Although the AAE had been developed as a print product, all of the text had been typeset using computer technology. The entire text existed as a machine-readable data base that was subsequently edited to eliminate nondisplayable characters as well as all references to the illustrations that are used in the print edition.

The data base was made commercially available in 1982 via Dow Jones News/Retrieval, and is now accessible to over 700,000 subscribers via some 12 additional on-line services, including CompuServe, The Source, Dialog, and BRS.

The on-line business is a viable one for Grolier. It's a business that will grow as the networking of computers continues to expand within the business and educational markets. It also has provided the company with a tremendous learning experience—particularly in terms of how different audiences, from young children to business users, access and use an electronic encyclopedia. We found, for example, that information searches were frequently frustrated by the unforgiving nature of the retrieval software programs—the interface between the user and the data base—that are used by the various on-line services. For example, the software of relatively easy-to-use systems such as CompuServe cannot handle slight misspellings or word transpositions in search terms entered by users, and the more powerful, professional services require a considerable understanding of the complex command language used by their software. Through this experience we realized the underlying importance of retrieval software, and how it can be adapted to better suit the needs of the encyclopedia user and to more fully realize the power of electronic media—issues that will be addressed later in this paper.

Our experience with on-line distribution of the data base has been helpful in other projects using various forms of optical storage as the delivery media. In 1984, Grolier worked with Laserdata Inc. to develop a prototype laser videodisc that stored the text of the AAE as digital data. That work was followed a year later by the commercial introduction of the *Knowledgedisc,* an analog videodisc edition of the AAE, and in 1986 by the introduction of *The Electronic Encyclopedia,* A CD-ROM edition of the same data base—both of these products were developed with KnowledgeSet Inc. (formerly known as Activenture).

The Encyclopedia Text Data Base:
Development Steps

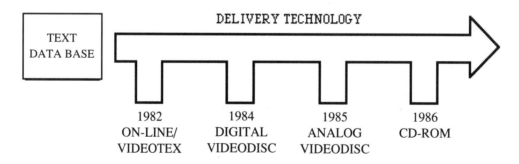

All of these developments have been viable in purely business terms, and each has been of significant value to the ongoing development and refinement of the data base. The text data base has in fact diverged considerably from its print parent: more articles have been added because, unlike the print edition, the electronic data base has no physical limitations. The electronic edition is also more current, with the on-line version being updated on a quarterly basis compared to the annual update of the printed set.

With the CD-ROM edition, we have also considerably enhanced the retrieval software, addressing many of the limitations of on-line services mentioned earlier. The success of a new distribution medium such as CD-ROM lies in its ability to be much more than a direct physical substitution for other delivery technologies. We have acknowledged that fact in developing the various editions of the data base, adding value to the information in ways that are not possible with the printed work.

Later in this paper, I will be reviewing how text information can be enhanced, but these enhancements are best explained by first examining how print encyclopedias are used, and then showing, through examples, how an electronic encyclopedia can better serve these same information needs.

The Role of a Print Encyclopedia

The primary role of a general encyclopedia is that of a reference source—a fact-finder—that is designed to meet many kinds of basic information needs across all fields of inquiry. In attempting to encompass all areas of knowledge (the circle of learning embodied in the word "encyclopedia"), the information contained within a general reference set must be carefully selected, and then distilled down to its essence. There are clear variables that affect this process: the physical capacity of the encyclopedia, in terms of words, pages, and illustrations; the targeted audience; the biases and skills of the many individuals who contribute to such a work; and the publisher's commitment to maintaining the currentness and effectiveness of the encyclopedia over time.

The ongoing value of encyclopedias continues to be that they are a microcosm of all knowledge—works that encompass all fields of human endeavor and experience in a convenient resource (though convenient is a relative term if you are working with a 30-volume set). In an age of increasing specialization in both the educational system and the work environment, encyclopedias endure as one of the few remaining sources of general information.

When seeking information in an encyclopedia, the user usually has a certain set of expectations about the work, in terms of how it is organized, the approximate range of the articles it contains, and the limited nature of its content (limited is also a relative term: a 10,000-word article on the American Revolution may be perfectly adequate for a 5th grader but inadequate for a college graduate). These expectations are ultimately either satisfied or not by the success of the encyclopedia in meeting the user's information needs, both in the primary role as a source of basic reference information, and as a vehicle for stimulating the user's curiosity to explore additional information within or beyond the encyclopedia.

Because their primary role is that of a reference tool, printed encyclopedias have been designed to facilitate information seeking. The alphabet is a powerful organizer (as we all know from our use of indexes, dictionaries, telephone books, and so on) and it is the method of organization used most frequently by general encyclopedias—you look in the N volume for articles on New York, and the C volume for information on California. (This convenient yet arbitrary arrangement of information can create some fascinating juxtapositions: Alvar Aalto, the aardvark, and Hank Aaron have almost nothing in common other than the double *a* in their spelling that's responsible for their proximity to each other in an encyclopedia. Yet this method of organization has a value, if only for the serendipitous discoveries it encourages.)

There is also an underlying organization that binds the alphabetically arranged articles to other topically related information. This is achieved within encyclopedia articles by the use of *cross-references* and *see-also listings,* which direct the user to related information elsewhere in the set, and through the use of the *index,* which usually contains listings under convenient topic headings. However, these devices for directing the user to topically related information do not eliminate the awkwardness of alphabetical organization of the information. For example, a child who wanted to see all of the articles on dinosaurs in the AAE would have to access 13 different volumes.

Limitations of Print Media

Clearly, a printed encyclopedia is limited because of the physical constraints of the print medium. The information on its pages remains fixed and cannot be dynamically rearranged to suit the needs and convenience of the end user. And of course the information cannot be updated or changed—short of writing directly onto the margins of the printed page. But printed encyclopedias have yet another limitation that is particularly relevant when one considers the encyclopedia's primary role as a reference source, and that is the inaccessibility of much of the information. For example, to find information on Mark Twain in the AAE, a user could either access the T volume directly, and turn to the article "Twain, Mark," or use the index volume. The AAE index lists six references to articles on Twain— the one principal article and five additional articles that have been selected by the indexer. In fact, a search of the electronic edition of the AAE reveals references to some *25* articles that are of relevance to Twain. The printed index is limited by size and the selection criteria of the indexer, and cannot direct the user to all the relevant information.

However, the printed encyclopedia has one advantage over the current electronic editions: It contains several thousand illustrations—photographs, maps, paintings, diagrams, etc.— none of which can be stored and distributed economically using the electronic distribution media described so far. But as previously stated, we plan to develop a complementary audiovisual encyclopedic data base, using the full range of audiovisual media to deliver an information experience that goes far beyond the fixed images of the printed book. I will describe this in a later section.

The next several pages of this paper show how a text-only electronic edition of the AAE can overcome many of the limitations of the printed encyclopedia, while also providing other enhancements that clearly demonstrate the ability to add value to preexisting information through electronic manipulation.

Limitations of Electronic Media

Before reviewing the advantages of an electronic edition of an encyclopedia, it would be useful to examine some of its inherent disadvantages when compared to a book. First, the computer screen can provide only the most myopic view of a large textual information resource, because a standard computer monitor displays approximately 300 words on the screen at a time, while a print encyclopedia can present *3,000* words across two facing pages. Because of its physical nature, the printed work can also provide a sense of scale and a sense of place: at the most basic level, everyone knows how to navigate in a book. An electronic encyclopedia cannot duplicate the physical dimensions and characteristics of the book; it requires a different set of navigational aids, and a completely different mode of interaction, as the following series of examples will demonstrate.

ENHANCING ENCYCLOPEDIA
INFORMATION IN ELECTRONIC MEDIA

The illustrations and examples used in this section show how one particular information quest can be aided by computer technology. It is assumed in the description that the reader is reasonably familiar with the user-interface conventions of Apple's Macintosh computer, in particular with the use of pull-down menus and the selection of options with a mouse.

In this simulated example, information in the encyclopedia data base can be located by direct searching or by browsing, using the various program options. In the first screen (Fig. 1), the user selects the encyclopedia data base from a "library" of reference tools, and chooses the mode of searching. Search options include the ability to search the encyclopedia by individual word, by article title, or by topic area. This particular example begins with the user typing in the article title "Mark Twain" and then clicking on "Search" (Fig. 2). Having found an article that exactly matches the user's request, the computer employs a split-screen technique to display an outline of the article's contents alongside the first "page" of text (Fig. 3). The user can then select any section of the article from the contents listing and view that directly, or remove the contents list (by clicking on the close box) so that the full screen of text can be displayed (Fig. 4).

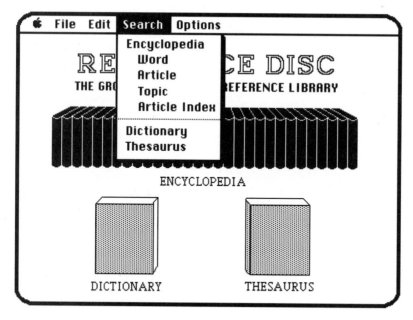

Figure 1

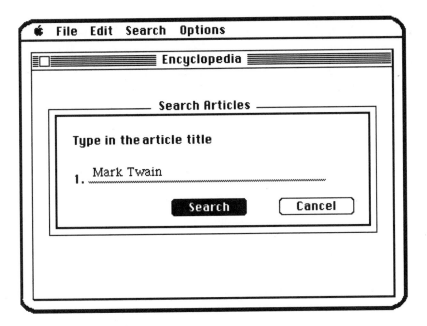

Figure 2

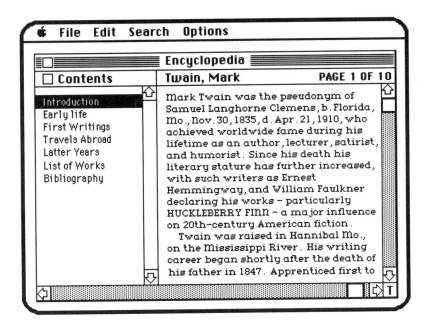

Figure 3

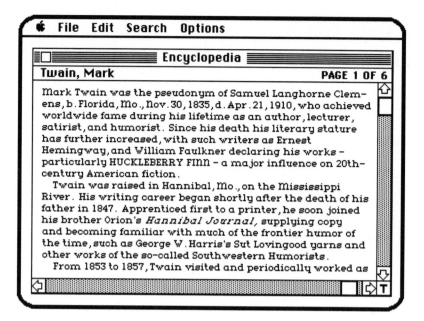

Figure 4

The vertical scroll bar can be used to view additional lines or pages of the article (the "page" convention is based on the portion of the article that is currently in view, hence the different number of pages listed for the same article in Figures 3 and 4). The horizontal scroll bar can be used to browse to articles that are adjacent to Twain in the alphabet, and it is possible to browse through different letters (volumes) of the alphabet by clicking on the current letter (Fig. 5), which changes the scroll bar into an alphabet from which other letters can be selected.

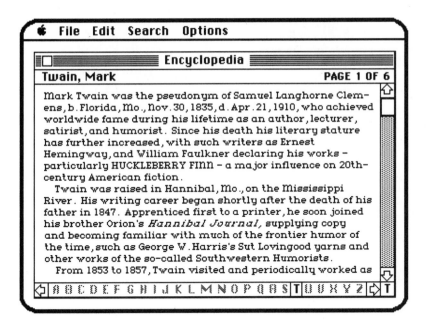

Figure 5

When viewing the text, there are a number of options available to the user, as the Options menu shown in Figure 6 indicates. These include the ability to mark and recall a specific page, to show the table of contents of an article, and to use a feature called "Search Trail," which automatically creates a list of all the articles viewed by the user during a single session with the computer. Other options will be explained through examples. The "Cross-Reference" option that is highlighted in Figure 6 enables the user to select a relevant cross-reference within the text (identified through the familiar book convention of capitalized letters) and then view the relevant article directly using a horizontal split screen (Fig. 7).

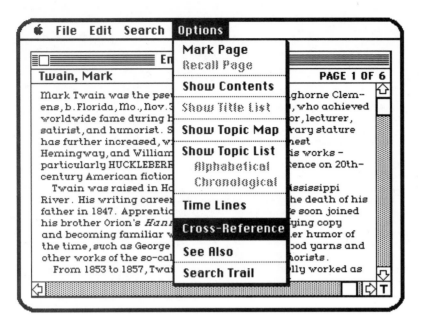

Figure 6

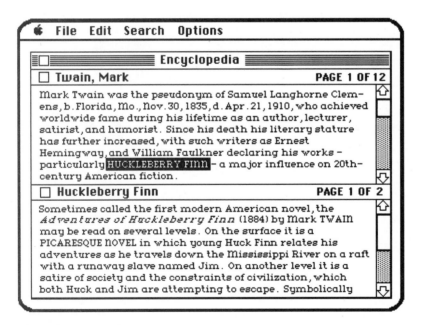

Figure 7

Selecting "See Also" from the Options menu creates a listing of all the titles of other articles in the encyclopedia that the author or editor has identified as being of particular relevance to Mark Twain (Fig. 8). Each of the articles listed can be displayed by highlighting the article title.

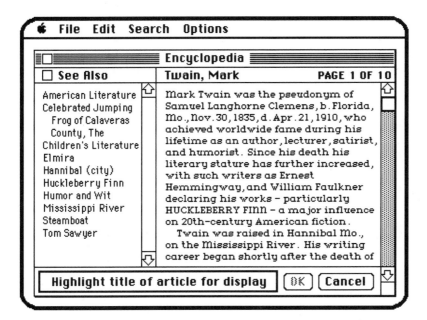

Figure 8

Another method for accessing information on Mark Twain would be to use the computer to search for every single occurrence of his name. Having established the particular search parameters (listed in the "dialog box" on the right side of the screen in Figure 9), the search reveals that the words "Mark Twain" appear 42 times in the data base, in 25 articles. A list of the articles can be displayed (Fig. 10) and any article selected (Fig. 11). The list of titles can be removed or redisplayed in the same way as the Contents and See Also listings described earlier.

```
┌─────────────────────────────────────────────────────┐
│  File   Edit   Search   Options                        │
│  ┌───────────────────────────────────────────────┐    │
│  │ ▢▤▤▤▤▤▤▤▤▤ Encyclopedia ▤▤▤▤▤▤▤▤▤▤ │    │
│  │                                                 │    │
│  │  Search For Words:        Words in same:        │    │
│  │      Mark Twain            ⦿ Article            │    │
│  │                           ○ Paragraph           │    │
│  │  and                      ○ Sentence            │    │
│  │  and                      ○ Proximity ▢         │    │
│  │  and                      ☐ Title               │    │
│  │  and                      ☐ Text                │    │
│  │  and                      ☐ Table               │    │
│  │                           ☐ Factbox             │    │
│  │  Words Appear:            ☐ Bibliography        │    │
│  │      42 Times in 25 Articles  ☒ All Sections    │    │
│  │                                                 │    │
│  │  ┌ Display ┐    ┌ Search ┐    ┌ Cancel ┐        │    │
│  └───────────────────────────────────────────────┘    │
└─────────────────────────────────────────────────────┘
```

Figure 9

```
┌─────────────────────────────────────────────────────┐
│  File   Edit   Search   Options                        │
│  ┌───────────────────────────────────────────────┐    │
│  │ ▢▤▤▤▤▤▤▤▤▤ Encyclopedia ▤▤▤▤▤▤▤▤▤▤ │    │
│  │ Word Occurrences/Article Titles/Number of Pages │    │
│  │  1/ American art and architecture / 32      ⬆  │    │
│  │  5/ American literature/ 29                     │    │
│  │  1/ Atlantic Monthly/ 1                         │    │
│  │  1/ Bock, Edward william/ 1                     │    │
│  │  1/ Brooks, Van Wyck/ 2                         │    │
│  │  2/ Celebrated Jumping Frog of Calaveras        │    │
│  │        County, the/ 1                           │    │
│  │  3/ childrens literature/ 13                    │    │
│  │  1/ Clemens, Samuel Langhorne: see             │    │
│  │        Twain, Mark/ 1                           │    │
│  │  2/ Connecticutt/ 35                            │    │
│  │  1/ Ellison, Ralph/ 3                           │    │
│  │  1/ Elmira/ 1                                   │    │
│  │  1/ Gilded Age/ 1                               │    │
│  │  1/ Hannibal (city)/ 1                      ⬇  │    │
│  │  ┌ Display ┐    ┌ Search ┐    ┌ Cancel ┐        │    │
│  └───────────────────────────────────────────────┘    │
└─────────────────────────────────────────────────────┘
```

Figure 10

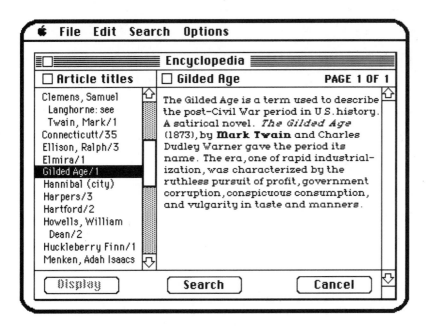

Figure 11

Information can also be searched for and displayed topically, using several different options. The "Show Topic Map" option listed on the menu (Fig. 12) allows the user to view a diagrammatic representation of a topic area (Figs. 13 and 14), which reveals the underlying hierarchical structure of the topic and the relative position of articles within that hierarchy. In this example, the Twain article is related to a series of topical groupings under the broad category of American Literature, which in turn is subordinated to a still wider grouping that encompasses all of the arts.

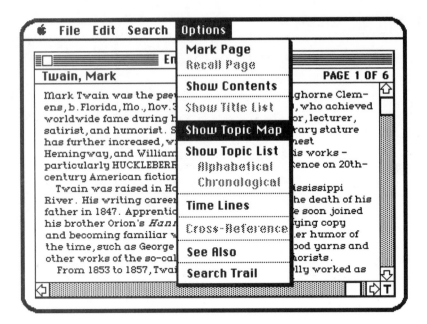

Figure 12

Figure 13

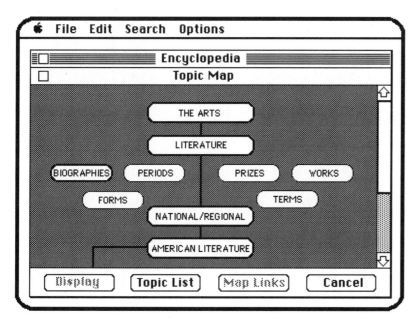

Figure 14

As the Options menu in Figure 12 indicates, topical information can also be viewed in a list form, in which the computer displays a predefined list of topically related articles. In the example shown (Fig. 15), Twain is listed in the context of other American novelists, but the article could also be viewed in the context of other categories of American writers, such as humorists or essayists. (In this example the pyramid icon in the top left corner represents the layers of hierarchy, with the levels that are currently being displayed shown in a highlighted form. Other levels can be selected by clicking directly on the icon.)

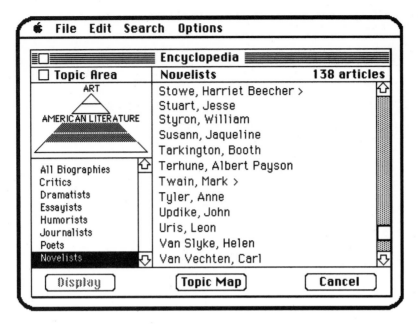

Figure 15

The alphabetical topic list in Figure 15 can also be displayed in a chronological sequence by selecting that option from the menu. The resulting display (Fig. 16) lists Twain and other American novelists in a chronological sequence, ordered by birth date—revealing at a glance Twain's contemporaries. Any article title listed can be selected and the text viewed, subordinating the listing to the window on the left side of the screen.

One final example continues the chronological theme but places Twain in a broader context. When the "Time Lines" option is selected from the menu shown in Figure 12, a diagrammatic representation is displayed, showing a period of time that coincides with the part of Twain's life (Fig. 17). In this example, the time line selected reveals key U.S. political events during a 30-year period of the 19th century. Other years, periods, or centuries can be selected using the horizontal scroll bar, and several different time-line options are available so that Twain (or any other individual or event) can be viewed in different contexts: from the point of view of political events, technological achievements, key events in the arts, and so forth. All of the events and individuals listed in the time line relate to articles in the encyclopedia. For example, the article "Mexican War" could be displayed by clicking directly on those words.

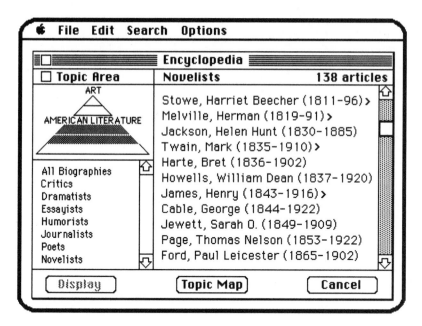

Figure 16

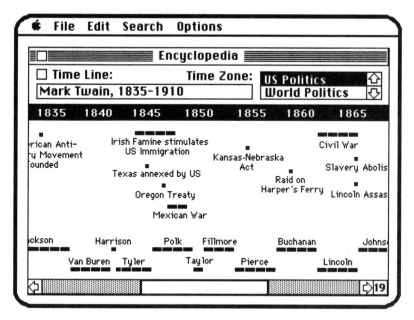

Figure 17

The purpose of showing and describing this series of examples (and I should emphasize that these screens represent a concept and not a commercially available product) is to reveal some of the many ways that a basic body of information could be linked, organized, and displayed. As I hope the Twain example reveals, it is possible to build a cognitive network and a navigational method that allow the user to approach an information inquiry from many different viewpoints, and provide a vehicle for truly dynamic exploration of the data base's contents *and* its underlying structure.

Other research work that Grolier is conducting is examining how best to link different data bases (such as the dictionary and thesaurus shown in the first figure of this sequence) and how to provide the user with easy and effective methods of manipulating and extracting information so that it can be used in a convenient form. All of these efforts have one single thrust—to enhance the value of our encyclopedic information, thereby providing a more useful, more valuable information tool—a dynamic encyclopedia that has been shaped to take *full* advantage of the technologies described earlier.

TEXT TODAY, MULTIMEDIA TOMORROW:
PLANNING AN AUDIOVISUAL DATA BASE

All of the work described so far has dealt with the development and enhancement of a text data base, but as I mentioned earlier, Grolier is also planning to develop a complementary audiovisual data base that will eventually merge with the text, forming a multimedia product. We had a head start with the text data base because the AAE already existed in machine-readable format and the development cost for the encyclopedia was primarily offset against the print edition. This is not the case with an audiovisual data base, because we have to start from scratch.

Two years ago, Grolier funded a pilot project to test the feasibility of using laser videodisc technology as the delivery medium for an audiovisual data base. The resulting videodisc prototype was a vehicle for examining the questions regarding contents and production dimensions that are involved with creating a viable videodisc series. Though the research was worthwhile, it revealed the enormous complexity and cost involved in creating an encyclopedic audiovisual data base. Nevertheless, our planning and research activities have continued, and have in fact intensified considerably in the light of renewed interest in the videodisc as well as the recent announcement of CD-I (compact disc interactive), a new audiovisual medium.

There are several distinct areas of audiovisual enhancement that we believe are valid for encyclopedia applications, including the use of audio, dynamic graphics, picture data bases, and full-motion film and video materials. The following paragraphs describe some of the potential audiovisual enhancements that we are investigating.

Audio Enhancement

Audio has many uses: music can best convey the essence of the works of composers and musicians, and what better way to describe a musical instrument than through the sound it makes? The use of recorded speeches is another interesting area; biographies of figures such as John F. Kennedy, Martin Luther King, Winston Churchill, and even Adolf Hitler can be brought alive through the vital quality of their speeches.

Dynamic Graphics

There are many kinds of graphics that can convey information in a much more meaningful way when they are dynamically controlled by the user. For example, historical maps can actually show the ebb and flow of history for subjects such as the rise and fall of the Roman Empire, the U.S. Civil War, Colonial Africa, and so forth. The rate at which events occur could be controlled by the user, as could the layers of detail that appear on the maps. Events and places listed on the maps could in turn be linked to text articles, and so on.

Other kinds of dynamic graphics include diagrams that illustrate different principles and concepts, such as how an internal-combustion engine works, the structure of the human eye, and how an aircraft flies. Again, each of these diagrams could allow for some degree of user interaction so that the underlying principles are better understood.

Picture Data Bases

Our encyclopedia application will contain many different image data bases in such areas as art, plants and animals, and peoples and countries. Each image in the data base can have certain attributes assigned so that the images can be reorganized to suit the needs of the user. For example, a data base of paintings might be viewed alphabetically by artist, or by date, region, media, style, period, or category (such as landscape or portraiture).

Motion Sequences

Motion can be used in many different ways: for example, movie and TV newsreels can show momentous historical events, such as the first moon walk; nature films can reveal the beauty of a humpback whale breaching, the speed of the cheetah, the elaborate mating displays of birds; and so on. Motion can also convey the complexities of sports activities that are impossible to describe through words or static images.

These examples show some of the ways in which we plan to use audiovisual materials. It is also our ultimate goal to build dynamic links between images, and between images and text—in much the same way as was shown in the Twain examples—that will allow the user to search for illustrations, and reorganize and manipulate them, in as many ways as possible. From our perspective, that is part of the ultimate appeal of multimedia technology—creating a truly flexible, dynamic medium that combines the stimulation and power of audiovisual information, the depth of layered text information, and the dynamic capabilities of the computer to manipulate both kinds of information.

In concluding, I want to reaffirm Grolier's commitment to keep pace with and use viable new information-delivery technologies. At the present time, multimedia technology is a promise, not a reality. That it will happen, we have no doubt; that it will be important to the educational community and other broader markets, we have no doubt. It is the when, and the how, that we cannot predict with the same degree of certainty.

Geography, Images, and Technology

Innovations in Education and Publishing at the National Geographic Society

George Peterson

GEORGE A. PETERSON

George A. Peterson is the Director of the Educational Media Division of the National Geographic Society.With a B.A. from Princeton and an M.S. in Journalism from Columbia University, Mr. Peterson worked as a freelance photographer, writer, and magazine designer before joining the National Geographic Society in 1970. Currently, Mr. Peterson directs the Society's creation and production of filmstrips, videodiscs, computer software, and classroom resource guides. Also under his direction is the Geography Education Outreach Program, a public service effort to improve geography education materials and teaching methods.

THE NATIONAL GEOGRAPHIC SOCIETY

In spite of its history of innovation, the Society has always respected the traditional and the familiar. But it is also characteristic of the Society that its leaders have never shied from the challenge of seeking the unfamiliar, whether it be found in the stratosphere or the depths of the ocean. And geographic and scientific exploration have always been closely paralleled by journalistic and technological innovation in publishing.

On January 13, 1888, a group of 33 geographers and scientists founded the National Geographic Society in Washington, D.C., and then launched *National Geographic* magazine, the aim being to increase and diffuse geographic knowledge. The first issue, put together by a volunteer staff in a small rented room, was short and technical. And it contained the names of all members, who even ten years later numbered only 1,400.

In 1897, Alexander Graham Bell became president of the Society. The organization was then $2,000 in debt. Bell hired the Society's first paid employees, among them his future son-in-law, Gilbert Hovey Grosvenor, whose $1,200 annual salary Bell paid out of his own pocket for nearly six years.

Under young Grosvenor's leadership, circulation expanded to more than 10,000 by 1905—the year the Society published its first photographic series, 11 pages of black-and-white pictures of the Forbidden City (Lhasa, Tibet). The first color series, hand-tinted scenes from Korea and China, was published in 1910. The magazine's earliest autochrome was published in 1914, followed in 1916 by the first natural-color series, depicting dancers Ted Shawn and Ruth St. Denis in an article titled "The Land of the Best."

By 1920, circulation was more than 700,000. Its increase during the war years, when the magazine concentrated on the geography of the battle-torn countries, was phenomenal. The magazine's maps, particularly one depicting the Western Front, were in demand all over the world.

Grosvenor's leadership continued to produce editorial and technical firsts. In 1926, a photographic team made the first natural-color photographs of life beneath the sea, immortalizing a hogfish and a host of other flora and fauna with the aid of blinding explosions of flash powder fired above the surface of the water. The first photographs from the stratosphere were taken in 1935 from aboard the gondola of *Explorer II,* which, on an expedition sponsored by the Society and the U.S. Army Air Corps, rose nearly 14 miles above the surface of the earth.

Grosvenor's editorial and business stewardship continued until his retirement in 1954. He was succeeded as editor and president by John Oliver LaGorce, his associate of more than 50 years. Then in 1957, Grosvenor's son, Melville Bell Grosvenor, became editor and president, the beginning of an era of dramatic change and growth for the Society.

When MBG, as he was known, decided to leave the Society's printer of more than 60 years, he announced to his staff: "This will be the first magazine to print color on every page." It is reported that a less imaginative officer moaned that this would be the demise of the *Geographic*: "He'll break the Society." Instead, Grosvenor more than doubled Society membership—to about 5 million—began a dynamic book program, published our first atlas and globe, and launched one of television's longest-running documentary series.

By 1960, the Society had moved into the era of electronic publishing, greatly expanding the means at its disposal to diffuse geographic knowledge, and at the same time dramatically enlarging both its audience and the impact of its message. When MBG retired as editor in 1967, he was followed by Frederick G. Vosburgh, who kept the momentum going and broke new ground as the Society continued to evolve and respond to members' concerns.

Gilbert M. Grosvenor, now the Society's president, describes some of the changes he witnessed in the decade (from 1970 to 1980) of his editorship: Our writers, photographers, and filmmakers were finding change everywhere they traveled, as timeless lands of nomads in the Middle East became battle zones and once-romantic jungle trails became highways to war in Southeast Asia and Africa. The need for geographic knowledge and understanding to help interpret these events grew with each year, as did our ability to meet the challenge.

> "Our fledgling book program blossomed into one of the largest publishing operations of its kind in the world, reaching new levels of quality each year. Our policy of diversification and lateral growth led us into an area in which I have taken a special personal interest. As members of the 'baby boom' of the 1940s and 1950s passed through school and into maturity, children seemed somehow to grow out of fashion as a topic of personal discussion. The Society had for half a century published the weekly *School Bulletin*, but I felt we could reach more children better with a different sort of publication. In 1975, we published the first issue of *National Geographic World*, a monthly magazine for children eight years old and up. Since its first issue, *World* has attained the largest circulation of any magazine of its kind.

> "Through our hundreds of educational filmstrips, films, videotapes, and multimedia kits, the Society has made available to schools high-quality materials in a broad variety of subjects at very reasonable costs. In 1984, we finally acted on the long-expressed desires of our membership for travel information that is at once educational and entertaining. We began publication of the Society's first new magazine for adults since 1888— *National Geographic Traveler*."

> *"Consider a snowflake,"* wrote National Geographic *editor Wilbur E.*

THE SOCIETY AND GEOGRAPHY

Garrett in his introduction to the magazine's most recent index, "as it touches your hand—intricate, delicate, beautiful. For one small moment it is present; then it melts into the past. Yet if you had caught the snowflake on a chilled glass slide and photographed it, that image would always live in the present, permitting you to study and enjoy it at your leisure— enhancing your appreciation of all future snowflakes. That is the essence of what the Geographic *has been trying to do since 1888—capture and preserve significant present moments with as little distortion as possible."*

The National Geographic Society ... to increase and diffuse geographic knowledge ... and is communicated through the creative use ... gether capture an image of the exotic, beautiful, ... rsteps and out of reach of our classrooms. Like ... raphy is characterized by diversity and, as ... mplex universe that can be exposed to study.

... ve discipline. Novelist James Michener noted, ... the more convinced I become that geography is

... the complex physical and social patterns of ... disciplines in the physical sciences (geology, ... ology).

... visual discipline. Maps are one of the primary ... ate professor of geography at Ohio State ... ive as one that "stresses, at the outset, where ... ps. No other academic subject begins that ... of the complexity of the contemporary world. ... h complexity. They cannot appreciate just ... arious parts of their own country are, or how ... f the world."

Maps help people to identify and analyze physical and human phenomena and the ways in which they are interrelated. The map is one symbol composed of many other symbols—a translation of perceived reality. Maps are made up of many symbols in the same way that essays consist of words, sentences, and paragraphs—a collection of symbols with accepted meanings, selected and organized by analytic and creative minds to communicate a reality too complex to reproduce in any other way. The photograph and the moving picture are also symbols, reproducing images of reality, frozen in time. Just as a black line—a thin trail of ink on wood pulp ground to paper—can become a highway to adventure, a photograph can be a key to geographic knowledge and understanding and a stimulus to further inquiry. Literally, geography means "writing about the earth." But it is perhaps better interpreted as a "way of thinking" about the earth. The visual image is an extension of that thought process. Some might even say the image precedes the thought. It is indisputable that the visual image is changing the way we think, the way we *see* the world around us, the way we *perceive* our relationship to it.

TECHNOLOGY, COMMUNICATION, AND
THE ROLE OF THE CREATIVE MIND

"Are creative people dinosaurs about to be imprisoned in hardware, captured in cable, shot with lasers and light beams? Will engineers—so brilliant in electronics but frequently so lacking in communications skills—control content? I submit to you that today there is greater need and greater relevance for creativity than ever. While today's capacity to transmit information is limitless, today's production of clear, valid, enriching information is practically nonexistent."

Society President Gilbert M. Grosvenor, in his remarks this summer before the World Congress on Education and Technology in Vancouver, British Columbia, reflected on the changing nature of technology, communication, and the role of the creative mind:

> "The sheer appetite and magnitude of communications today will make it impossible for the average family not to OD on electronic junk without the inspiration of the creative mind to correct, to modify, to elevate, and to enlighten a viewer. We must seek out the magic of creativity.

> "The kind of magic I have in mind comes in on a beam of light from some unknown somewhere else. I think of J.R.R. Tolkien. The year is 1928. He sits in his study at Oxford correcting a student's thesis. His life to that point? His father's death in South Africa when Tolkien was a child; his mother's religious conversion, subsequent separation from her family, and her premature death; his years as an orphan, under a guardian who forbade him to see the woman he loved; his friendships at school, blown away during the first day on the Somme, when the stupidity of generals took 20,000 lives in a single day. All of this is behind him as he sits reading the thesis. The student has, for some reason, left a page blank. When Tolkien comes to it, he picks up his pen and writes on the blank page: 'In a hole in the ground there lived a hobbit.' Thus launched one of the great literary careers of our century.

> "No machine, no electronic wizardry, can replace the single act of creation, the inspired moment that arrives in its own time, at its own speed, and from its own unknown source. It is what drives all the rest of it; industries are built upon it. Regardless of how technology increases the speed, the volume, and the nature of communication, the value of the content—the very essence—will begin and end with the creative personality.

"In a way, technology is no stranger in the classroom. The printed page is a technological teachers' aid. But why haven't we advanced further? Why do we still rely so heavily on traditional media and fail to take advantage of computers? Why do we continue to rely on filmstrip projectors when the television monitor is so much more powerful? Television is after all universally acknowledged as the second teacher—an electronic teacher whose magical moving images capture children's attention with an ease unmatched by even the most mesmerizing storyteller. Computers with the right software can work magic, too.

"If we can harness them intellectually, I am convinced that the television monitor, the computer, and the telephone are destined to transform the way we learn and the way we teach, and I intend to put my money where my convictions are. The technologies are available, and the costs are predictably dropping."

THE NGS AND EDUCATION

The National Geographic Society's mission to increase and diffuse knowledge in the geographic sciences can be fulfilled only if we do our best to support improved education in the classroom. We bring to this task our skills and reputation as an educational publisher, our success and experience in the development and distribution of classroom materials in science and geography, the highest standards for editorial content and production quality, and a commitment to the application of innovative technologies to classroom education.

We would like to see a videodisc player in every classroom, and we would like to see it hooked up to a computer. Imagine how much knowledge a teacher could impart using a videodisc of every photograph ever published in *National Geographic* magazine. Imagine a geography field trip under the control of the student—a tour of California, for example, that permits an inquisitive mind to explore freely across space and time to experience, instantaneously, relationships between places and interactions between peoples and landscapes.

We are convinced that we're on the threshold of a dramatic breakthrough that will see a proliferation of creative, educationally sound software for computers and videodiscs—and we're committed to playing an active role in developing that software. We've already produced one interactive videodisc, "Whales," which combines motion-picture footage, stills, and text frames—and there will be more discs in the near future.

For computers, we're now working on several software programs to be released in 1987, covering a range of subject areas and grade levels. These programs will be fully integrated with richly illustrated reading materials. Our goal is to produce simple, flexible programs appropriate for typical schools, utilizing the worldwide resources of the National Geographic Society and the best of traditional educational materials and methods.

We believe these efforts are a transitional phase to an era when more fully interactive educational programs will be as common as books on library shelves. Toward that end, we're making major investments in developmental projects involving telecommunications networks and highly interactive computer and optical technologies. One of our goals for the not-too-distant future is to publish an interactive atlas of the world.

But there is much to be done before that vision becomes a reality. It is clear that excellence of materials, by itself, will not ensure adoption by our nation's schools. We will need to forge alliances across a broad spectrum of interests if we are collectively to have an impact on the improvement of teaching methods and materials. We will need partners. We will need to join forces with policymakers at the federal, state, and local levels. We will need to work with school systems and with hardware manufacturers.

We are determined to commit the Society's resources to those projects that promise maximum impact and stand the best chance of attracting additional outside funding and support. We cannot do it alone and, even if we believed we could, it would not be a wise course. We are convinced that only through partnerships will we be able to generate the energy, the enthusiasm, and the financial resources necessary to put technology to effective use in the classroom.

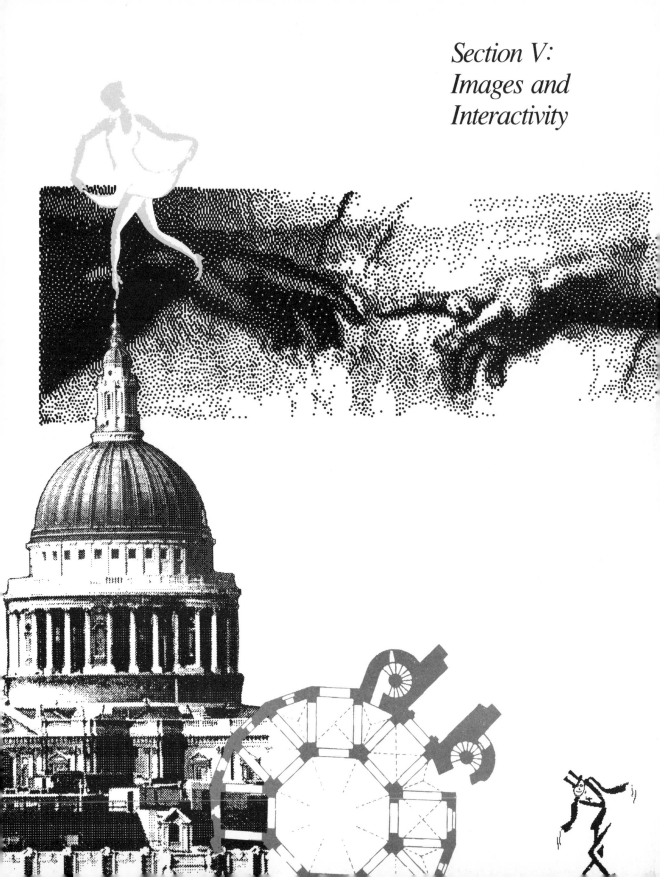

A growing community of individuals are focusing deliberately on interactive multimedia experiences as a central area of discussion and development, rather than as an extension of experiences or of traditional expertise. **Steve Gano** is consciously addressing the development of new, personalized image-based media, for example. He notes that although the technological capabilities are now available, or at least coming quickly, people are understanding slowly the potential impact of the visual communication enabled by these technologies. When you can prepare an interactive display for your mother as quickly as you can write a letter, will you? What tools will you need in order to make this attractive, and what skills will you need to make this exercise fun and effective? Even if you have available the greatest images of the world, will you be able to tell your story or deliver your intent? And how might you use text to best advantage? Or sounds? How can digitizing cameras and sound recorders easily help you "capture" the world around you to elaborate your stories and ideas? Will you end up generally making linear presentations for your friends, relatives, and business associates? Or will you create personalized experiences for them, more as a museum exhibit designer than as a great author?

Questions. There are so many questions that arise when addressing these new issues straight on. **Doug Crockford's** persistent question is "Are we having fun?"—his interest in multimedia interactivity is in the entertainment area. More specifically, he wants to create engaging experiences for people, as have great entertainment people in the past. Yet he wants to extend this concept to include education, work, and other typically nonentertaining areas. His criterion for a great multimedia presentation is not whether it is interactive or technical; rather, his focus is on the phenomenological experience of the moment, and its success. Video games do indeed provide successful experiences, in a very limited range of experiences for a limited audience, and hence provide a good background example. However, it is the expansion of this fanciful engagement in material that needs to be the focus of these video games, not the specifics of a particular "look" or purpose.

Suzanne Ropiequet presented a demonstration of the Microsoft Multimedia Encyclopedia (MME) at the conference, providing a valuable demonstration of a specific implementation of ideas described throughout this book. Since the conference, Microsoft has developed its concepts of multimedia. The final chapter of this section by **Sally Brunsman**, **John Messerly**, and **Susan Lammers** demonstrates Microsoft's recent perspective on this topic.

Multimedia Technology Is for Casual, Everyday Use

Steve Gano

STEVE GANO

Steve Gano has been a designer and builder of inter-active systems for 10 years. He received undergradu-ate degrees in psychology and computer science, and apprenticed in systems programming before joining MIT's Architecture Machine Group for graduate work. At MIT, Steve developed novel ways of interacting with images, created artificial talking heads with videodiscs, and produced electronic books with movies for illustrations. At the Atari Sunnyvale Research Lab, he developed prototypes of interactive systems for appropriating multimedia objects from large data bases for personal use. Now at Hewlett-Packard Laboratories, Steve is applying advanced computer graphics and video technolo-gies to design new qualities of human-computer and interpersonal interactions.

This paper proposes that multimedia technology can be used by ordinary individuals casually and frequently for very commonplace purposes. The implication is that multimedia technology will join the basic repertoire of techniques for individual self-expression, along with speech, gesture, and writing. This proposal is examined from three perspectives:

One: Multimedia technology for personal use is at hand. On the shelf, or on the near horizon, are tools that make the materials and techniques of cinema available to any individual.

Two: We may be disinclined to imagine the personal uses of multimedia technology because of the overwhelming presence of electronic media, such as broadcast media, in our culture.

Three: Personal multimedia technologies will provide individuals with entirely new means of reflection, investigation, and self-expression.

One: *Multimedia technology for personal use is at hand. On the shelf, or on the near horizon, are tools that make the materials and techniques of cinema available to any individual.*

Video Recording

Thirty years ago, the first videotape recorders were available (from Ampex) for broadcast use. They used two-inch tape (about a mile of it to record an hour's worth of video), cost several hundred thousand dollars, and were about the size of a catering truck. Today, over 30 million homes in this country have videocassette recorders (VCRs) that outperform those first recorders in every respect, and cost only a few hundred dollars.

Home VCRs are used primarily for watching rented movies and for "time-shifting"— recording television shows for later viewing. The 30-million-owner mark is a significant one for video producers, because it represents a base market large enough to justify made-for-home video production.[1] And it's a base large and varied enough that video publishers can consider projects for smaller, specialized audiences, in the same way that book and magazine publishers do.

Manufacturers are also providing consumers with more opportunities to *use* video as well as watch it. Compact video cameras with built-in recording decks have been available for several years. Now Sony has introduced an 8mm video system that includes a "Handycam," a camera and recorder about the size of a cigar box. The Sony system also includes something new for the home market: a video editor that allows people to electronically assemble their home movies. The system is advertised as a way to take "moving snapshots," suggesting simple operation and frequent, casual use.

Optical Videodiscs

Optical videodiscs, introduced to the home market in the late 1970s, provide two significant advantages over magnetic videotape. First, laser-read discs are a mass-producible, virtually indestructible *archival* medium for cinematic materials. Second, the videodisc is a *random access* medium: the laser read head can quickly jump to any spot in the program, while videotape must be laboriously wound and unwound to access a particular spot on the tape. These two qualities make optical videodiscs particularly useful for publishing cinematic reference materials.

Videodiscs also provide unique ways for people to access and use cinematic materials. Random access, coupled with stable still frame and variable-speed play, allows people to probe and peruse a videodisc as they might a book. As Nicholas Negroponte observed in the first days of the technology, the distinction between books and movies "will become thin as soon as we envisage 'books' whose photographs are movies and whose diagrams are animated, or as we embed more and more still-frame material into 'movies.'" [2]

Videodiscs were developed as a redistribution medium for theatrical movies, but the VCR, because it can also record video, has overwhelmingly outsold videodisc players in the home market. Still, some distributors offer videodiscs that introduce viewers to the possibilities of the medium. For example, Voyager Press of Los Angeles distributes a "coffee table" videodisc depicting the city of Vancouver through historical photos, posters, maps, and time-lapse journeys through the streets. Knowledge Set of Monterey, California, produced a videodisc containing—on printed video frames—the entire text (and, ironically, none of the illustrations) of Grolier's *Academic American Encyclopedia*.

Another provocative videodisc offering is the *Video Encyclopedia of the 20th Century* from CEL Communications of New York. It contains 75 hours of indexed primary cinematic source material beginning with footage shot by Thomas Edison at the 1893 Columbian Exposition and proceeding through coverage of disasters, wars, presidents, riots, moon-walks, and other events up to the present. To have this kind of material for personal use, available as readily as a dictionary or almanac on the shelf, is a very new and exciting possibility. It gives children the opportunity to explore and vividly experience the events that shaped the world as it is today. What might be the outcome of giving a student such video source material, a VCR, and the assignment to put together stories for Eyewitness News?

Compact Discs

Over the past three years, consumers have embraced a new technology for recorded music: the digital compact audio disc. Unlike the videodisc, which represents its images and sound in a continuous, or analog, form, the compact disc (CD) stores its information in discrete, digital bits.

Both videodiscs and CDs can store images, sound, and text. The digital format of CDs is more economical for text, computer programs, and data bases; the same Grolier encyclopedia that, as printed video frames, occupies an entire videodisc side, takes up only one-fifth of a digital compact disc. On the other hand, a videodisc can store more images (54,000) in its analog format than can a compact disc (500–4000); more significantly, the videodisc can store and play moving images. Add to this the fact that videodiscs can also store high-density digital information in several formats, including CD format, and it's clear that the videodisc is the more potent technology.

However, the public's reception of videodiscs has been lukewarm, largely because the marketing focus for videodiscs as a movie redistribution medium has been overshadowed by videotape. It appears that the compact disc is in a better position to become the first interactive multimedia device to be established in the home, in part due to a better-organized industry push for software standards. The compact disc-interactive (CD-I) format supported by Philips, Sony, and others gives developers a standard format for images, sound, and data—something that interactive videodisc producers have never really had.

Although the compact disc cannot reproduce live motion to any useful degree, it has some important elements of a cinema machine. Its vast capacity for storing data can be used to offset the modest microcomputing capability of a home machine. For instance, it can store all of the pre-rendered cells of an animation that a more powerful but less capacious machine might have to draw anew each frame. Also, limited "camera movements," such as a slow pan across a landscape, are possible through well-known digital image-buffering techniques. And, of course, there is abundant high-quality audio to provide a temporal dynamic with music, sound effects, and voice-over narration.

This is not the stuff MTV is made of (yet). But consider a public-television-style historical documentary or science program that is made up entirely of still photos and paintings, animated diagrams, the voice-over narration of the field experts and host, and perhaps an opening pan across a mood-setting landscape with a bird or two flying overhead. A properly designed and outfitted CD-based system could conceivably generate such a program. Moreover, the program could be interactive, paced and structured by the viewer, with megabytes of supplementary information available instantly.

Digital Video Effects

Videotape and optical discs are multimedia technologies that have made the journey from research laboratory to industry to the home in a generation's time. If we can also apply that progression to technologies being developed today, then within the next decade we should expect to have digital video manipulation capabilities in the home. This would exponentially enhance the features of current technologies, and serve as a catalyst for new technologies, such as electronic photography.

Digital video effects—images that flip and tumble through space, or curl off-screen like the pages of a magazine—are now commonplace on television. These video tricks are accomplished by turning analog video images into digital data, applying geometric transforms on the digital images, and then turning the digital data back into analog video, at rates of 30 frames per second, with one million bytes per frame. The image transformations require that a substantial amount of arithmetic be performed on each and every point of every frame, and be performed extraordinarily quickly. The high-performance devices available today to work this magic (for example, Ampex's ADO and Quantel's Mirage) cost from $100,000 to over $500,000. But the core technologies of digital video—huge, fast digital memories and fast, special-purpose microprocessors—continue to get bigger, faster, and less expensive.

Early results are available today. ITT, for example, manufactures a television that can display video from two sources at once: a normal full-sized picture from one source, and a quarter-sized picture from the other source, inset in the larger picture. The underlying digital video capabilities are few but significant: The ability to instantly crop, scale, and position live images anywhere on the television screen, and to overlay them.

Even these simple capabilities change how people can use videotape and videodiscs. With a digital video display, a viewer could simultaneously examine material from the beginning, middle, and end of a video source.

This would allow, for example, having several "volumes" of the CEL video encyclopedia open and spread out at once, just as one might with a print encyclopedia. Digital image techniques will also enable people to "cut and paste" video material from different parts of a source, and from different sources, to create entirely new material. This would constitute a personal creative medium that is more expressive and more flexible than anything previously available to individuals.

Two: *We may be disinclined to imagine the personal uses of multimedia technology because of the overwhelming presence of electronic media, such as broadcast media, in our culture.*

Simple access to new technologies cannot by itself guarantee us a brighter future. We have to know what they can do and how we might use them in order to tap their liberating potential. We can either project a new context for the new technologies, or misuse them in old contexts. That is the present situation for electronic media, which have evolved in an industrial, mass-consumer context, and have so exaggerated the attenuated role of the individual that we may neglect to dream about how these technologies might serve us as individuals.

The role of broadcast media in our culture is a novel one. There has never been anything like it in the past, nothing as compellingly real and immediate, and certainly nothing as omnipresent (except perhaps the church in past ages). For example, in the United States over 98 percent of all households have at least one television set; the average "on" time is over seven hours per day.[3] This is an unprecedented, almost unfathomable, sphere of influence—and one that, aside from the token presence of noncommercial public television,[4] is entirely in the service of commerce.

In order to sell products, the broadcast image is made to appeal to the largest number of people possible. Regional traits are homogenized out of television's oratorical standard: Local newscasters around the country, for example, are essentially interchangeable. In its worst (and all too common) moments, commercial television projects its own needs for a buying public on its audience. Through its programs, and particularly through its advertisements, television celebrates the role of the individual as consumer. In the mythology of commercial broadcasting, an individual achieves success and satisfaction not through wit or hard work, but by buying the right products.

This kind of use of television is not inherently unhealthy. In fact, it's probably an inescapable aspect of a free society. What's culturally debilitating is to concede exclusive use of this powerful communications medium to special interests. It would be tragic if we could not at least *imagine* a society where everyone has a voice in this new electronic marketplace of ideas, or if we did not consider what we might become if we were to live in such a culture.

Downscaling technology gives us the opportunity to rethink the use of electronic media, to turn them into something Ivan Illich calls *convivial tools.* "Convivial tools are those which give each person who uses them the greatest opportunity to enrich the environment with the fruits of his or her vision. Industrial tools deny this possibility to those who use them and they allow their designers to determine the meaning and expectations of others."[5]

From this perspective, broadcast media are industrial tools, for they offer viewers no opportunity to interact with their information environment or to enrich it with their personal views. The meaning of the individual in the electronic media environment today is as a demographic unit in the numbers games played by networks and advertisers. On the other hand, in the democratization of electronic media technology there's at least the potential for individuals to define their own roles in the society.

With tools for appropriating information in various rich forms (images, sound, computer data) from various sources (on-demand data bases, correspondence from friends, trusted free-lance information hunters, broadcasts), an individual can be an active participant in information gathering. With tools for manipulating multimedia information, for arranging it and reconstructing it like the pieces of a puzzle until a clear picture emerges, an individual can be a powerful analyst, and can concretely re-create the many different points of view from which events and ideas might be understood. With tools for recording and redistributing multimedia information, an individual can achieve a voice in the electronic marketplace of ideas, and help sustain the flow of information that keeps a convivial society alive and spiritually prosperous.

Three: *Personal multimedia technologies will provide individuals with entirely new means of reflection, investigation, and self-expression.*

The impact of personal multimedia technologies on the individual is difficult to predict because there aren't any precedents for the casual, *everyday* use of such powerful technologies. My intuition is that we are near the beginning of an intellectual revolution as sweeping as the one that accompanied the advent of the printed book. For the first time, ordinary individuals will be able to create and arrange events in space and time, and design direct experiences for themselves and for others. What has been the expressive medium for a very few can now join speech, gesture, and writing in everyone's repertoire of personal expressive forms.

Rather than speculate haphazardly on the nature of these changes, I will close this paper with three scenarios that suggest some possible personal uses of multimedia technology. The settings for these scenarios are purposefully mundane, to emphasize the casual, everyday use of the media. None of the systems described exist today; however, they could be built, if not yet for the home, as laboratory prototypes that anticipate home use.

Data Base Search Keys from Life

Well, Hillary had certainly caught one this time. It was a large bug, over an inch long, with yellow and orange stripes around its body, and two pairs of wings. Unfortunately for it, one of its wings was broken, which is how Hillary had caught up with it on the windowsill.

"What is it, Mom?"

"I don't know, dear, but please don't wave it in my face. You should go look it up in the encyclopedia."

"OK," said Hillary, and she ran to the family room and inserted the encyclopedia disc into the reader. Holding her prize tightly in one hand, she zipped through the index until she came to the "I" section, and then slowly homed in, first on "insects," and then on the "insect identification" section. She had been there many times before to use the "build-an-insect" classification table.

Hillary selected parts from the table that matched her new prey, and as she did so, the encyclopedia assembled, on screen, a reasonable likeness of the creature in her hand. "This is a member of the sawfly family," the encyclopedia narrator said, just as the assembled illustration of the creature began to crawl around on a green, leafy background. "A primitive relative of the ant, bee, and wasp. Some species are considered pests because their larvae bore into the trunks of weakened or dead deciduous trees."

"Oh-oh, better tell Dad about that," Hillary thought, and paused long enough to print out a picture of the sawfly and its caterpillar-like larva and a paragraph about its feeding habits. Her father had been wondering lately about the elm in the backyard.

The next page of the article showed a close-up animation of the female sawfly cutting into a maple leaf and depositing her eggs. The printed text explained that the saw-like egg duct of the sawfly had developed into the stinger of wasps and bees. Hillary decided that her next science report for school was going to be about the strange things insect mothers have to do to find a place to lay eggs, so she copied the animated page into her electronic notebook and typed a note on it to remind herself of some other species to look up later.

A Little Dialectical Montage Between Friends

Brian was feeling a little outclassed by his Japanese video pen pal, Ichiro, who had sent him a fastidiously assembled videotape of his mother preparing the evening meal. Brian was scanning through his own video that he had taken this evening to send to Ichiro, and he felt a little embarrassed at how crude and ordinary everything seemed. Where Ichiro's mom had artfully sculpted carrots into maple leaves to float in the soup, Brian's mom had used the Cuisinart to shred things for the slaw. Where Ichiro's mom had laid out everything in separate dishes, arranged in a quiet, formal way (which Ichiro displayed proudly with an overhead pan, a "sky-cam" kind of shot), Brian's mom had pretty much just piled the roast and potatoes on a big platter. (Brian scanned in a more picturesque version of the meal from a cookbook and spliced it into his tape; he typed over it in big yellow letters: "This is what it was SUPPOSED to look like.")

All at once he had the insight that would let him trump his Japanese friend. He would assemble the two tapes together to show both the differences and the similarities of the two cultures: their delicate vegetable carving versus his Cuisinart; their steaming oshibori versus the paper towels he used for napkins; their pickled eggplant and burdock root versus (or almost just like!) the pickles and olives on his table. Brian cruised through his videotape with the joystick, hitting the "fire" button to mark the beginning and end of each shot. For every shot he marked, a small icon appeared on the computer screen. Then he began stringing some of the icons together, like beads, into a sequence, alternating shots from his tape with shots from Ichiro's. As he watched the editor assemble his video pen-pal letter, Brian grew more enthusiastic about his new technique. He was a little disappointed that the result wasn't quite as smooth as he wanted, like the things he saw on television. But still, it told his story, and he knew Ichiro would be impressed and would probably come back with something new himself.

Post-Vacation Photography as Reverie

The snapshots from the trip to Barcelona were back from the photo lab, but to Zeke, they seemed sadly empty of the experience he and Nancy had there. The scale was wrong: The spires of Gaudi's Sagrada Familia cathedral had seemed so imposing, even as they stood at the entrance, unable to see the entire façade. Zeke loaded the PhotoQuick European Travel disc into the mnemotography machine, and quickly scanned to Spain, and then to the Barcelona section. There he found pictures of all of the buildings of Gaudi, with their ornate, organic forms, that they had visited in Barcelona. The cathedral, like all the others, was present in two forms: in postcard-photo style and in a series of photographic projections showing all faces, interiors, and landscaping simultaneously—like a cut-out, pop-up dollhouse ready to be assembled.

Zeke selected a view of the exterior of the nativity façade, where they had stood and smiled while the friendly old man took that blurred photo of them. He grabbed the view into the digital picture easel. The catalog view was bright and sharp, but it had been overcast when they were there, so he selected "overcast" from the ambient-light menu, and the picture took on a more subdued cast.

Next he brought in photo-mannequins of Nancy and himself from their own home photo album. He couldn't remember what he had been wearing, but he knew that Nancy had worn her khaki dress and "sensible" shoes for all the walking they would do that day. And, she was carrying that oversized leather handbag stuffed with maps and travel guides. Zeke would tease her about having her nose buried in the travel guides instead of experiencing it all firsthand and uninterpreted. So he collaged their photo-mannequins on the steps of the cathedral, with Nancy sitting on the steps, her face hidden behind the Michelin guide, with him excitedly pointing skyward to the colossal nativity scene. He had to scale down the façade so that the scene was visible in the picture, which made him effectively 20 feet tall or so, but it was still quite a plausible picture.

The scene in the picture never took place, yet it held more of the experience that he had there than any of his actual photos. He saved the photo on a new optical disc he labeled "Spain," and also printed it out on the color printer to tack on the refrigerator so Nancy would see it when she came home. For a few minutes, he had been back to the steps of Sagrada Familia with her, and he wanted to share the souvenir.

FOOTNOTES

1. Matthew White, "Is made-for-home video finally making it?" *Videography*, Volume 11, No. 5, May 1986.

2. Nicholas Negroponte, "The impact of optical videodiscs on filmmaking," MIT Architecture Machine Group, 1978.

3. U.S. Bureau of the Census, *Statistical Abstract of the United States: 1986* (106th edition), Washington, D.C., 1985.

4. "About 95 percent of the audience's viewing time is spent watching commercial television. American television is essentially synonymous with commercial television." National Institute of Mental Health, *Television and behavior: ten years of scientific progress and implications for the eighties,* Volume 1, p. 73, 1982.

5. Ivan Illich, *Tools for Conviviality,* New York: Harper and Row, p. 21, 1973.

Stand By for Fun

Experience and Interaction

Douglas Crockford

DOUGLAS CROCKFORD

Douglas Crockford is a product of our public school system. A registered voter, he owns his own car. He spent two years at Atari, Inc., and is now working at Lucasfilm Ltd., where he is designing interactive media and experiences for entertainment and education.

Lamppost

Before I begin to get to the point of this article, which is about Experience in the context of "home interactive theater," I'd like to share a little story with you. It is a well-known story, so stop me if you've heard it before.

There's a drunk on his hands and knees under a lamppost. A guy walks up and says, "What are you doing?" and the drunk says, "I'm looking for my keys. I dropped them over there." So the guy asks, "Then why are you looking over here?" and the drunk says, "Because the light's better."

The point of that story should become clearer as we expose the issues of interactivity and experience to the illuminating lamppost of reason.

I am going to be talking specifically about entertainment products. Any educational products that I produce will also be entertainment products, even if they happen to be about geography. I need to say that at the beginning in order to make this all seem to be relevant.

Another Revolution

We are standing here at the dawning of another one of those technical revolutions. This one is the next major breakthrough in interactive entertainment and education. There is activity all over the place in new media which promises to deliver valuable experiences to the folks at home and the kids at school. The most visible examples are the Philips CD-I system and its obvious enhancements and imitators. Expectations for these new systems range from a gimmick for trying to trick people into buying unnecessary home computers again, to the next-to-last significant step in the social evolution of man. The new media will offer neat images and sounds in an interactive format.

We are exploring the capacity of these new presentational media to entertain people, not just as novelty (although we are not above that) but as a new kind of storyteller, telling a new kind of story, and telling the oldest story in a new way.

The biggest surprise is that it is much harder than it looks. You would like to expect that you simply make the story *interactive,* and that's enough to get the big payoff. You would also like to expect that everything gets neater as the delivery technology gets neater. Unfortunately, neither is necessarily the case.

The technology must be delivering messages which are more interesting than *"High-tech is a great gimmick."* The delivery medium does you little good if you are using it to deliver experiences that nobody wants. In the long run, audiences will not be judging you on the "highness" of your tech. This is equally true in education, unless it is your intention to teach Technology Appreciation.

We need to beware of the technology traps, the seductive things that technology can do for you that don't really have anything to do with delivering a compelling experience.

So, taking the moral of the lamppost story to heart, I have spent the past year wandering around in the dark, looking for fun. I can do that because Lucasfilm makes fun and not light bulbs. Lucasfilm is not a technology company, it is an entertainment company, and so when confronting a new technology, I can ask, "Is it *fun* enough?"

Technology and the Quality of Experience

Is it ever the case that an improvement in technology brings along an improvement in the experience? The answer is often yes. Obvious examples include color television, Cinemascope, and stereo. But there are also counter examples, including 3-D, videodiscs, and colorizing of classic movies.

Obviously, a lot of this stuff is subjective. There have been attempts to quantify "fun," such as how many stars a movie rates, but generally such systems aren't very scientific. The best of the rating systems is the Crockford Scale, which rates movies on an integer scale between 0 and 1. If I found that a movie was worth seeing, I gave it a 1. I find it quite reliable, but then, that could just be me.

In order to discover the truth about interactivity, you need to separate technology from the experience, which is difficult because sometimes technology *is* the experience. Does recorded music get better as you turn the volume up? Often it does. Audiophiles know this, and by their tedious manipulation of subtle reproduction parameters, are able to trade psycho-acoustics for some other kind of psycho-experience.

The Video Game Experience

Most of our experience in interactive entertainment is in video games. There is much we can learn by reviewing the Video Game Age, which we do in the same way you might relive an automobile accident. Sure, we're stuck in the '80s, but we've learned a few things, which I'll share with you right now.

Right off the bat, the desktop metaphor of interactivity is inappropriate to real-time entertainment. The game experience is usually more direct. It is more like being in a spaceship than using a "user interface." But it goes deeper than that.

Let's turn the Wayback machine back just a few years. Video games are a major force in American culture. They are everywhere, threatening the very existence of the movie and music industries. Video games are big business. Video-game revenues are used to make military-spending programs look reasonable by comparison.

This pretentious new little art form held an incredible fascination over this country, which was followed by a unanimous rejection in the winter of 1982. Why were video games such a big deal, and why did they then become such a little deal?

The second part of the question is easy to answer. Video games became a little deal because they did not really do anything for people. Most video games involved some level of learning and skill building, but the things you learned and the skills you built didn't help you in living your life, or even in playing other video games.

The first part of the question then becomes a real puzzle. If video games didn't do anything for people, then how did they become a big deal in the first place?

I think much of the original attraction was in its promise. Here was computer technology, *hands on*. The science fiction fantasies were coming true. "Get a head start on the brave new world for just a quarter." The same naïve *Popular Science* enthusiasm that sold those millions of computers into closets also glamorized video games. That enthusiasm will not be rekindled until someone can tell the folks at home what home computers are good for.

But there was more going on than that. Video games were an exciting way to play for the children of the Television Age. It was TV that responded to you. It was a new form of fun, a new kind of experience. But ultimately, it was not satisfying, and people stopped playing.

The response of the game makers was interesting. The game makers responded to the public's complaint "Is that all there is?" with "Here's more color! Here's better graphics!" But it didn't do anything to stop the erosion in demand for the games. Videodiscs were expected to revive the withering industry. We saw one novelty hit, *Dragon's Lair,* and the decline continued. So here is your clearest example of improvements in technology not necessarily delivering the goods.

So what were the goods? What did the people think they saw when they first tuned in? What was it that they discovered was lacking when they asked "Is that all there is?" and tuned out?

If we want to make a new mass market for interactive media, then we should figure out what the video-game fascination was about, what people thought they were being promised, and find a way to deliver on the promise.

Whatever it was, it is somehow different from what we thought it must be. While the presentation capabilities of the technology are very important in constraining the experience, they do not define the experience. *Space Invaders* was experientially lacking and ultimately boring. The evolution of the succeeding games added complexity and polish, but failed to enrich the experience.

Interactivity

We know that the best new trick in computer technology is that it can be interactive, and we believe that there must be some important fun potential in computer technology. But we don't really know what interactivity is or what it's good for.

Interactivity is not by itself experientially important. Being able to branch and so being able to select the left door and then die because you didn't pick the right one does not work as great entertainment.

My model is the "home interactive theatre." I am telling a story, and inviting the interactor to become involved in it. I am not inviting them to change the outcome, because if it is an important story, then structurally the story must retain its integrity to the end. (And besides, it's my story.) The interactor instead gets a little slack, a little room for self-expression in the context of some interesting events, much as you might get when you hear a story told well while you sit around the campfire.

The experience should be safe. As much as possible, all technological anxiety should be relieved. Even Mom should be comfortable with it.

Everyone should win. The experience may be an ordeal, but we want only survivors. Whatever it takes to help people along will be dispensed as needed.

You should care. Even though it is fixed that you will win, there must be room for doubt. You don't really affect the outcome, because the outcome is success. The outcome is not what is important.

The presentation will be tailored to you based on your responses. Your choices don't affect the outcome, they affect the presentation.

There are some contradictions in the goals of the experience versus deliberate choice in the interactive environment. This paradox in the relation between freedom and interaction is known as Crockford's Paradox. It can be resolved by redefining the meaning of interaction. *Interaction should have more to do with taking part than in making decisions.* It is joining the dance around the tribal fire. It is not choosing to fire a gun into a crowd. It is finding the rhythm in the structure of the experience and resonating with it. It is not playing your horn in the middle of the violin solo.

Another model for interaction, which is not necessarily distinct from the one I just outlined, involves kinesthetic participation in a psychologically safe co-creative fantasy with powerful metanoic consequences. (See "Fun with Metanoia," an unwritten article by Steve Arnold.)

Reader Participation

This is the end of the article. I am making it interactive by letting *you* determine the outcome. Please write your conclusions in the space that follows:

Publishers, Multimedia, and Interactivity

Sally Brunsman, John Messerly, Susan Lammers

Sally Brunsman, John Messerly, and Susan Lammers work in the CD Consumer Group of Microsoft Press, a division of Microsoft Corporation. Their group is charged with the task of creating interactive, multimedia products for the consumer and educational markets.

Publishers, encouraged by the vanguard of private and public research, are ready to explore the exciting territory of interactive multimedia publications. Hypermedia—multimedia publications that use hypertext software—contain information that a user, or traveler, can view in an interactive, nonlinear way. Hypermedia exploit a full complement of media—sound, image, text, animated graphics, and so on—to fulfill their mission of conveying information while also allowing a traveler to manipulate that information. Successful (and entertaining) hypermedia products will present text, sound, and image as dynamic, synergistic companions. Stored on compact discs and other high-capacity storage devices, hypermedia can be accessed from relatively inexpensive microcomputers.

For example, a Sports disc could contain how-to guides for every imaginable sport and provide comprehensive supplements for each. The coverage on game fishing might include sketches of wildlife; text listings of species information, habitat, and mating patterns; a graphic atlas of trails and maps; a text almanac listing state-by-state licensing requirements; and an audio describing how to clean fish and prepare delectable recipes with the big catch.

Suppose a traveler's particular interest is trout fishing. She selects the trout category from the Sports disc and images of trout swim placidly on screen to the sound of Schubert's *Trout* quintet. Our traveler clicks on a swimming image to identify its species and learn its habitat, nicknames, and which flies are most attractive to it. To learn about Idaho's abundant trout streams, she selects a list of maps and statistics. The traveler locates the Northern Idaho panhandle and plans her next fishing expedition. Next, she wants to know about other species of fish in this region, so she goes to the Northwest freshwater fish section for a list. After this excursion into ichthyology, she listens to an audio about fly-fishing techniques. She becomes curious about books on fly fishing. Searching for a list of such writings, she discovers an amazing body of literature, including Izaak Walton's *Compleat Angler,* Richard Brautigan's *Trout Fishing in America,* and Norman Maclean's *A River Runs Through It.*

Interactivity by Design

Interactivity of this caliber does not happen by accident, however. Publishers must responsibly and consciously design and author their on-line publications; they can provide serious interactive tools that promote learning through lateral thinking and that also stimulate the traveler's creativity. Travelers will use well-considered hypermedia tools to construct cohesive, *meaningful* experiences by making choices.

As did our traveler through the trout section, any traveler should be able to browse freely through topics and media. The publisher of hypermedia should aim to maximize a traveler's ability to pursue individualized associations so that she or he can seek detail on a topic or pursue a caprice of imagination. Although a publisher may impose an information structure, the traveler should also be able to reconstruct that information and present it in a variety of contexts. An ideal hypermedia publication would allow a traveler to jump with ease from one subject to another—and from one medium to another.

The significant potential for rich hypermedia experiences demands flexible and powerful publishing systems. A publishing system consists of the informational tools, the equipment, and the software that together produce an on-line document. Achieving interactivity mandates that a hypermedia publisher consider not only a publication's content but also what presentation methods and tools to use. The publisher will need to make technical decisions early in a project and abide by them. Technical decisions have a lasting impact on how data will be used and interpreted in authoring a publication and long after. As you will see, deciding how to access information in the authoring process of hypermedia is an essential first step.

Choosing the appropriate internal logical data structure and coding scheme for the data base is vital to an efficient publishing system. Hypermedia require an internal logical data structure that organizes discrete parts (atoms) tagged for identification (and meaning), into groupings (modules).

In the print medium, tagging passages with key words or phrases is the job of cross-references. In the hypermedia production process, publishers need tags to identify audio, animations, images, and active objects. Tags are the regulated currency of a data base that can be exploited in a number of ways. Tags are the first level in creating different contexts and can be used to track information on hand and to locate where it can be shared and where it is currently in use. For example, after Schubert's *Trout* quintet is digitized, it could be tagged with "Schubert" and "quintets." Because *The Trout* is by Schubert, the atom also inherits all relevant tags to Schubert, such as "Romantic music" and "music of Austria." It could then be stored as an atom in the data base, available for use in any of these contexts.

An atom can be grouped with any number of other atoms to make a module (Figure 1). For example, an image of a brown trout could be grouped with a caption and a descriptive audio segment; each item—text, audio, and image—is tagged as an atom, but the sum of the parts forms a module.

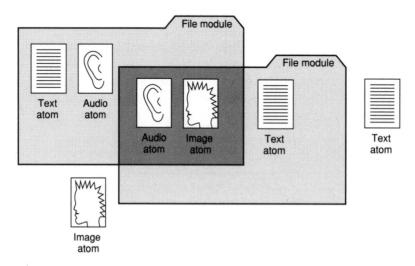

Figure 1. *Atoms and modules.*

Structuring as much information as possible at the atomic level gives maximum mobility and flexibility for sharing and interchanging an atom among different modules. For example, as publisher of the Sports disc, you might want to publish a disc that contains only trout information and images and no audio. You can draw out the text and images tagged as "trout" and then compose a new disc, perhaps with different sequences of events and new material, without dismantling hard-wired information.

The beauty of a well-planned publishing system is this ability to share atoms in a data base. The internal structure of the data base allows the publisher to store information in a generic, neutral form, separate from restricting structures or hard-wired links. The result is that atoms can be reused in any number of contexts. If a publisher has astutely identified atoms with tags, editors can create links with minimal effort. Besides functioning as identification devices, tags are useful for tracking and reporting; editors can identify what tags have been "borrowed" from the data base's library, how many times the atom has been used, and in what modules. In this new, interdisciplinary medium for the marketplace of ideas, tags become the coin of the realm.

Publishers *must* adopt standards for text markup, such as Standard Generalized Markup Language (SGML) as adopted by the Association of American Publishers (AAP). SGML is a means to define applications of markup and methods of treating document collections. It is a mechanism for document interchange that lets a data base be neutral; an SGML document can be ported to various systems and output devices (printers, CRTs, and so on). SGML is appropriate for identifying and marking parts of an electronic manuscript (text) so that computers can distinguish the parts; it may also be possible to adapt SGML to define instances of interconnectivity of images and audio with text. Implementing an SGML standard allows the system to define interconnective occurrences consistently, without the need for external structures. (Of course, we look forward to the day when hypermedia has its own language.)

Tools of the Trade

If we hope to see on-line publications become living documents—that is, true associational structures in which the same information can be presented in several contexts—we must develop tools to work with the new media.

After a data base is prepared, one of the next steps is storyboarding—using sequencing techniques, borrowed from the movie industry and localized to hypermedia, to arrange modules into narrative structures. In other words, a publisher uses storyboarding to impose a structure on the data base. With a storyboarding tool, an editor or a nontechnical person can build sequences and coordinate events. (Storyboarding is not to be confused with the manuscript development and copyedit phase, which, when possible, should coincide with preliminary data-base preparation.)

The most powerful storyboard tools will derive from tools used by hypermedia's nearest cousins, video and film. Directors use storyboards to visually map out sequences—how they look and how they synchronize with soundtracks, action, and dialogue. Sophisticated video mixing boards, with multiple tracks, or streams, of media, allow explicit control in postproduction—the phase the multimedia editor will be in when using the storyboard tools. By the storyboard stage, all images are scanned; the music, narration, and sounds are digitized; the text has been updated; and data has been converted from print to electronic form.

When a storyboarding tool uses a graphic interface, abstract and often complicated relationships can be represented and understood. Significantly, the relationships can be manipulated by someone with little or no technical expertise, so what would otherwise be expensive author tool training is affordable to publishers. Arrows indicate relationships, the meanings of which depend on the context the author selected.

In Figure 2, the arrows describe relationships and point from causes to effects. For example, an arrow from the time elapsed (relative to the beginning of this segment) says to play the Balletti Chorale ten seconds into the article. Similarly, an arrow dragged from the end of the Balletti Chorale to the end of the image above it is a cue; when the music stops the picture will no longer be displayed.

In a different context screen, arrows represent other relationships. In a formatting context, an arrow from a button to a section of text means (as set by format option) to position a button adjacent to the text, to position it over the text, or to insert it into the text. Clicking on items on the screen gives information about them: type of link; which tags are attached to them; number of words in a text passage; other uses, if any, being made of the item; and so on. Information must be viewable in a compressed format so that sequences spanning a number of frames can be displayed.

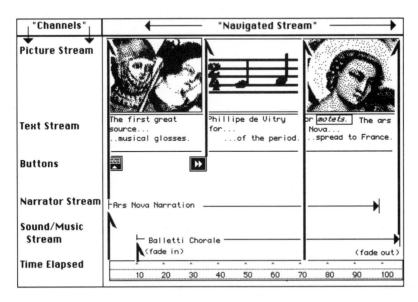

Figure 2. *Displaying events that control sound and images.*

The Information Path

We have just described a purely linear structure, which in a non-hypermedia environment is probably the most common way people access information. Therefore, it may seem at first to be the most desirable structure for a hypermedia traveler. However, just as the film industry at first borrowed heavily from stage idiom and then moved toward creating its own, both the creators of and the audience for hypermedia will move beyond highly serial, noninteractive sequences. Storyboard tools must represent nonlinear, highly interactive sequences, such as those employing a museum metaphor. In such a segment, a traveler must be able to leave one "room" through one of several "doors" leading to different interest areas. In the storyboarding tool, columns of media slide vertically, displaying these "rooms" and the events that give entry to them. Rather than restricting a traveler from freely associating images, sound, and text, authors act as trailblazers through the wilderness of information to map out what they consider interesting contextual paths.

We envision the day when a "programmable publication" feature will be included with hypermedia. A publication is "programmable" if flexibility is inherent in the modular or atomic structure of the data. Eventually, if tags can be assigned a precise "meaning," an expert rule-based system, acting as a reference librarian, could compile lists of potential links among tags (useful to editors and travelers). For example, when a new trout image is entered into a data base as an image atom, it could be tagged with various classifications so that a link is automatically (that is, without editor or author intervention) available to that specific image as well as to the other objects with the trout subject tag, such as text atoms in which a trout is described and audio atoms in which, perhaps, the trout's anatomy is explained. In an intelligent retrieval system, the search engine ought to take advantage of these classifications.

Publishers and authors should welcome the possibility that their information may be supplemented by third-party researchers, authors, artists, or purveyors of intellectual information who develop add-on products. Third-party add-ons, which can impose alternative structures on an existing publication, will be loaded in from a diskette. Potential add-ons include commentaries and margin notes, new articles, tour guides, complex webs of association, filters, eventually even natural-language routines that attempt to parse the meaning or significance of a data-base item for the traveler.

For example, to our Sports disc a naturalist could add on a product that augments the existing data base's sketches with pictures of the evolutionary development of trout, including supplementary articles and instructional exercises written for seventh graders. Publishers and authors will be gratified to note (and will profit by) the way their electronic corpus can be used to further interact with a variety of audiences.

Summary

Hypermedia's strength is its vast capability for interactivity and random, nonlinear associations. In many ways, fixed-function publications will pale in comparison with programmable hypermedia. Hypermedia can create a wholly new reality based on the dynamic combinations of visual and aural phenomena. Hypermedia will be truly context-sensitive and will actually reinforce the traveler's perspective. There is one caveat, however: The success of hypermedia presumes that the information structure is ever-changing, depending on the whims and needs of the traveler. The first step toward maximizing true interactivity between traveler and information is the commitment to the idea that individualized associations are the greatest good. Publishers must constantly remind themselves that achieving interactivity requires vigilant attention both to how their system will manipulate content and to how travelers will manipulate that content. If systems and publications support the goal of true interactivity, publishers can devote themselves to the promise of the fantastic potential uses of hypermedia.

Palimpsest is a term we can apply to how we view true hypermedia. Palimpsest, common before the invention of the printing press in 1450, was writing material, such as parchment, paper, and tablets, so prepared that the writing could be erased and the material reused. A palimpsest manuscript often contained two or three earlier writings that had been erased and written over, with traces of those earlier texts remaining. Palimpsest was the ancients' method of interactivity. In traditional print publishing and also in many interactive or hypertext documents described today, the publisher imposes a structure and fixed links on the material, but it is a palimpsest structure that will let the traveler deviate from the structure provided by the publisher and create an individualized path. The granular, or atomic, structure of information will let the publisher and the traveler move freely through material—rubbing it out or interacting with the existing data structure or restructuring it to suit themselves.

For further information on SGML:

Association of American Publishers, 1986. Standard for Electronic
Manuscript Preparation and Markup (Electronic Manuscript Project).
Association of American Publishers, Inc., 2005 Massachusetts
Avenue, N.W., Washington, DC 20036.

SGML Users Group. TAG (SGML Newsletter). SGML Users Group, 105A
Carpenter Drive, Sterling, VA 22170.

Section VI:
Thought Pieces

A number of issues raised at the Conference did not form the central theme for any paper. Many of these were raised in our formal discussion sessions or in hallway discussions. Others were raised by individuals who attended the Conference but did not present papers.

In order not to lose these perspectives, Conference attendees were invited to write "thought pieces," which summarized their personal perspectives on these "extra issues" in a few pages. These are included in this section.

Assuming That…

Anne Nicol

New technologies—in particular, the integrated sorts of systems described in this book—hold great promise for learning. Their linking capabilities invite individually customized and inquiry-driven approaches to knowledge acquisition. Their interactivity encourages problem-solving activities. And their capacity for vast storage and quick retrieval puts whole domains of visual and auditory information within reach. Potentially, they become the tools that enable people to learn in a most meaningful and effective way—by discovery.

Somehow, we all know that discovery learning is "good" learning. Things that we have found out for ourselves take on special importance; the knowledge we gain is bolstered by personal and emotional content. We remember what we have discovered longer, and we are more likely to pay attention to new, related information. But discovery is not always the most effective way to learn a particular concept or to achieve a given learning objective. And even when it is, circumstances in the situation may obstruct the natural learning process. As designers, we need to carefully examine and test the assumptions that underlie both the "what" and the "how" of our projects.

Jerome Bruner, an eloquent advocate of discovery learning, reminds us that "discovery favors the well-prepared mind" (Bruner, 1962). His argument is that there are relevant prerequisite experiences that, in any domain, make discovery more likely. Let us explore briefly what the implications of Bruner's statement might be for our new interactive multimedia projects.

Because the users of these systems will often be learning how to use the system at the same time they are learning the curriculum delivered by the system, there are really two classes of prerequisite experience that need attention. First, navigating through a complex learning environment will require an understanding of how navigational features of the user interface may correspond to the organization of information in the system. For example, the use of arrows to move through levels of information is intuitive only to the learner who already knows that the information might be organized in levels and who knows something meaningful about the relationship between levels. This kind of knowledge need not be specific to the discipline or to the organization of the particular data base. It may come from previous experience in using other information systems, or from a good advance overview or map of the system at hand.

A second class of assumptions has to do with relationships between the learning process and the subject matter. Most programs that encourage an inquiry approach assume that learning begins with a learner's question. But as experienced teachers know, students new to a subject are rarely able to formulate the questions that will lead to fruitful research. Questions of that sort must be based on hypotheses, and it takes some practice and some knowledge of the field to generate useful hypotheses. The system needs to have ways of modeling the inquiry process for the learner in the same way that good instructors lead their students to ask appropriate questions.

Also, in designing responsive systems, we make assumptions about the motivation and interest of learners. Taking full advantage of the opportunities made available by new technologies requires "mindfulness" on the part of the learner. "This mindfulness—the deliberate employment of nonautomatic processes—is partly determined by learners' proclivities, perceptions, expectations, fears, and self-perceptions, and partly by their immediate experiences with the computer" (Salomon, 1985). The latter we can have control over; the former, we must be ever mindful of ourselves.

Once one develops expertise in an area, it is always difficult to remember what one "didn't know then." But we can get lots of help by trying out our systems with "real" students and by working with "real" teachers throughout. We can do the same sorts of task analyses that curriculum writers have always done, in which we identify prerequisite concepts, both cognitive and procedural, for each important learning objective. To conclude, this is a call for continuing, formative evaluation of our design work, in which we test our assumptions about learners as well as our program content against educational goals. In this way, we ensure that the tools we create will truly enhance the learning process for all learners.

REFERENCES

Bruner, Jerome. (1962) *On Knowing: Essays for the Left Hand.*
Cambridge: Harvard University Press.

Salomon, Gavriel. (1985) "Information technologies: What you see is not (always) what you get." Paper presented at the Annual Meeting of the American Educational Research Association.

Anne Nicol *is an educational psychologist whose research interests are children and television, children and computers, and human-computer interactions. She has taught kids of all ages how to use computers and is currently directing the Human Interface Testing Laboratory at Apple Computer, Inc.*

A Layered Theory of Design for Optical Disc Software

Mike Liebhold

INTRODUCTION

The following paper is a summary of thoughts after the Multimedia in Education conference at Apple Computer in 1986.

Most applications of CD-ROM are transformed network-information-retrieval products. Interactive videodiscs, on the other hand, have been principally designed for structured computer-aided instruction (CAI). Both, however, neglect the promise and ultimate power of the technology.

CD-ROMs that help a user merely find *facts* may not offer added value over print and network services. The media and computational technology are clearly well suited for *decision aid*. New models of productivity imply more intelligence than mere search and retrieval.

Videodiscs that have been hard-wired, tree-structured CAI programs ignore the vast archival capabilities of the format. A videodisc, for example, with 27 minutes of discrete video sequences still has a capacity for 5,400 still frames—a capacity rarely utilized. *Videodisc is a data-base technology* that may also be used as an instructional resource.

The Four Layers:
An Approach to Optical Disc Software Design

In this paper, I propose a design approach that combines the archival power of optical media with the intelligence and flexibility of computer software. This approach entails four layers:

- Data
- Index
- Browser
- Intelligence

Data Layer

Any combination of five principal data types may be combined on a compact or LV (laservision standard) disc:

Text (usually ASCII)
Graphics (including fax, bit maps, vector drawings, and GKS)
Motion (animation, video [ntsc, pal, secam, hdtv, digital])
Sound (speech, music, sampled sound)
Code (computer programs, machine instructions)

The key words for this layer are *appropriate* and *coherent*. Obviously, if you are planning a disc on medieval history, footage of the *Voyager* planetary flyby would not be useful.

Index Layer

A *data-base* management system of the data on the disc constitutes the index layer. Following Ted Nelson's Xanadu hypertext concepts, the system should permit *annotation, updates,* and *personalization*. Imagine a photograph of the earth taken from a satellite in 1978. A modern meteorologist who understands a previously unknown cloud formation because of recent research would clearly want to update the data-base record for the optical disc image.

A personally annotated version of the library card catolog is also possible. Since we are considering read-only media, the *differential files* will have to reside on a magnetic-media floppy or hard disk. You wouldn't be carrying the entire card catalog around on your floppy, just the *pointers* to the cards you have annotated.

Browser Layer

Any disc-based information system may include a wide range of tools or methods such as the following for finding or navigating through data:

- Key word (Boolean) search
- Alphanumeric search
- Topical browsers
- Graphic browsers
- Intelligent browsers

Key word (Boolean) search.
An example would be "Find Saturn *and* moons" or "Find Lincoln *not* automobile." This is a technique fairly familiar to librarians and network data-base searchers. The most commonly developed application for CD-ROM, it really needs an intelligent thesaurus and natural-language understanding to be fully effective in other words, supporting the *DWIM* command (*Do what I mean!*).

Alphanumeric search.
As in a book index, you have **abacus** under A, **baseball** under B, and **captain** under C. You need to know the name of what you're looking for in order to find it.

Topical browsers.
A table of contents is a topical browser. Vast files of data on a CD or videodisc may be comfortably navigated by chapter, unit, and section or by various subject or theme topics. Using various pull-down and pop-up menu schemes on Xerox and Symbolics Lisp machines, Steve Weyer has demonstrated great examples of sophisticated, structured topical-browsing systems.

Graphic browsers.
Maps, diagrams, and charts are all potentially useful as an interface to data. Point and click on Chicago, Illinois, on the map, and the appropriate data-base record or picture pops up. Filevision is an early example of this technique. The MIT movie manual projects produced by Steve Gano, Andy Lippman, and others illustrate the rich variety of applications of digitized images for browsing and instruction.

Transparent graphic-overlay in an interactive video environment may, in the future, permit running video objects to be directly manipulated. As a video object moves across the screen, a transparent "cursor target" follows: hypermedia! New 3-D graphics systems also suggest a new opportunity for direct manipulation of screen "objects."

Intelligent browsers.

Real-world knowledge is not linear. Three-dimensional arrays or *concept networks* of common-sense links are closer to the way humans organize thoughts. Ted Kaehler calls them *semantic networks*. Here's Ted's example:

- A *fern* in the forest >
- A *tree* in the forest >
- A *logger* cuts the tree >
- The tree is taken on a truck to the *sawmill* >
- The tree is cut into *lumber* >
- The lumber is used to construct a *building* >
- The building was designed by an *architect* >
- The architect has a computer >the computer has a CRT > > > etc.

We've traveled from a fern to a CRT in comfortable, lateral steps.

Although some work is being done at MCC and elsewhere to automate construction, accumulation of these links will most likely be an incremental manual and social process for some time. The emergence of common hypertext environments will permit communities of scholars to aggregate their knowledge into machine-readable formats. Greg Crane's Perseus project at Harvard is a fine example of scholars (in this case, Greek history scholars) collaborating to construct a hypertext and hypermedia representation of a discipline.

The Intelligent Layer

Any of the following types of applications may be layered on top of an optical-disc-based reference system:

- Instruction
- Simulation
- Productivity
- Creativity
- Serendipity
- "Expert"

While most videodisc producers have ignored potential reference value of the browser layer and gone straight for interactive instruction, most CD-ROM creators have stopped at the browser layer—short of productive applications other than information retrieval.

Clearly, the future of optical disc information systems rests in the development of new *data-rich* models of productivity. A *hyper-spreadsheet* model of world financial phenomena, if well designed, would be far more useful than a CD-ROM almanac of financial facts, and an encyclopedia with curriculum-coordinated courseware more useful than a basic reference. A stand-alone page-layout program would be considerably enhanced by a library of images, an *intelligent data-base agent* would be more helpful than a vanilla terminal program, and a *simulation* of a living biosystem more compelling than a collection of photos and files.

Mike Liebhold *is Manager of Optical Media Applications in the Advanced Development Group of Apple Computer, Inc. He is developing hardware and software systems for optical media-based information products. Previously he developed publishing relationships for optical media products with publishers, data-base companies, and optical software developers. Before joining Apple Computer he was responsible for advanced market development at ByVideo Inc., a transactional videodisc system vendor. At the Atari Division of Warner Communications, he was responsible for the Strategic Systems Research Laboratory and its work on optical information systems.*

Links or Stories— A Compromise

Bernard Frischer

All designers of multimedia computer systems for education have to confront a basic question at some point in their work. Should end users be able to range freely through the various data bases, like scholars in a library, making whatever connections, or "links," they wish between the data, or should they be led along a predetermined path through the material to be mastered? This question is, of course, but a specific form of the fundamental question all teachers must answer—no matter what subject they are teaching or what technology they are using—about whether a student learns better in a free or a structured environment.

The advantages and disadvantages of freedom versus structure are well known. Freedom enables students to find themselves, and nothing is more important to individual development than that; structure can be counterproductive because it forces students to learn what they may not yet be interested in learning. Structure ensures that students learn *something*, however unwillingly; freedom entails the possibility that students will never get off the mark and find either themselves or their way through the desired material. And so on.

It seems clear that the major advantage of computers is precisely their programmability, or their flexibility to interact with users in ways that traditional tools cannot. A riveting hammer cannot become a machinist's hammer—let alone a basin wrench—just because the job demands a different tool. Obvious as this observation is, it has, I daresay, been frequently ignored in computer applications to education, perhaps because of the genesis of CAI in theories of managed instruction.

In computer-managed instruction, "individualization" is defined simply as giving students the power to make their way *at their own speed* along a predetermined route.[1] Individualization might, however, also be defined as determining how a student best learns before deciding whether to impose structure or permit freedom. Assuming that a choice must be made between self-directed and structured learning on the computer, then good instructional design ought to begin with a profiling of the student to see which approach is appropriate *for that student at that time for that subject*. The absence of such profiling is a major factor, I think, contributing to the otherwise puzzling failure of most CAI to show statistically significant results. By imposing "one right way" on all students, most CAI measures up as a wash because it turns students on or off in about the same percentage of cases.

---

[1] See F.B. Baker, *Computer Managed Instruction. Theory and Practice* (Englewood Cliffs, N.J. 1978) 56.

Profiling students before setting them loose in a computerized learning environment is one way of overcoming the opposition of freedom versus structure. Another way involves a different conception of the student's role. When we put students into a highly structured curriculum (whatever the technology used for packaging and delivery), we cast them as immature—not to say irresponsible—children. When we put students into a situation of freedom, we cast them as mature, budding scholars who are able to make their way responsibly through the material, different from the true master of the subject only in degree, not in kind.

A third role is also possible, at least in many humanistic disciplines—that of explorer. Explorers, whatever their age, are people who have invested their limited resources of time and money in travel to a self-selected place that they wish to get to know better. To this end, they typically put themselves into learning situations that are sometimes structured and sometimes unstructured. For example, before embarking, the typical explorer will consult with others who have already made the trip and will read books on a variety of topics and levels. That is, the explorer will consider a variety of structured approaches to mastering the subject and may well put together a personal synthesis of them all. Once arrived at the destination, the explorer continues to seek out structured learning—for example, a guided tour—while also continually breaking out of this routine by freely exploring the environment, making connections and discoveries along the way.

Applying this to multimedia computer programming, I would conclude by claiming that "links or stories" is an unnecessary choice—one we are not, in fact, forced to make. If the user is viewed as an explorer—not as a "student"—then at every moment, both guided tours ("stories") and free exploration ("making links") should be options provided by the program. The explorer metaphor is, of course, especially appropriate for a project such as the one I am working on (Cicero), where the student is, quite literally, an explorer sent back in time to a re-creation of ancient Rome. However, *mutatis mutandis* (as the Romans said), there is no reason why the metaphor could not be applied in many other contexts, even where the world of the program is not an imaginary trip to an exotic time and place.

Getting a Boost from the Real World

Ted Kaehler

"Direct manipulation" of things on the screen is a powerful idea, because it draws on experience we have in the real world. Once a person "gets it" that they can drag icons around on the Macintosh screen, you don't have to explain the details. They already know what to expect. Moving a file from one folder to another is very much like moving groceries from a paper bag to the refrigerator. We unconsciously make up little algorithms to do these tasks, and when we see a direct analogy on the computer screen, we can transfer our knowledge. We stop thinking out every step and start doing the actions unconsciously.

Programming languages have gotten a similar boost from the real world, but at a more abstract level. An "object" is a package of data and procedures that belong together. Object-oriented programming encourages the programmer to think of each part of his or her system as a "thing." When the programmer has divided the system into the right set of parts—the set that corresponds best to how he or she thinks about it on a visceral level—writing code becomes much easier. When the objects are aptly named, they behave as one would expect, and the programmer can skip a level or two of abstraction and mental translation. A package of data and procedures named a "push-down-stack" is much easier to use when it acts like a single "object," behaves as a stack should, and can be created simply by saying "make me a new stack."

One of the problems with object-oriented languages is that objects are difficult to edit directly. Objects are exactly what you want for constructing a card catalog for a library. However, it is very laborious to edit a card from the programming language (the program to change one field is more complex than the card). The time-honored solution is to build a specialized editor, so that the user can directly manipulate the data on the card. However, building a specialized object editor is difficult—in fact, often harder than writing the original program. Since objects are hard to manipulate, they are scarce. The programmer is in the awkward position of wanting to play in a universe but having to create every blade of grass.

A hypertext system combined with an object-oriented language is a fusion of these worlds. All around you is a wealth of objects—paragraphs, links, documents, pictures, and spreadsheets. These objects are there because they are actually being used. At last there is something real to talk about, and with an object-oriented language, the talking is the best we know how to do. A little fragment of code is all one needs to say, "When I click on this button, check that this field contains a date and that this field is a legal call number for a book." Many objects, such as paragraphs, records, and pictures are already there in full bloom. The hypertext system provides a good editor "for free."

Laura Gould and Bill Finzer's Programming by Rehearsal and Dan Ingalls's Ariel are two early systems that allowed programmers to directly manipulate an object as soon as it was created (without building a specialized editor). Systems that allow the object-oriented ease of description and programming but that also have the richness of data and the highly honed editors of a hypertext system will be quite compelling. I hope this fusion will help us to complete the unfulfilled vision—what the average person thought of when he or she first heard the words "personal computer."

Ted Kaehler, *a Senior Engineer at Apple Computer, was educated at Stanford and Carnegie-Mellon (M.S. in Computer Science). He was a member of the SmallTalk group at Xerox PARC for 14 years before joining Apple in 1985. Currently he is a member of the Advanced Technology Group at Apple.*

Authoring with Hypermedia

Carol Kaehler

With hypermedia, authors have the capability to create large and complex learning environments that users can easily navigate and annotate. Two challenges in designing an interface for such an environment are:

1. Showing users of the system where they are in relationship to the rest of the system—answering the inevitable question: "Where am I? Show me a map."

2. Preventing readers from being overwhelmed by the amount of information available.

An Ever-Present Map

Hypermedia applications such as HyperCard both cause these problems and offer solutions for them. Because of the branching nature of most hypermedia systems, it's easy, as you go down a path, to lose sight of where you came from. You might be able to look back one level, to retrace a single step, or even to see a map of the system. But a better solution is available: the system designer can model an interface that includes an ever-present map which changes as the reader traverses it to show the current location in the system. The tabs on the notebook in the HyperCard Help system are the system's "map."

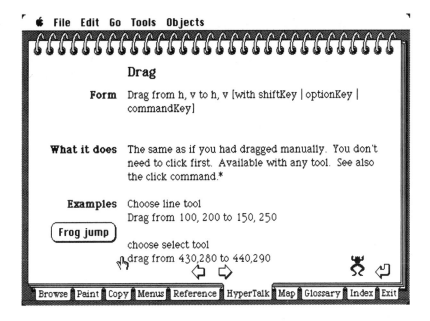

When you click on one of the notebook tabs, you go to that part of the system, and the appropriate tab pops forth, showing which part of the system you're in. So the form of the Help system becomes its own map, changing as you traverse the system and creating the illusion that you're in a geographical location of a book—the reference chapter, the index, or the map, for example.

Hiding Complexity Within a Simple Structure

The second problem—making a large amount of information seem negotiable—is a natural outcome of using omnipresent maps such as the notebook's tabs. The user sees not 1000 forbidding pages of text, but rather a simple, graphic notebook with seven or eight subjects. The structure belies the complexity within.

Hypermedia also brings serendipitous discoveries. Entering the realm of hypermedia, authors might worry that readers will feel uneasy when they don't know exactly how much of the book remains to be read. Readers are used to judging what they have yet to conquer in a subject by how many pages are behind them and how many still are ahead. But instead of this anticipated problem, hypermedia authors have discovered that hiding volume behind a simple interface can be an advantage. For example, in the above illustration, nearly half of the Help system is devoted to the language—HyperTalk. A reader who saw the bulk of a book devoted to programming might be intimidated and immediately put the book down. But tucked behind an innocent tab, the programming information isn't very threatening. And so readers who might be overwhelmed by a thick book (or 800 KB of information) see only a small, easily navigated notebook.

Carol Kaehler

Carol Kaehler is a Senior Technical Writer at Apple Computer. She was educated as a musician (M.A. in Music Theory and Composition) but joined Apple in 1982 to write Macintosh, the owner's guide for the Macintosh computer. She also wrote the manuals for MacPaint and MacProject. Her most recent work at Apple has been in developing a hypertext help facility.

Section VII:
Summary

Multimedia in Education

Summary Chapter

Kristina Hooper

KRISTINA HOOPER

Kristina Hooper was trained as a cognitive scientist at Stanford (A.B.) and the University of California at San Diego (Ph.D.). In her research over the last 15 years, she has extended this perspective into the areas of picture recognition, imagery, and visual technologies. Her early activities included a postdoctoral fellowship in architecture, a faculty position at the University of California at Santa Cruz, a DARPA project on geographic information systems that led to a visiting faculty appointment at MIT working on the Aspen Project, and an NSF grant to study the use of computer graphics in teaching calculus.

With the birth of her son Matthew, Hooper moved to the Atari Sunnyvale Research Lab where she became director of R&D, and Matthew became the resident "developmental prototyke." Her daughter Erika was born as the Atari dream ended, and Hooper moved on to Apple's Education Research Group. Jocelyn was born in the midst of the preparation of this manuscript, as Hooper formed the Multimedia Group at Apple with Sueann Ambron. The plan is that this book will help to generate multimedia materials in the near term for these inquiring minds, as well as for many others.

As the old saying goes, "you had to be there." The June Conference on Multimedia in Education, on which this book is based, was an exciting affair. We talked about more issues than I can even recall, all of which seemed central at the moment to the main topic. We discussed issues that had been raised years ago—hypertext, augmentation of human intellect, the opportunities of videodiscs in an interactive environment—wondering once again why these notions hadn't already "taken off." We mused about past projects and future plans. And we decided that "now is the time" for the multimedia revolution, and that among all of us in the group we had the insight and perspective to "pull it off" ("it" being a combination of marketing, educating, designing, computing, visualizing, cognizing, saving the world, and making money).

And then we all rested, for it was as exhausting as it was exhilarating to engage in all these important ideas and plans.

The chapters you have just read represent the efforts of all the participants after they had rested, after they had taken a step back from the excitement of the moment and come to the task of putting down on paper what they thought were the major issues in this (once again) newly focused field.

Different Perspectives

As you probably have noted, the perspectives of all these people are quite different. Such was the intent of the Conference. For the perspectives of a large number of constituencies—including educators, computer scientists, TV producers and broadcasters, entertainment companies, hardware developers, software designers, dreamers, realists, publishers, engineers, and cognitive theorists—are all required for the successful development of the computer-based multimedia revolution that was addressed in our Conference and that is considered in this book.

The current issues are just how these traditions can merge, and the kinds of experiences that are available once this is done. Interestingly, it is difficult to describe the hoped-for experience from these multiple perspectives. And it is hard to describe the nature of the products that result from these perspectives. They are somewhat like books, but not quite. Sometimes they are more like movies, but then they change in character to become more encyclopedic or interactive. Occasionally, these presentations are compared to educational software, yet the high production values available from optical media (such as sounds and images) make it clear that though these new presentations share "interactivity" with this software, there are great differences that require mention.

In time, we will probably stop describing such experiences according to other models with which we are more familiar, and we will begin to call them by their own names (which are yet to be determined; "multimedia presentations" is only a current, inadequate, working title). In addition, more and more people will focus their activities on this class of experiences, without explicitly acknowledging that the roots of their interests or talents are in computer science, television, or other well-established disciplines. When this happens, we will know that the revolution in interactive multimedia experiences has occurred.

Varied Projects

A major criterion for selection of attendees at the Conference (in addition to a sense of humor and a keen insight on the issues) was that they be involved in specific activities in the general area of multimedia. The reasoning was that to understand this new area one needs to be working directly in it. More centrally, it seems that people have been talking about this general field extensively over the last few decades, without producing many highly visible examples that can be scrutinized and learned from. And it seems like the time has come to deliver on the (excellent) rhetoric, and try to "make it happen" (and along the way find out what "it" really is, as well as to honestly assess whether "it" is worth the effort).

The specifics of the projects with which Conference attendees are involved are typically elaborated in the chapters. However, it is also useful to acknowledge the range of these projects in order to appreciate the generality of the class of presentations and experiences that technologies in the multimedia/computer area allow. It is also a useful exercise to contemplate the concrete examples described apart from all the reasoning described in the chapters; this provides a reality check on the entire multimedia endeavor.

Doug Engelbart's Augmentation System was functioning years ago, providing the core for a research community, enabling collaborative work on complex problems. His current work at McDonnell Douglas is an attempt to reinitiate such work and experiment in the use of technology in communication and problem solving. Norm Meyrowitz's Hypermedia Project at Brown University is clearly about to take off; it is available now to students in a number of classes. Steve Weyer's early work at Xerox for browsing a history text, as well as his work at Atari using the Grolier encyclopedic data base, makes explicit just how browsing can be incorporated into the use of large-scale data bases. The NoteCard System, developed by Frank Halasz, is now a product available through Xerox, and a specific example of how linkage systems might be designed.

Larry Friedlander has completed a graphical simulation of theatrical performances on a computer for use by his students at Stanford, and has successfully demonstrated a prototype of a videodisc-based system to explore still and moving images of theaters and performances. Bernard Frischer is moving quickly, with the assistance of UCLA, to produce a travel system for teaching the Classics. And Robert Campbell and Patricia Hanlon have produced an example of the kinds of presentations a teacher might make to a class from available materials related to *The Grapes of Wrath*.

Sam Gibbon at Bank Street College has already distributed a television series and supporting print and computer materials in the area of science and math education (Voyage of the MIMI) and is in the midst of preparing a second series (Voyage of the MIMI II), which will incorporate videodiscs. Tom Anderson has demonstrated his concepts of reuse of physics material very effectively, and is actively involved in productions based on this demonstration.

The CD-ROM Encyclopedia product provided by Grolier is still a major example of a working CD-ROM system; Peter Cook's recent work will clearly expand the capabilities of this product to include more flexibility and imagery. The National Geographic Society is now committed to developments in computer software and extensions of their past optical media efforts in enhancing geographic understanding, as described by George Peterson.

Steve Gano's ideas about personalized imagery are surely providing the basis for a number of systems at Hewlett-Packard, some of which we hope to see in the public eye soon. Similarly, Doug Crockford's version of fun will probably be available to a wide audience soon. And as stated earlier, Microsoft's multimedia encyclopedia demonstration, described by Suzanne Ropiequet, is already highly visible, providing a very useful example of a computer multimedia experience for all of us to examine and enjoy.

Prior to reading this book, one would think there was little in common among Shakespeare, physics, *The Grapes of Wrath*, and the Classics. Similarly, television and print publishing may have seemed quite unrelated, as did encyclopedias and entertaining storytelling, broadcast television and personalized imagery production, collaborative work environments and classrooms, and sophisticated hypertext systems and classroom computing. I hope that this book has made it possible for you to see the interconnections of these very different efforts, as well as notice that new technologies can provide augmentation in all these areas, expanding our personal experiences and improving our capabilities (and those of our schoolchildren).

Ten Themes

There are a number of themes that pervade many of the chapters, most of which are the same themes that hallway and dinner conversations focused on at the Conference. Important among these are the following:

1. What is the nature of interactivity? Are linear presentations obsolete?

It is currently quite fashionable to be in favor of interactivity. In a related vein, concepts like "personalization," "browsing," "manipulable," "divergent thinking," "response-contingent displays," and "discovery learning" have gained great mileage in the computer education revolution. And this is only appropriate.

The computer (which now comes in many flavors and many different forms, many of which are simultaneously reasonably priced and quite powerful) allows for the realization of dreams that address these concepts in pragmatic terms. We truly can now reflect on our own intuitions of our thought processes—what William James at the turn of the century described as the "perching and flights" of consciousness—and we can dream of machines that can mimic these processes, as well as machines that can assist us in making good use of these mental ramblings.

Yet when one seriously attempts to design "interactive experiences" that incorporate the aforementioned concepts, it becomes less and less clear just what we mean by the word "interactive" and whether or not we are all talking about the same thing. More critically, it becomes unclear whether interactive necessarily implies something that is good (and conversely that linear presentations are necessarily bad).

Anyone who has looked at run-of-the-mill computer software or branching videodiscs that continually interrupt the viewer with multitudes of unappealing choices understands that interactivity is not a sufficient condition for a good experience. Similarly, those of us who have sat on the edge of our seats in lecture halls and theaters, enjoying a nonpassive experience even though we have no control of outcomes or opportunity for any interaction, must acknowledge that there really is something to the crafts of rhetoric and storytelling.

Looking at this seriously, it becomes clear that we must start to understand what the most important aspects of interactivity are, and how complex interactivity has to be in order to produce experiences that are qualitatively different from noninteractive situations. We must, for example, have a crisp answer to questions like the following, the answers for which are based on analyses rather than "religion":

- Isn't most of "interactivity" gained by the ability to start and stop, review and preview, presentations?

- Are videotapes then the major innovation in interactivity, not computers?

- Aren't too many choices distracting?

- Isn't the personalization provided by self-selection artificial?

- Where does interactivity fit into classic theories of narratives, and of the importance of beginnings, middles and ends, in determining the impact of an experience?

- Where is the correct place for the artistic expression of an author in an interactive presentation?

- How can an author create resolution for a viewer in an interactive environment?

- What marks the end of an interactive opportunity?

We must develop a common vocabulary to discuss these questions, including a set of well-defined words to describe agreed-upon concepts, as well as a set of common exemplars to which we can refer in our analyses.

In sum, we need to give up the simplicity of the equations that proclaim interactivity as good and linear presentations as bad. We can then focus on our task of using new technologies to create effective and engaging experiences, taking advantage of all past experiences (in interactive and noninteractive areas) as well as all available media (digital and analog).

(See chapters by Anderson, Crockford, and Gibbon.)

2. What can be done with all the imagery made possible with videodiscs and the sounds enabled by compact discs? Is any of this really new?

Frequently, one is struck with the feeling of having "heard it all before," particularly if one spends much time in the field of education. The pessimistic interpretation of this is that everything is a fad, and that most of what we are hearing lately about new technologies is all hype. The optimistic interpretation is that good ideas stay around, no matter how badly they are handled, and that, eventually, they will garner the appropriate momentum to be "done right."

The idea of using images and sounds in education is clearly age-old, an idea that has been the basis for the development of a range of audiovisual technologies and materials running the gamut from overhead projectors to television, slide shows to elaborate movies. And the notion that "since images and sounds are available cheaply, they should be used in education" has clearly been overworn in the educational community.

Yet the use of multimedia computer presentations to solve problems that cannot be addressed effectively in any other context is extremely appropriate, as well as exciting. This direction of motivation and development—presented often in this Conference—is highly compelling and convincing vis-à-vis the importance of these new AV presentations. What we still need, however, are fully developed examples that make this obvious—to remove this issue from academic argument and let it face the scrutiny of potential audiences. We need examples that make explicit the wide range of ways that sights and sounds can add to educational experiences, and specific evaluations showing how these contribute to the learning process. Our current psychological theories argue that multisensory learning should enhance understanding, though few of the studies available address interactive situations. It will be interesting to find out just what differences these presentations can make when they are under user control.

In doing this it is important, however, to realize that there are a large number of components that will need to be in place if examples are to be effective. The existence of new hardware and new hardware standards—be they CD-I or DV-I or LV-ROM or CD-ROM or videodiscs—do in fact provide an opportunity not available to even the most talented designer before. For the sheer amount of information is at a scale hardly imagined possible before, a scale that makes possible highly textured information environments which very few of us have ever experienced. And the variety of information allowed by this scale of information storage—for music and images in particular—makes possible the intertwining of different presentations, presentations that are manipulable, in new and exciting ways.

Similarly, new software tools and new ideas for interfaces in a range of application domains—many of which are described in this book—are surfacing frequently of late, many of these offering direct access to information by teachers and other noncomputer professionals.

The interactions of hardware, software, and interface innovations can provide for some long-lasting and solid changes in educational environments. Changes in scale of information, in the tools for information manipulation, in the cost of widely distributed data bases, and in the "appearance" of information, promise revolutions in the human processing of information; education can focus on human thought and thoughtfulness in a range of media, and defocus from the memory of textual facts as the current very new potentials are realized.

(See chapters by Campbell/Hanlon, Friedlander, and Anderson.)

3. Are emotional presentations appropriate to education? Or should technology efforts be used primarily to present "factual data" in educational settings?

At the Conference, there were interesting arguments presented for both sides of this issue. A number of people couldn't believe that others thought emotions were inappropriate and manipulative in the classroom. They argued that emotions are already present in classrooms, and that emotional involvement is critical to make materials relevant to students and to allow any depth of understanding or interest in a topic.

People on the other side of this argument insisted that emotional manipulation of students was "unfair" and inappropriate to the pedagogical enterprise. They found the techniques of the theater and the movie screen highly dangerous in a learning environment; they found the use of music to increase the impact of a political message very unsettling, for example, as they did the theatrical embellishment of a personal discussion/argument portraying controversies. Typically, these people argued that the task at hand, for them anyway, was not to polarize arguments or to use readily available multisensory techniques to arouse and convince. Instead, their task was to accumulate available data and to provide tools so that people could access these.

It is unclear which approach is appropriate. It is clear, however, that as multisensory presentations and tools for their organization are made available by new technologies, people will need to learn to use them and to interpret them, much as they have already done for textual presentations. It is also clear that there will be many controversies about the appropriate use of these technologies in educational institutions (which is not so surprising).

4A. Is the central task in the design of educational presentations to link large amounts of information? Or is it to "tell stories"? Should presentations emulate libraries as reference centers or classrooms (as teaching centers)? Is there a significant difference between encyclopedias and textbooks and TV documentaries and novels and lectures?

4B. What balance is required between directed search and browsing paradigms? Can one count on individuals to bring their own questions and research strategies to their tasks, or must the technological environments provide these?

A number of the presentations at the Conference focused on hypertext systems, systems that enabled the linking of various sorts of available data. Similarly, a number of these presentations dealt principally with encyclopedic presentations, presentations deliberately designed to put a very broad range of information "at the fingertips" of the viewer.

These emphases are extremely exciting and are realistic given technological advances, including general extended memory and increased speeds of processing, as well as advances in software design and existing and expected advances in knowledge representation.

People often paused at the Conference to consider this approach in some detail, however, remembering that there are already large amounts of data available that they don't use very often. Also, reflecting on how they do their own work, they remembered how particular situations and compelling stories and people had led them to their profession, and that these same elements continued to motivate them in their activities. And they began to discuss just how poorly prepared most students are for schooling, and how few of them seem interested in anything.

In many conversations people then argued that even the best-presented "linkage map" would not be enough to engage learners' interests, that it was very important to provide "motivating overviews" and "engaging situations" to people so that moving through these webs of information would be compelling. And it was suggested that this was the prime opportunity of multimedia presentations that should not be ignored. Similarly it was argued that the "nodes" of a linkage system should frequently be highly engaging, often providing elements of surprise and humanness in the presentation of both factual and conceptual data. The argument was that cognitive activities and affective activities are not mutually exclusive, and that in fact affective presentations were not mere accompaniments to "serious presentations" but were in fact their very essence.

In other conversations people argued that the first task was the provision of large data bases, principally of existing materials, and that the incorporation of new media presentations and of affective elements could be a task at a later time, after this large task was accomplished. Similarly arguments were made that suggested that systems should be modeled on motivated individuals first, that the study of these individuals could be of the most help in the design of initial systems. As the proficiency of systems increased, they could be modified to account for the generation of initial curiosity.

The general sense of the Conference, and that of the chapters in general, is that these different approaches are highly compatible, and that on reflection, probably both are critical for the success of any system. What was also acknowledged is that some people will work on systems that emphasize one approach, given their beliefs, and others will work on the other. Optimally, at some point there would be a merging of approaches; designers would learn from the successes of each approach and incorporate them in new examples.

(See chapters by Weyer and Meyrowitz and Thought Piece by Frischer.)

5. What will it require to make the presentations now quite familiar in research laboratories available to the general community? Why is it seeming to take so long?

Doug Engelbart's work in the general area of "augmentation of human intellect" was very nicely demonstrated in the 1960s in his SRI Laboratories. He organized a community of workers who used a system to keep track of itself. He demonstrated hypertext systems and systems for collaborative activities. He developed the mouse (as well as a range of other input devices) and showed how they could be used. He set up working videoconferencing systems, with computers as central elements.

A lot of this work was followed up at Xerox PARC, as systems were developed that combined text and graphics, and that showed the advantages of an object-oriented programming language (Smalltalk). Interfaces were developed that made the powerful computing resources accessible to users, including programmers of these new systems and individuals involved in education.

J.C.R. Lickleider and Craig Fields extended the multimedia character of work that focused on human-usable computer systems in their ARPA funding programs. Negroponte's Architecture Machine Group projects were extremely important for this class of activities. The Aspen Project, for example, made clear that videodiscs could be used under computer control to do things that were never before possible—in this case, the apparent travel through a town. The Movie Manual project provided a specific example of just how text, moving and still images, and sounds could be made available to users under interactive control. The Bicycle Repair Manual provided another example of multimedia projects made possible by the combination of optical media and computers. The "Put That There" demonstration also made explicit just how multimedia input devices—voice and direct, manual pointing—could complement large-screen presentations of data. And the SDMS (Spatial Data Management System) demonstrations made explicit how these different multimedia techniques could be used for "navigation through information space," extending the usability of large data-base systems.

Yet even with these explicit examples, multimedia experiences have seemed to be stuck in the imaginations of researchers and in the special environments of flourishing research laboratories. For example, videodiscs generally have been quite unsuccessful in entering marketplaces. Though CD audio has been widely accepted in the marketplace, it is unclear whether CD-ROM will be able to build on this success, or whether computer/CD-ROM combinations (in whatever form) will find tasks beyond reference works that show their potentials.

"The chicken and egg" problem is blamed for a lot of this: if there is no hardware, there will be no applications; or if there is no successful application, there will be no hardware investment; and so forth ad infinitum. Standards issues and multiplicities of hardware options are also blamed; until there is a standard CD-ROM format, investors are uncomfortable in using this medium very seriously given the risk involved. And the general digital *vs* analog encoding argument also seems to get in the way of coherent action; computer folks are slow to understand why video is anything more than a nuisance, and video and graphic designers see little motivation to work very hard in cumbersome digital media on short-term projects.

And so the conversations go on in limited communities, and very little gets done that is visible to many people. In addition, given the lack of funding for projects, few people are given the opportunity to take on the challenge of multimedia presentations, and so few are trained in the multiplicity of areas required to address the design of such presentations. Even fewer people are involved in the integration of the huge number of issues that must be addressed and simplified to produce coherent products. More and more potential becomes available—interruptibility, interaction, individualization, consistent interfaces, sounds, images, moving images, dynamic computer graphics—and still there are few success stories.

No one will probably ever know why this is all taking so long, though clearly we all have our pet hypotheses. (My pet notion, incidentally, is that our culture fundamentally does not know much about the personal manipulation of information, particularly sound and image information; we are consumers of complex media, but not generators. This provides a great block in "convincing people" of the worthiness of multimedia presentations; it also results in a limited set of experiences on which designers in this new media can draw.)

What is important is that conferences like our June Conference and documents like this book keep trying out the ideas again and again, gathering momentum for some great successes. For indeed, the potential is certainly sitting there awaiting our cleverness.

6. What do we know from cognitive theory to mold our efforts in designing with new multimedia interactive systems?

Fundamental to the entire field of cognition is the finding that unless people engage a task, they will not learn from it. William James pointed this out at the beginning of this century, and research over the last 20 years has provided elaborations of this basic point.

The interactive nature of the multimedia presentations discussed as well as the emphasis on browsing modes will encourage active involvement by users, and therefore, it should enhance learning. Interactions with high-quality sounds and images will be unique in these presentations; more traditional media, including most existing computer software, simply do not provide learners with access to changeable images and sounds. This capability should enhance learning in ways we have yet to anticipate.

Another fundamental finding is that materials that are rich in sensorial content—especially visual displays—are quite effectively remembered. Moreover, the use of visual materials in learning situations—diagrams as well as photographic images—has been shown to enhance learning consistently.

Finally, the entire investigation of knowledge representation—in computer representations as well as in mental models—emphasizes the importance of the interlinking of conceptual materials, something that is a major focus in work on hypermedia as well as simpler hypertext systems. Though we are still naive in matters concerning how users will interact with capabilities for the interlinking of materials, as well as with materials that are presented to them in interlinked contexts, it seems that this approach to the presentation of materials should make explicit to learners the importance of interrelationships of ideas, and therefore enhance learning. These experiences can then emphasize "metacognitive skills," which are showing themselves again and again in basic research investigations to be critical for important learning.

And so the basic research in cognition supports the notion that multimedia presentations should be highly effective in learning.

From a slightly different perspective, multimedia presentations will allow cognitive researchers to study multisensory and interactive learning in ways that have been prevented in the past, given technological difficulties in image and sound presentations as well as the lack of tools for observing complex user responses. And so we can look forward to some valuable interactions between the field of cognition and multimedia approaches, each enhancing the other.

(See chapters by Anderson and Gano.)

7. How will multimedia educational "stations" fit into schools? Or will they?

Schools will be required to invest in new hardware in order to deliver the multimedia experiences discussed in this book. This obstacle will prove to be extremely large for some school districts, whereas it will be minor for others. Recent histories of computer purchases in schools suggest optimism; schools will find new ways to finance hardware when it is shown that the materials delivered with these technologies are important to their business of teaching and learning.

In addition, teaching staffs will need to adjust their methods of presentation in order to take advantage of multimedia presentations. Though experiences with audiovisual materials and with computers will help in this adjustment, there will be clear shifts in emphasis that are suggested by multimedia presentations.

Some of these shifts may be well beyond the curricular guidelines in certain areas, and in advance of the training of individual teachers. In addition, they may well be inconsistent with policies designed to maximize standardized test scores.

The challenge to the multimedia designer in all these regards is to create some applications that are clearly attractive and superior to materials now available. Unless there is a clear superiority demonstrated, there will be no motivation for making substantial classroom changes.

Of course, some teachers will grab hold of new materials and expand them in ways that make it obvious how these new materials both suit standard criteria and expand the opportunities for teachers and students. Clearly, new multimedia presentation designers need to work with these kinds of teachers to encourage these elaborations, and to suit the presentations to classroom realities. Given the pendulum shifts typical of the educational establishment, there is a clear chance that these new presentations can catch on in classrooms. Whether or not they stay in classrooms will be a function of just how good they really are, and just how accessible they are for individualization by both teachers and students.

(See chapters by Campbell/Hanlon and Gibbon.)

8. How can we best develop a language to describe the "experience" of a technology-based presentation? How can we both focus on the hardware/software required for the delivery of this experience and be sure that the experience is the primary motivator and criterion for developments?

The intrigue of new hardware and software developments is highly exciting and compelling. Processors are faster, software is more accessible, and the quality of possible presentations is ever higher. It is extremely tempting to take on these issues for their own sake.

For a different group of individuals, the development of new experiences in the learning and work environment is of paramount interest. New techniques for engaging students as well as engaging one's own mind are central to the interests of this group; a new technology is interesting only because it offers a new opportunity for human thinking/entertainment/etc.

Both perspectives are key to the development of multimedia experiences, as both the technologies and the experiences of users are critical to the success of these presentations. At the moment, the description of the experiences of users seems to be the gaping hole in dialog necessary for co-development of these perspectives. The current approach is the explicit demonstration of experiences that can be directly evaluated. Such an approach typically requires a large technological and financial investment, however, which means that there are not very many public articulations of what the goal is of a multimedia learning environment. Similarly, there are few instances in which these demonstrations are of large enough scale to allow much systematic analysis and testing.

So one is left only with the approach to make as many examples as possible, and to develop some that can be widely available and widely tested. With experience, we can hope to develop a descriptive (if not prescriptive) language to "get better at all this" more systematically.

(See chapter by Crockford.)

9. Will there/should there be a standard interface to multimedia experiences? What is the appropriate metaphor for this interface? Is it the familiar desktop? The understandable spatial map? A task-oriented environment? A set of research tools? A number of construction kits?

The Apple Desktop Interface provides an attractive interface for a wide range of tasks. More critically, it provides a consistent interface for a range of applications, thereby providing users with easy access to many materials without new training for each one. This allows users to focus more quickly on the task and materials at hand, and to use computer tools easily and intuitively. It also allows developers access to a range of conventions of interactions, allowing them to focus on particular applications rather than on new and different interfaces for different tasks. And it provides developers with a constituency that does not require training and explanations from the most basic level.

This interface should therefore serve an important role in the development of multimedia applications; it provides a flexible beginning for a range of user interactions.

However, as multimedia applications develop, there will clearly be elaborations to this interface, and most probably some extensions that are quite significant. As Friedlander finds in his application, a task-oriented metaphor is central to some educational situations. Campbell and Hanlon, as well as Meyrowitz and Weyer, suggest that a linking framework is key to the use of sophisticated text as well as image and sound browsing and manipulation. Frischer is betting that a spatial metaphor will suit his students' explorations of ancient civilizations. Cinematic metaphors are suggested by Gano's analyses. The Microsoft encyclopedia clearly relies on the metaphor of a book, and the specific organization of reference books. And other metaphors—including sets of research tools, agents, and construction kits—clearly represent other quite viable alternatives for user accessibility to multimedia presentations.

It's currently unclear which of these approaches is most generalizable or most useful. The sense is in fact that until we have examples we won't really know which way to proceed most confidently. Over the next few months and years we will begin to see each of these kinds of metaphors and more and less elaborate interfaces that make use of them. It will be interesting to see which approach—if any—proves to be the favorite for this new class of applications. It will also be interesting to see how the Apple Desktop Interface can stretch to include all of these requirements and approaches.

(See chapters by Cook, Frischer, and Friedlander.)

10. What happens when you combine the traditions of movie making, graphic design, computer education, encyclopedia development, text publication, public television, computer workstation design, classroom teaching, library organization, entertainment, and psychology?

Can it possibly be boring? Will the results be something new?
Will the results be significant educationally? Will they be entertaining? Can they possibly be both?

Will "multimedia experiences" be similar to the experiences of watching a finely crafted movie, writing a heartfelt letter, having a tantalizing conversation, visiting a great library, hearing a fine lecture, attending a symphony, listening to your favorite grandmother, viewing great old newsclips, playing the violin, opening a brand new book you've been waiting for, browsing in your favorite bookstore, effortlessly painting a great picture, reading your favorite magazine, working at a flexible word processor or a spreadsheet, playing a great videogame, winning at Monopoly....?

Or will they be more like taking exams in school?

It is bound to be an interesting next era in the multimedia applications business!

Since our conference, Bill Atkinson has contributed a new product for multimedia work. Titled HyperCard, it's a tool for making the kinds of presentations discussed throughout this book an accessible reality on Apple Macintosh computers. As the following epilogue describes, HyperCard lets each of us explore and build multimedia presentations without requiring that we become computer programmers or that we work in well-supported research labs.

This book and HyperCard have become quite irreversibly intermingled, as Apple participants at the Multimedia Conference have actively worked with HyperCard. For example, the contributors to the "Thought Piece" section of this book were major participants in HyperCard developments. Ted Kaehler was a principal contributor to the programming of HyperCard. Carol Kaehler produced HyperCard's innovative on-line Help system. Anne Nicol conducted the basic research on the effectiveness of the HyperCard interface in laboratory tests. Mike Liebhold created one of the first HyperCard applications, showing impressively how this tool can be used with optical media to create multimedia applications. And the editors of this book have formed the Multimedia Group at Apple, which has created a number of HyperCard prototype applications for use in classrooms.

The revolution has begun (again)!

Epilogue: HyperCard

Michael Jay Markman

On August 11, 1987, Apple Computer, Inc., introduced HyperCard, a software tool that radically broadens the capabilities of Macintosh computers. HyperCard achieves fundamental breakthroughs in two realms. The program provides new ways to organize, display, and navigate through information. And it gives non-programmers the capability to design and write their own applications. In combination with a level-3 videodisc player, HyperCard becomes at once the simplest and most flexible tool available for authoring multimedia presentations. The application so simplifies the mechanics of creating presentations that students and teachers now can make this type of presentation a routine classroom activity.

This remarkable software deserves attention not only for what it can do but also for the way it goes about it. On many levels, HyperCard exemplifies the fusing of technology, showmanship, and teaching that is the essence of multimedia. The software is the culmination of a three-year team effort led by Bill Atkinson, the developer of QuickDraw and MacPaint. In the details of its design, HyperCard reflects attention to style, presentation, and function.

Like other multimedia programs, HyperCard presents information vividly and gives us the capability to explore the information through associative and interest links. HyperCard realizes a dream that goes back more than four decades. In a 1945 article, "As We May Think," Vannevar Bush envisioned a desk-size appliance called Memex. Crammed full of microfilm, machinery, and optics, Memex was to record and retrieve information with an agility that reflected the way our minds create and recall thoughts. The program would not only store vast amounts of data, but would also give users the capability to jump from item to item along free-ranging trails of association. The trails themselves could be recorded, providing a way to exchange not only data but also insights. Given the same body of information, different people might create different links and trails reflecting their own viewpoints and understanding.

Memex was an intriguing fantasy, but its capabilities now can be realized through Hyper-Card.

Because this software is included with every Macintosh, hundreds of thousands of people have the opportunity to work with HyperCard. And many of those people have done remarkable things already.

They have created hypertext course materials that assist students in exploring subjects ranging from the humanities to electrical engineering to anatomy. Non-programmers have developed and marketed commercial programs. Filmmakers have created interactive multimedia tours through videodisc collections. Hopeless pack rats have organized their personal, business, and financial information. Ordinary mortals have taken their first hesitant steps toward computer programming, and, soon after, made confident, ingenious leaps in programming. Managers have created business presentations and children have designed games. And all sorts of people have built directories and indexes of books, records, projects, prospects, clients, associates, and friends.

In short, people have done thousands of serious and frivolous things with HyperCard. They have marveled at it. They have been exasperated by it. And they have formed a community that eagerly trades HyperCard documents (known as "stacks") along with programming tips.

And, along the way, these people have showered Bill Atkinson and his team of developers with suggestions, wish lists, and demands for making the next version even better.

Before the program's release, trying to define HyperCard was a full-time job for dozens of Apple product managers, marketing mavens, designers and copywriters. Since HyperCard's release, the press has taken up that unending quest with full vigor. The *New York Times* may have come as close as anyone ever will to defining HyperCard with a headline that read, "It's, well, HyperCard."

If you ask Bill Atkinson what he was trying to accomplish in creating HyperCard, he will tell you that one of his chief purposes was to teach, and that another was to engage people through the aesthetics of the program.

HyperCard embodies some impressive advances in its algorithms for searching text and some neat tricks in its compression of bit maps. But the technical side is not what captivates people. The winning side of HyperCard is the program's style…the showmanship…the soul.

And the soul of HyperCard, like the soul of all great teaching, is in sharing. It's the impulse that grows out of knowing something wonderful that is just too good to keep to yourself—the same impulse that drives us, when we hear a great joke, to run and tell it to someone. With HyperCard, Bill set out to teach the world something about what he knows is possible.

Like a master teacher, Bill designed a smooth, gradual path to draw a person into his subject. You can make your first foray into HyperCard with no training at all. You simply point to something on the screen, click with the mouse, and watch what happens.

Information comes to you a screenful at a time, or, in the program's metaphor, a "card" at a time. The buttons on the screen link the current card with another when you click them. Some buttons perform activities such as dialing a phone, doing calculations, or controlling a videodisc player. Bill Atkinson's concern for aesthetics and showmanship is reflected in bit-map graphics and filmic visual effects such as dissolves and wipes that are supported by music and sound.

As you work with HyperCard, the interface discloses itself to you step by step, and you dicover more ways of controlling and customizing your information. Take a second step, for example, and you can modify existing stacks by typing your own data on new electronic cards. At the next level, you can gain access to HyperCard's painting tools, with which you can add illustrations to your stacks.

The two highest levels of the interface offer fuller control over the workings of the program. Advance one level, and you can customize your stacks by creating buttons, making new links, and exploring new paths through your information. At this level, you also can copy a useful button from one stack into another. For example, you might copy a phone-dialing button from your address file into your ToDo list. And finally, at the highest level, you can peer behind the buttons to see and modify the scripts that make them work.

When you reach the highest level of the HyperCard interface, you have, by gradual stages, come to HyperTalk, an object-oriented language that reads very much like simple English. With HyperTalk, you can create custom stacks in which information can be linked with cunning sophistication. You can build your knowledge of HyperTalk gradually, beginning with simple commands such as "Go to next card." As you progress, you can devise complex scripts that perform such things as conditional branching, mathematical calculations, and text searches.

As it unfolds its levels of interaction, the program invites you to make new discoveries and gain greater mastery. You can go as far as you want. There is never a high threshold to cross before you can make the program useful.

Compare that to traditional programming languages, which can require a year or more of training and practice before you can do rewarding things with them. To help you learn HyperCard, Apple includes a Help Stack, written by Carol Kaehler, which is a model of pedagogy—and of presentation.

HyperCard is not simply, as Apple marketing calls it, "a toolkit for information." It is an engine for stimulating creativity and for fostering collaboration and sharing among a community of explorers. Of course, if Apple marketing told you that, you might not believe it. But if you look at what is happening, you'll find the claim is true.

The success of HyperCard should be a reassurance and a challenge to anyone worried that bringing technology into the classroom will mechanize and dehumanize teaching. Hyper-Card proves that a string of some 300,000 zeros and ones can convey personality so strong that people respond to it personally and emotionally. The program also conveys its creator's enthusiasm.

Multimedia in teaching—at its root—is not about media; it's about teaching. And, like HyperCard, multimedia is about sharing. It is a way of recording and publishing deep insights about how the world goes together—how something that happens over here connects with something else over there. Multimedia is about creating an environment in which learners can make and record their own discoveries and then pass them along.

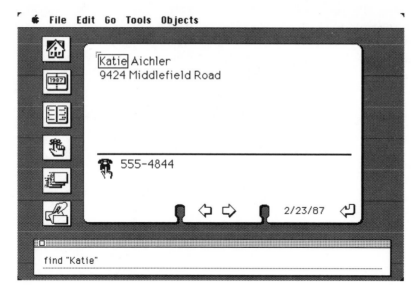

An address card styled to look like a Rolodex. This card is from one of the stacks that Apple distributes with HyperCard. Buttons along the right of the screen will go to the Home Card, dial the number of this card, link to a To Do list, scan through all the cards, and sort them.

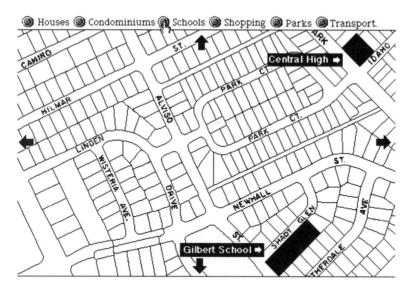

A real estate office might use HyperCard to create a dynamic map. In this card, for example, buttons along the top of the screen will bring out buildings or facilities in each category (here we're asking it to show schools). Clicking on any building will disclose more information. The arrows along the border lead to adjacent map quadrants.

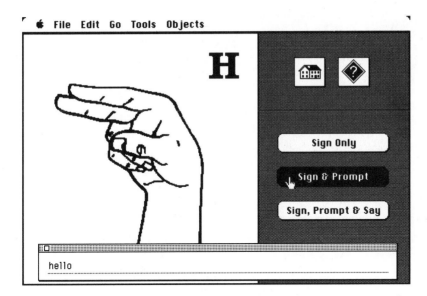

FingerSpell by Joe Williams and Cliff Guren. This stack helps teach how to sign letters of the alphabet. Type any word into the box at the bottom of the screen, and the hands will spell it out, prompting or even speaking the letters according to which button you click.

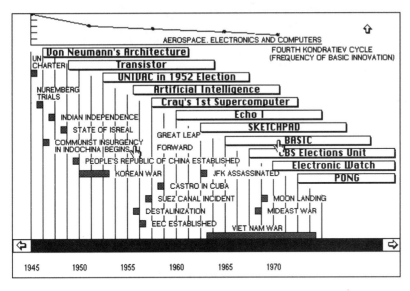

"The Timetable of Computing and Broadcasting" is part of an ambitious, multi-disc set, "Timetable of History," offered as a commercial stack by Xiphias. Clicking on a technology or event in bold type will disclose more information. Here we are clicking on "BASIC."

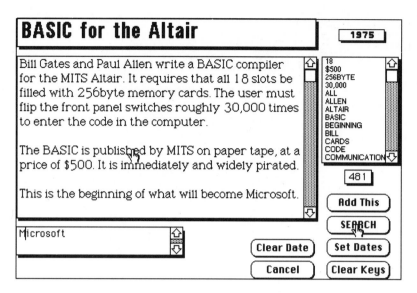

The next level into the "Timetable of Computing and Broadcasting." Navigating through information about BASIC discloses this history card.

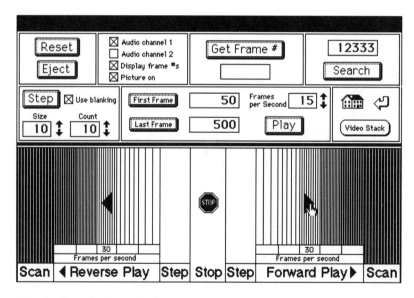

Videodisc Controller designed in HyperCard by Kristee Kreitman. The lower part of the screen works like a joystick. As you drag the mouse across the card, the video will run forward or in reverse at various speeds. The upper part lets you call up specific frame numbers or sequences, as well as control stepping and other functions.

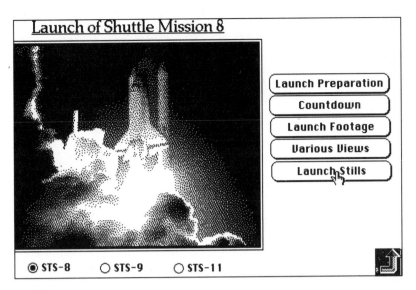

An example of a HyperCard tour of a videodisc. This stack is a guide to the NASA disc, "Shuttle Downlink: Repair of Solar Max" from Optical Data Corp. The buttons on this card allow you to select a mission and then review various phases of the launch. Other cards in the stack deal with crews, experiments, and equipment on the shuttle.

The manuscript for this book was prepared and submitted to
Microsoft Press in electronic form. Text files were processed
and formatted by Rick Bourgoin using Aldus PageMaker™
for the Apple® Macintosh™.
Text composition by Microsoft Press in Times Roman output using
Adobe Postscript™ to the Linotype L300 Laser Imagesetter.